Creating Safe Space

CREATING SAFE SPACE

VIOLENCE
AND
WOMEN'S WRITING

EDITED BY

TOMOKO KURIBAYASHI
AND JULIE THARP

STATE UNIVERSITY OF NEW YORK PRESS

Published by
State University of New York Press, Albany

Printed in the United States of America

Cover art: "A Safe Place" by Barbara Harman. Used by permission of the artist.

For information, address the State University of New York Press,
State University Plaza, Albany, NY 12246

Production by Diane Ganeles
Marketing by Nancy Farrell

Library of Congress Cataloging-in-Publication Data

Creating safe space : violence and women's writing / edited by Tomoko
  Kuribayashi and Julie Tharp.
      p.   cm.
    Includes bibliographical references (p.   ) and index.
    ISBN 0-7914-3563-6 (alk. paper). — ISBN 0-7914-3564-4 (pbk. :
  alk. paper)
      1. American literature—Women authors—History and criticism.
  2. English literature—Women authors—History and criticism.
  3. Women and literature—United States.   4. Women and literature—
  Great Britain.   5. Child abuse in literature.   6. Sex crimes in
  literature.   7. Feminism and literature.   8. Violence in literature.
  9. Women—Crimes against.   10. Incest in literature.
  I. Kuribayashi, Tomoko.   II. Tharp, Julie Ann.
  PS147.C74   1997
  810.9'9287—dc21   97-1723
                                                              CIP

10 9 8 7 6 5 4 3 2 1

Contents

Introduction

This collection of articles has grown out of a rather simple, though earnest, interest in writings by women—many of them unknown to the reading public—who have experienced degrees of sexual abuse, most typically incest. *Voices in the Night*, edited by Toni McNaron and Yarrow Morgan, and *I Never Told Anyone*, edited by Ellen Bass and Louise Thornton, came out almost simultaneously in the early 1980s as a result of writing workshops organized by and for women survivors of childhood sexual abuse. The editors of both volumes point to the therapeutic benefits of writing about one's experience of childhood sexual abuse as an indispensable step towards genuine healing. In their introduction, McNaron and Morgan emphasize "the necessity and excitement of rendering women's lives into art as healing, enriching and affirmative experiences," since "otherwise this huge reality for one-third of all women will be romanticized or buried or trivialized or mocked" (17–18). Bass and Thornton define their goal in putting their book together thus: "to help give the sexually abused child a voice. She had been studied, evaluated, re-evaluated, and compiled into numerous statistics and case studies. But had this child ever spoken for herself?" (17). Supporting these beliefs, psychologist Judith Herman in her 1991 book, *Trauma and Recovery*, recognized the importance of "reconstructing the trauma story" as one of the major stages of the healing for survivors of traumatic experiences since "when the truth is finally recognized, survivors can begin their recovery" (3,1).

Herman defines the first stage of recovery in the context of counseling as that of "establishing safety" and the second stage as that of "reconstructing the trauma story" (3). But the process of writing about violence as described by McNaron and Morgan and by Bass and Thornton seems to indicate that creation of safe space occurs simultaneously as the telling/writing of the story. When women write about their experiences of violence, then, safe space is not a prerequisite, but something that comes out of the writing process.

Our 1993 Midwest Modern Language Association Meeting session titled "Women's Writing As Creation of Safe Space" was a rather casual offshoot of such knowledge and exploration as these books made possible of the relationship between women's sense of safety and their writing. We simply wanted to gather papers that would illustrate ways in which survivors of sexual violence

1

used their writing to create a safe space from which to speak, in order then to create more safe space, perhaps to be shared with others. This seemed to be by itself a worthwhile cause to base our session on, as we daily faced reports of various sorts of violence against women and our own increasing sense of personal danger.

The paper abstracts we received in response to our one-page call for papers in the spring of 1993, however, opened our eyes to larger possibilities. The scholars who wrote to us addressed the issues of childhood sexual abuse, ensuing trauma, and survivors' efforts to overcome the sense of imminent danger through writing. They also proposed to examine other related topics such as social violence against women, emotional abuse, definition of audience for and by survivor discourse, as well as linguistic and literary problems surrounding women's writing about experiences of violence. The session, which eventually became a double session, far outreached our initial expectations, growing into a multifaceted colloquium, with presentations including various eras—seventeenth to twentieth centuries—and various nationalities—American, British, Canadian, and German.

The range and number of paper topics proposed for our session only reminded us of the prevalence of violence against women in many societies, past and present. If one needs any "academic" and "professional" evidence—as if news reports are not depressing and convincing enough, or because they are too sensational to warrant level-headed contemplation—a number of recent publications provide proof of the widespread violence and demonstrate how such violence is condoned or even encouraged by the cultures and societies in which we live.

In *It Could Happen to Anyone: Why Battered Women Stay*, Ola W. Barnett and Alyce D. LaViolette quote statistics from the late 1980s that say "approximately 20%–50% of all female emergency patients (not just trauma victims) are battered women" and "women make 1,453,437 medical visits per year for treatment of injuries resulting from an assault by a spouse" (xvii–xviii). According to Ann Jones in *Next Time She'll Be Dead: Battering and How to Stop It*, all the attention paid by media and legal efforts made in the recent years have not helped to decrease domestic violence. "A few years ago the FBI reported that in the United States a man beats a woman every eighteen seconds. . . . Now [i.e., in 1992] it's *twelve*" (6, author's italics). The most reliable count, the number of homicides resulting from domestic violence against women, says that such violence is on the increase: "In Massachusetts, in 1989, one woman was slain by her husband or boyfriend every twenty-two days . . . in 1992 it is happening every nine days" (Jones 7).

In *Transforming a Rape Culture*, edited by Emilie Buchwald, Pamela Fletcher, and Martha Roth, the preamble defines "a rape culture," which is the culture in which we live, as follows:

What is a Rape Culture? It is a complex of beliefs that encourages male sexual aggression and supports violence against women. It is a society where violence is seen as sexy and sexuality as violent. In a rape culture women perceive a continuum of threatened violence that ranges from sexual remarks to sexual touching to rape itself. A rape culture condones physical and emotional terrorism against women *as the norm*. (vii, authors' italics)

Ellen Bass corroborates that "we live in a society where men are encouraged to do violence to women and children, subtly and overtly" (25). According to McNaron and Morgan,

approximately one out of every three girl children experiences sexual abuse in her family, and with figures that approximately 97% of all victims of sexual abuse are girls and not boys, we begin to place incest within the context of a sexist culture. Anything that happens to one out of every three girls is neither random nor exceptional. (14–15)

In an interview with *Ms.*, Ann Jones links domestic violence against women to the popular concept of romance and love: "The problem is that so much of men's controlling behavior is absolutely synonomous with what is described as signs of love in the 'true luv' [i.e., romantic myth widely circulated through popular literature and media] kinds of literature" (60). In *Interrogating Incest*, Vikki Bell also suggests that "normal sexuality, normal power relations and the normal family are implicated in incestuous abuse. The men who are known to have abused children are not perverted, but 'normal,' everyday men" because so much of the sociocultural norm of male sexuality is linked to aggression, domination, and violence (82). In the face of such cultural and societal assumptions (however hidden) that women are to be controlled by men even (or especially) with the use of violence, women do write both creatively and theoretically to have their voices heard and to create safe space.

Relevant to such societal acceptance and encouragement of violence against women, one crucial question emerged as we organized our session on women writing to create space: Can acts of writing—and their products—be dangerous for women who write to overcome their experiences of violence and ensuing trauma?

Historically, writing has been both a means of empowerment and a source of anxiety for women. Feminist scholars of earlier women writers agree that women writers had more obstacles to overcome before they could write than their male counterparts. Some scholars believe that it was a path of thorns even for more successful women writers. Scholars of eighteenth- and nineteenth-century British women writers, for example, assert that women who attempted to write did suffer considerably from the incompatibility between the contemporary definitions of the nature of writing and the socio-cultural ideals of femininity of their time. Writing was an act of self-assertion, a characteristic alien to behavior expected of women, especially well-bred ones. In *The Madwoman in the Attic*, Sandra Gilbert and Susan Gubar argue that creation of literary texts was considered an exclusively male domain from which women were biologically barred; it was believed that "because they are by definition male activities . . . writing, reading, and thinking are not only alien but also inimical to 'female' characteristics" (8). Consequently, "those women who were among the first of their sex to attempt the pen were evidently infected or sickened by just the feelings of self-doubt, inadequacy, and inferiority that their education in 'femininity' almost seems to have been designed to induce" (59–60). Elaine Showalter, in *A Literature of Their Own: British Women Novelists from Brontë to Lessing*, concurs that "early women writers' relationship to their professional role was uneasy. Eighteenth-century women novelists exploited a stereotype of helpless femininity to win chivalrous protection from male reviewers and to minimize their unwomanly self-assertion" (17).

Other scholars emphasize the happier examples while acknowledging the difficulties women writers faced. In *Literary Women,* Ellen Moers discusses how Elizabeth Barrett (Browning) and George Sand "made those difficulties [that plague women's lives] into resources" (5). According to Moers, Barrett (as well as Sand) had it all: "She [Barrett] wanted fame: published in her teens and twenties, her poetry was hailed round the world, and she was nominated for the laureateship. She wanted a share in the normal masculine literary life, and . . . she saw that life come to her. . . . She wanted love as well. . . . She wanted more love; and it came, it came—" (7).

We probably should not forget either that for many a woman such as Harriet Beecher Stowe, writing was one of the few options, if not the only one, for earning a wage large enough to support herself or her family. These women wrote mainly or partly out of an economic necessity, rather than—or not only—out of a desire or a need for artistic self-expression. In such cases, writing as a means of economic independence, even with its own drawbacks, must have been empowering to the women themselves.

Today's scholars of women's writing echo the scholars cited above when considering women's relationship to the printed word, sometimes choosing to magnify only one of the two potentials of writing: the danger or the empowerment. Bass and Thornton optimistically observe that in their book "women . . . have tranformed themselves, like phoenixes rising from the ashes, through their own words" and that "in this book, survivors of childhood abuse use the power of speech to transform, to fuse secret shame, pain, and anger into a sharp, useful tool, common as a kitchen knife, for cutting away lies and deception like rotten fruits, leaving the clean hard pit, that kernel of truth" about incest (22,59). In contrast, McNaron and Morgan hesitate to celebrate the coming of their book unquestioningly:

> Often we wept deeply, not from content, but from uttering the taboo words in a safe, supportive environment. To write those same stories as narrative is a second and huge step because we put form around what has seemed so chaotic, we make public to strangers the most intimate truths about ourselves. We also give up control because we cannot know how a given reader will respond to us. (19)

Herman also recognizes the danger of self-exposure: "Those who attempt to describe the atrocities that they have witnessed also risk their own credibility. To speak publicly about one's knowledge of atrocities is to invite the stigma that attaches to victims" (2). As Thornton argues, many children do not speak up about their abuse because they believe that their "word alone will very likely not be honored" (18). A woman/child can be labeled liar when speaking the truth, and thus have that calumny of dishonesty piled on the previous pain and trauma.

In this volume, a number of articles address the question of the danger of speaking up. Diana Swanson considers Woolf's ambivalent relationship to a medium that both sustains her and renders her terribly vulnerable. Brenda Daly and Susan L. Woods both discuss the particular vulnerability academics open themselves up to when they write autobiographically. All three articles purport to discover why, if writing is risky, women still continue to try to write. Sonia Apgar's article details the recovery process undergone by women writing about past trauma. Other answers to the question are proposed by nearly all of the essays in the collection, most being psychological, but some even economic.

This question later grew into another, yet more complex one. Are women co-opted into the oppressors' group when they write their way into the mainstream, by accepting and even using the power dynamics that oppressed them in the first place? While this question lurks behind many of the essays, Annalee Newitz discusses it more directly in her consideration of the incest and pornography in Anne Rice's enormously popular fiction.

The concept of safe—or unsafe—home is inseparable from the act of writing for the purpose of creating safe space, because the home is a central spatial element to many women's lives and also because much of the violence women experience takes place in their home, belying the social myth that the home is safe space for all residents. Home is supposed to be, but often is not, safe for women, as is attested by the number of women battered at home and children sexually and otherwise abused by their family members. Mary Jo Dondlinger argues that a number of Emily Dickinson's poems can be read as symptomatic of just such a homelife. In some cases the family home or private acts of writing such as journaling may appear safe, but in fact are not. Certainly Dickinson is very protective of her writing, even within her home. Could the appearance of safety be a reflection of the deceptiveness of society's paternalistic attitude towards women? Are victims of incest in some ways privileged in their comprehension of this?

When the home itself is threatened or transplanted, a new set of problems arise, as we discover in Lisa Logan's discussion of Harriet Spofford's fictive captivity narrative. The American frontier was a difficult place to maintain any sense of safety whether at home or abroad. Mary Sylwester's analysis of Rebecca Ketcham's trail diary reveals a woman desperately seeking a sense of home and security on the westward trail. One solution to the dangers of home suggested by Willa Cather is seclusion in a convent, a space which Linda Karell examines.

Another important question is this: Is writing—language—as dangerous to women as many homes are, or is there a kind of writing that is particularly safe? For example, does so-called women's language, valued and sought by feminist writers like Luce Irigaray, provide a safer medium for women writing about their experiences of violence? How much safer are journaling and more private types of publishing, such as magazines like *Ms.* that are geared towards a self-identified feminist audience or small circulation journals? Don't these publications also have their own codes of acceptability so that some writers may get censored and/or criticized when they have expected more sympathetic reception? If writing—language—and publishing have long been male-dominated and any changes that women may make are still only grafted onto the cultural base that condones or supports violence against women, could women ever find or create a safe home by writing at all?

From the anthologized articles focusing on nineteenth-century and early twentieth-century writing, it would seem that women have attempted many different strategies of voicing their experiences—encoding, symbolism, allegory, plot machinations—in ways that also protect them from discovery by all but the most sensitive or informed reader. The very secretive nature of much of women's early writing suggests a knowledge of its power and danger. Susan Anne Carlson explains how Charlotte Brontë's novelettes were originally written in script so small they require a magnifying glass to read.

More fundamental questions arise concerning the body—more specifically, the female body—space and writing and their interconnections. What kind of space can possibly be created by writing, and what is the process by which one creates it? Tomoko Kuribayashi proposes that Sandra Cisneros creates safe space through bilingualism, creates a house where neither the poverty and sexism of her Chicano home nor the violence and racism of the Anglophone world can hurt her. How does writing also relate to the body, when the wish to have a safe haven for their bodies is one of the reasons these women are writing? All of the twentieth-century authors under consideration in this anthology address these concerns, although perhaps none so felicitously as Alberta Hunter who, according to Kari Winter, wrote blues lyrics as a playful language of the body which in fact protected Hunter's lesbian identity. Unlike Hunter, Joy Kogawa, according to Julie Tharp, connects the sexual trauma of her young protagonist to racial/ethnic oppression, in this case the oppression of Japanese Canadians during World War II. For both authors, however, a reclamation of the body's integrity is central to their writing.

Recently the newspapers have been flooded by reports on trials in which a parent previously accused of incest sues his/her child—and often the child's psychologist—for false charges and is granted monetary and other compensations. What alleged victims of abuse say or write is cast into dubious light by mass media. Articles and books published on the subject of false memory syndrome, such as Michael D. Yapko's *Suggestions of Abuse: True and False Memories of Childhood Sexual Traumas* and Mark Pendergrast's *Victims of Memory: Incest Accusations and Shattered Lives*, do address important issues that are potentially beneficial to authentic survivors of abuse. Retractors' newsletters and associations for parents falsely accused of sexually abusing their children do provide valuable help. The same can be said for books like *Wounded Innocents: The Real Victims of the War Against Child Abuse*, by Richard Wexler. But these can also lead to the assumption that what women—or children—say about their experiences of violence should always be taken with a large pinch of salt, if not downright suspected as false or exaggerated. Twenty years ago, women speaking out about the abuse they suffered were already not believed. According to Ann Jones,

> Once feminists encouraged battered women to 'speak out' and tell their stories, as women in the antirape movement had done, the circumstances of the battered woman and of the rape survivor proved remarkably alike. Both were doubted and disbelieved, both were charged with making false accusations, both were blamed for provoking violence, both were said secretly to enjoy it, both were blamed for not preventing it themselves, both were shamed into silence. (8)

While the current atmosphere, created by the backlash against women working to stop violence against women, would seem to be a dangerous one in which to bring forth a book of this nature, the work done here provides needed affirmation of the efforts undertaken by women to survive and recover from genuine trauma.

The essays in this volume are arranged so as first to introduce the reader to theoretical frameworks that may help her better understand the following sections. The second section contains essays about nineteenth-century and early twentieth-century writers, and the third section focuses on mid to late twentieth-century writers. The essays also happen to share thematic and rhetorical similarities, however, in that the earlier writing frequently reveals a survival mentality in which women write of these matters only at great risk to themselves; and the later literature reveals women writing from a more secure place certainly but still with the problems and ambivalence expressed by their foremothers.

Such is the range of issues addressed by the essays included in this anthology. Together the essays question, and explore, what safe space for women is, how women define and try to create it through writing, and how it can be dangerous to women writing at all. Which may, or may not, lead to creation of safe space within this volume.

Bibliography

Barnett, Ola W., and Alyce D. LaViolette. *It Could Happen to Anyone: Why Battered Women Stay*. Newbury, CA: Sage Publications, 1993.

Bass, Ellen, and Louise Thornton, eds. *I Never Told Anyone*. New York: HarperCollins Publishers, 1983.

Bell, Vikki. *Interrogating Incest: Feminism, Foucault and the Law*. New York: Routledge, 1993.

Buchwald, Emilie, Pamela Fletcher, and Martha Roth, eds. *Transforming a Rape Culture*. Minneapolis, MN: Milkweed Editions, 1993.

Gilbert, Sandra, and Susan Gubar. *The Madwoman in the Attic: The Woman Writer and the Nineteenth-Century Literary Imagination*. New Haven: Yale University Press, 1979.

Herman, Judith Lewis. *Trauma and Recovery*. New York: Basic Books, 1992.

Jones, Ann. *Next Time She'll Be Dead: Battering and How to Stop It*. Boston: Beacon Press, 1994.

———. "Where Do We Go From Here?" *Ms.* 5.2 (September/October 1994): 56–63.

McNaron, Toni, and Yarrow Morgan, eds. *Voices in the Night*. Pittsburgh and San Francisco: Cleis Press, 1982.

Moers, Ellen. *Literary Women*. 1976; New York: Oxford University Press, 1985.

Pendergrast, Mark. *Victims of Memory: Incest Accusations and Shattered Lives*. Hinesburg, VT: Upper Access, Inc., 1995.

Showalter, Elaine. *A Literature of Their Own: British Women Novelists from Brontë to Lessing*. Princeton, NJ: Princeton University Press, 1977.

Wexler, Richard. *Wounded Innocents: The Real Victims of the War Against Child Abuse*. Amherst, NY: Prometheus Books, 1990.

Yapko, Michael D. *Suggestions of Abuse: True and False Memories of Childhood Sexual Trauma*. New York: Simon and Schuster, 1994.

Theorizing Our Lives

Over the last two and a half decades, women in western and non-western societies have started to vocalize the aspects of their lives that had long been ignored, devalued, or misrepresented by mainstream discourses. This newly claimed area of public discourse has included women's experiences of sexual violence, a powerful tool by which women had long been silenced and "kept in place" in patriarchal societies. Women's accounts of sexual violence have also brought to light other kinds of violence, exposing a societal system, previously invisible, of brutalization, intimidation, and oppression. In telling their individual stories of sexual violence from the survivor's perspective, women have also found validation of their experiences and viewpoints, which has led to their liberation from the sense of shame that sexual violation often evokes in the survivor. Women narrators have, however, encountered hostile and damaging criticism from those who do not grant credibility to their accounts.

Academic feminist discourse, which has grown out of the same need and desire for affirmation and freedom as these life-stories have, not only has prompted and eased the birthing of women's first-person narratives, but also illuminates ways in which women can use their stories to empower themselves and those they wish to protect. For example, feminist theory can help give credence both to the women narrators themselves and to their potential audience. Feminist theory can also identify an audience that will be receptive or affirming instead of doubtful or condemning. In turn, these women writers have nourished academic feminist discourse, by providing the evidence of women's reality to generate and validate theory. The relationship between feminist academic discourse and women's accounts of their experiences is that of mutual understanding and nurturing. One cannot exist without the other.

The following section contains three essays which illuminate such crossroads of women's stories and feminist theory, one on the benefits and dangers of writing autobiographical academic articles; one which demonstrates how autobiography and theory can flow in and out of each other in one narrative; and one which theorizes, from a psychoanalytic and linguistic point of view, on the process of empowerment in contemporary women's writings about sexual violence. All three essays offer frameworks, at once autobiographical and theoretical, from which to better understand women's accounts—both contemporary and of earlier eras—of their experiences of violence.

9

I Stand Here Naked, and Best Dressed in Theory: On Feminist Re-fashionings of Academic Discourse

Brenda Daly

Is academic writing a "safe space" in which to tell personal stories? For a well-established, tenured professor, the answer may be "yes," but for women students, especially those who want to tell stories of sexual trauma, the answer, though still "yes," comes with this qualification: those who have such secrets to tell should reveal them, at least initially, only to those who will bear witness to their suffering. Despite this cautionary note, I know how liberating it can be for a survivor to bring the issue of sexual abuse into the academy, especially when she claims the right to theorize her own experience. Nevertheless, since writing that synthesizes the autobiographical and the theoretical violates the conventions of academic writing, it can be risky. Hence, the ambivalence of my metaphors: shall I stand here naked in autobiography, or shall I clothe myself in theory? Yes, it is possible to protect one's self with layers of theoretical clothes, to establish authority and distance through formal apparel, but it is also possible to shed too many layers of clothing, to become overly personal, to lose one's authority through intimacy. Therefore, this paper asks the following pedagogical questions: 1) how do feminists establish a new dress code when, in fact, we are actively engaged in transgressing the conventions of academic attire? And 2) how do feminist teachers establish ground rules for students who wish to attempt this synthesis of genres? I open with a discussion of anxieties that surfaced as I began writing autobiographical academic essays; then, with insights gleaned from my experiences, I turn to the issue of establishing guidelines for a pedagogy of the personal.

During the 1980s, my feminist teachers at the University of Minnesota, Shirley Nelson Garner, Toni McNaron, and Madelon Sprengnether, provided assignments and occasions for integrating autobiography and literary criticism. During this period, however, I would disclose my personal trauma only in private and only in the company of trusted friends. Even though traumatic childhood experiences had determined the topic of my dissertation, I didn't think it wise—given the intense competition for tenure-line positions—to risk writing an autobiographical dissertation. Nevertheless, while in graduate school, I did transform one formal academic paper, initially written for a linguistics course, into an essay about my mother's "feminine" speech. Later published in a feminist journal with the title, "I VIVIDLY REMEMBER, pretty well: A Witness Against Her Self," this essay dramatizes my ambivalence toward my mother's feminine helplessness, as well as ambivalence about violating the academic taboo against any use of the personal. Although it felt liberating to integrate linguistic theory and feminist insights, in retrospect, I view this piece as a betrayal of my mother's trust. Even though she gave her permission to use the trial transcript of her testimony on the witness stand, I didn't show her the essay because, I rationalized, I didn't want to hurt her feelings.[1] As this example illustrates, self-revelation can be risky, not only for the writer, but for those written about. Teachers should remember this.

Only after completing my degree did I finally write a fully self-disclosing autobiographical-academic essay. In "My Friend, Joyce Carol Oates," first presented at the University of Minnesota's Center for Advanced Feminist Studies, I briefly mention that I had chosen to write a dissertation on Oates because of her ability—though she did not know me—to authentically portray my personal pain, the pain of an incest survivor. I recognize, in retrospect, that I was using this autobiographical essay to build a life raft of words that would enable me to survive the ego-crushing rejections that occur during a job search. During this search, the family secret I had carried all my life exacerbated my sense of inadequacy, but I had finally found a safe feminist place in which to break my silence. Yet, it was one thing to present the paper before a visibly friendly audience, quite another to publish it for an invisible audience which would, in all likelihood, refuse to believe me. After all, even Freud had determined that when "hysterics" accuse their fathers of violating them sexually, they are lying. Primarily because of my concern with audience, I revised "My Friend, Joyce Carol Oates" a number of times before it appeared in a collection called *The Intimate Critique*. I was, I confess, relieved that the collection was not published until after I was tenured, for I was once again concerned about audience: not only about those in my English department who would review my work, but also about scientists on the college committee who would be even less likely to value autobiographical writing. The pedagogical point here is that teachers should be aware that, depending upon the audience and the timing, survivors of sexual trauma may actually be traumatized again if required to write autobiographically.

I expected, after achieving tenure, to feel less anxiety about writing autobiographical criticism. To test this newfound sense of security, I responded to a call for autobiographical-criticism by writers from a variety of disciplines for a collection called *Nexus*. This time, in an essay called "My Father/My

Censor: English Education, Politics, and Status," I decided to confront directly my ancient (and perhaps exaggerated) fear of being punished for truth-telling. To my surprise, the old ambivalence returned with a vengeance: yes, I felt my "soul at the white heat" while writing the essay, but I also felt threatened by the real possibility of negative consequences. This time it would not be my father who would punish me (in fact, my father is dead) but THE FATHERS. "The fathers," as I have internalized them, are the powerful men, the Wizards of Oz, who run institutions. These fathers always privilege "masculine" theory over "feminine" pedagogy; they assume that professors are always smarter than high school teachers; and they create and enforce the professional conditions that require others, who also want professional status, to conform to their views. More specifically, since "My Father/My Censor" analyzes how institutional hierarchies affect my current teaching position, I still anticipate anger from some members of my own English department. But I have grown tired of splitting myself into two separate curriculum vitae—one featuring literature, the other English education—depending upon the academic positions of my anticipated audience. This strategy has been necessary because elitist members of this profession regard my background in high school teaching as automatically disqualifying me to teach or write about literature. This snobbishness, practiced by some but not all English professors, still makes me angry.

Fortunately, I liberated myself from this debilitating anger during the process of writing "My Father/My Censor." Writing this essay also enabled me to recognize a recurring theme in all of my autobiographical-critical essays: the importance of reading in my life. Even during my adolescence, when I was unable to stop my father's abuse, reading helped me to keep alive some faith in my ability to act and think independently. Later, inspired to read women writers by the women's movement, I discovered a community of women writers and characters who could understand and even sympathize with my point of view. Moreover, many women in this community had suffered abuse—sometimes even sexual abuse—but they had survived and, in some cases, had managed to become authors. I decided, therefore, to examine the effects of my language arts education on my ability to author my own life and writing. This project was a way of joining with feminists engaged in the collective struggle to revise a sexist and racist language arts curriculum. To research this autobiographical-theoretical study, which I call *Authoring a Life*, I visited English classrooms, from grade school to graduate school, where I was once a student or teacher. In particular, I asked what changes, if any, had been made in language arts classrooms since the women's movement. Were women writers now being taught in high school English classrooms and, if so, what difference did this change make in the lives of women students?

What I have learned is that high school students continue to read few, if any, works by women. If we accept the testimony of many feminists, that women read novels and autobiographies to learn how to plot their lives, then the traditional language arts curriculum, still firmly in place in most high schools, continues to deny young women opportunities to imagine and analyze their narrative options. Traditional plots are inequitable, as Joanne Frye points out: "The paradigmatic plots based in the qualities of strength, autonomy, and aspiration seem reserved for male protagonists; the paradigmatic plots based specifically in female experience seem to confine women in domesticity and apparent passivitity" (1). To counter the gender constraints of traditional plots, I recommend teaching fiction that re-visions old plots— fiction that Gayle Green defines as meta-fiction. By comparing plots and counterplots, students of both genders will learn a wider range of narrative options. It is also possible that such activities—activities that invite students to engage in re-visionary reading and writing—will prompt more women to actively theorize their own experience, rather than leaving this important task to others. Regardless of race, as bell hooks argues, women must resist the impulse to leave the theorizing to white men, for theories which have not been tested by the experiences and insights of women can, of course, be used to oppress them. In short, I believe that despite conflict and tension, a new synthesis of the theoretical and the autobiographical is emerging in academic writing. It is now possible to be both "naked" and "dressed" in the same essay. And despite the risks, young women and men should be encouraged to participate in this life-altering form of writing.

My own work is a good example of the synthesis of autobiography and theory, but feminists, beginning with the poet-critics, have practiced this synthesis for some time. Adrienne Rich and Susan Griffin are two of the earliest and best known examples; more recently, Lynne Z. Bloom, Diane Freedman, Jane Gallop, bell hooks, Nancy K. Miller, Sharon O'Brien, Jane Tompkins and others have synthesized autobiography and theory. Nevertheless, despite numerous models of successful autobiographical writing by feminists, my doubts and anxieties continue to surface as I write autobiographical criticism. One reason for my insecurity is that the synthesis of autobiography and theory varies greatly—ranging from Jane Gallop's confessions of uncertainty while reading Lacan to the situational dynamics of television talk shows that often deny the power of theoretical analysis, or expertise, to survivors of sexual violence.[2] At least for a feminist audience, Gallop's revelation of uncertainty makes her authorial stance seem less godlike and more appealing; by contrast, revelations of uncertainty by an unknown incest survivor may automatically disqualify her as an expert on the topic. The status of the speaker, and the context in which she speaks, make all the difference. As a survivor of father-daughter incest, I know how vulnerable one can feel when acknowledging such a history; at the same time, I believe it is terribly important for survivors to claim the right to theorize and thereby change a culture in which such violence occurs. Linda Alcoff and Laura Gray address this very problem in an article called "Survivor Discourse: Transgression or Recuperation?"

Alcoff and Gray use a synthesis of autobiography (they briefly acknowledge the fact that they have been victims of sexual violence) and theory (Foucault corrected by feminist insights) to analyze the problem of confessional modes of discourse. They are most concerned with those confessional discourses that involve sexuality—including rape, incest, and sexual assault. After analyzing a variety of discourse situations, including television talk shows, they conclude:

> Our analysis suggests that the formulation of the primary political tactic for survivors should not be a simple incitement to speak out, as this formulation leaves unanalyzed the conditions of speaking and thus makes us too vulnerable to recuperative discursive arrangements. Before we speak we need to look at where the incitement to speak originates, what relations of power and domination may exist between those who incite and those who are asked to speak, as well as to whom the disclosure is directed. (284)

Alcoff and Gray argue that in their "struggle to maintain autonomy over the conditions of our speaking out if we are to develop its subversive potential" (284), survivors must claim the right of "obstructing the ability of 'experts' to 'police our statements,' to put us in a defensive posture, or to determine the focus and framework of our discourse" (284). This analysis by Alcoff and Gray, as well as the work of bell hooks, has helped me to articulate why it is imperative that trauma survivors maintain authority over their own confessional discourse. The question is, if students are assigned autobiographical writing, can they maintain authority over their own discourse, even in a feminist classroom?

As I know from experience, even when the occasion to speak out is provided by feminists, it is difficult for a survivor to strike the balance of self-disclosure and self-censorship, or between autobiography and theory. For example, when I sent "My Father/ My Censor" to Diane Freedman, co-editor of the *Nexus* collection, she asked me to revise, omitting some textual references and providing more autobiography. Initially, because this request made me feel as if I were being asked to take off more clothing, I struggled to determine whether, by complying, I would be giving up authority over my own discourse. I finally recognized that Freedman's editorial recommendations would actually improve my essay, for in this case I was trying to hide behind theoretical/textual analysis. It was a strategy for armoring myself against the vulnerability I felt when writing in the confessional mode. As I wrestled with this issue, I determined that for me to speak with authority requires that I speak clothed in theory, whereas to speak strictly autobiographically means to stand naked, defenseless, exposed. This conflict—a conflict with myself, not with Freedman—forced me to acknowledge that I sometimes use theory as armor to protect myself and/or my audience from the embarrassment of emotion. The confessional mode (And why should I confess? Am I guilty of something?) prompts my fear of loss of control, or loss of authority; however, a synthesis of confessional and theoretical modes stimulates a different kind of fear: the fear of rejection.

I worry, for example, about rejection from feminist friends who have criticized the use of the personal in academic essays, describing it as self-indulgent or exhibitionistic[3] or simply irrelevant. Daphne Patai says, for example, "I doubt that I am the only one who is weary of the nouveau solipsism—all this breast-beating, grandstanding, and plain old egocentricity. Where does it all leave us?" (53). She replies that autobiographical writing leaves us "with nothing more than a shared awareness that scholarly works do not descend from heaven, but are written by human beings" (53). Perhaps Patai is right. If I write an essay about the sexual abuse of children, what difference does it make that I, like many women, actually experienced such abuse? In fact, for some readers, personal revelation would only weaken my argument against male violence since, presumably, I lack the objectivity of a detached observer. At the same time, I also consider possibility of rejection by feminists who resist theory, as for example, Nina Baym does in "The Madwoman and Her Languages: Why I Don't Do Feminist Theory," or by feminists who embrace theory, as, for example, Laurie Finke does in "The Rhetoric of Marginality: Why I Do Feminist Theory." Controversy, especially among feminists, threatens my need for affiliation. Even fictional depictions of conflict between women—such as Joyce Carol Oates's *Solstice* or Margaret Atwood's *Cat's Eye*—are painful for me to read. In other words, I am concerned about a possible loss of authority when I write autobiographically—because most women need more authority, not less—but I am even more concerned about a possible loss of affiliation. If women start airing their emotional differences in public, will anger drive us apart?

If what many of us seek is more a sense of community than of prestige, then this societally conditioned fear of conflict must be confronted again and again. Unfortunately, as Lyn Mikel Brown and Carol Gilligan demonstrate in *Meeting at the Crossroads*, adult women actually teach girls to avoid open conflict—with the result that by the age of thirteen many young women have lost their voices and their self-confidence as knowers. All of these concerns make me wonder whether, as a teacher, I should provide occasions for students to write autobiographically. Yet when I introduce theory, whether to undergraduate or graduate students, they almost always write more effectively when allowed to test new ideas against their own experiences, as well as the experiences of their peers. Therefore, I will describe the virtues and risks of some of my autobiographical writing assignments, beginning with a discussion of undergraduates and concluding with a discussion of a graduate student who has, courageously, chosen to write an autobiographical thesis.

One argument for encouraging undergraduates to write autobiographically is that, in the process of synthesizing the personal and the theoretical, they internalize new concepts more readily, integrating them more fully and criticizing them with more authority. Peter Elbow makes a related point in "Reflections on Academic Discourse: How It Relates to Freshmen and Colleagues" when he argues that "the use of academic discourse often masks a lack of genuine understanding" and may allow students to "distance or insulate themselves from experiencing or really internalizing the concepts they are allegedly learning" (137). I see such masking of genuine understanding, as well as distancing and insulating, in the writing of those students who have taken our newly required undergraduate theory course. Suddenly, many of these students seem to lose the capacity to write honestly. When this dysfunction occurs, I encourage students to write autobiographical essays about theory. For example, after introducing reader-response theory in a senior seminar on the canon debate, I asked students to write about the place of reading in their lives, suggesting that they reveal or conceal as much as they chose. (Women, I have noted, tend to be more self-revealing than men.) I recommended that, in these narratives about their lives as readers, they reflect upon why and how they read in order to prepare themselves for raising questions about the assumptions, stated or unstated, in assigned theoretical essays.

To further stimulate self-analysis and theory building, I then ask students to exchange and compare their reading autobiographies. What similarities and differences do they see? Are these differences based upon gender, race, religion, age, geography, or generation? This assignment moves students from response to analysis, usually enhancing their ability to read the assigned theoretical essays more critically. As Elbow says, "Often the best test of whether a student understands something is if she can translate it out of the discourse of the textbook and the discipline into everyday, experiential, anecdotal terms" (137). Elbow cites other authorities who advocate the integration of formal concepts with everyday experience: "Vogotsky, when he describes the need for what he calls 'scientific' or 'formal' concepts to become intertwined in the child's mind with 'everyday' or experienced concepts; Bakhtin, when he explores the process by which people transform 'the externally authoritative word' into the 'internally persuasive word'" (137). It is my hope that, after taking my courses, students will feel competent to read theorists and critics, not submissively, but critically. However, assignments requiring students to integrate the theoretical and the personal must be carefully designed and monitored.

Such assignments must be especially well designed and carefully monitored for use in public secondary schools. As I explain to future teachers enrolled in my undergraduate methods course, it is sometimes politically risky to ask students in middle school or high school English classes to write personal essays or journals. Since students are often surprised to learn that the practice of assigning journals or personal narratives may anger some parents, I illustrate this point with a copy of the *Phyllis Schlafly Report* which bears the front-page headline, "Parents Speak Out Against Classroom Abuse." Schlafly's article quotes from letters written by angry parents, all of whom object to classroom discussion or writing about any "personal" topic, such as suicide, death, drugs, shoplifting, teen pregnancy, and abortion. "Who are the Typhoid Marys," Schlafly asks, "who carry such poison into the classroom?" (1). This inflammatory question implies that knowledge of such matters is what causes children to act them out. To counter such efforts at censorship in public classrooms, I argue, as James Moffett does, that the chief characteristic of the censoring mind—"agnosis," or the desire not to know—is illustrated by Schlafly's argument, which is based upon the highly dubious notion that if young people do not know about social ills, such as teen sex, they will escape such problems.

As Moffett demonstrates in *Storm in the Mountains*, the objections of some parents to the use of the "personal" by classroom teachers may lead to community violence. Moffett reports that in Kanawha County, West Virginia in 1974, the wife of a fundamentalist minister, Mrs. Moore, objected to the state's attempt to adopt Moffett's co-edited series of language arts textbooks, *Interactions*. In her objections to *Interactions*, Mrs. Moore explained that she followed these guidelines:

> Textbooks must not intrude into the privacy of students' homes by asking personal questions about interfeelings [sic] or behavior of themselves or parents . . . must recognize the sanctity of the home and emphasize its importance as the basic unit of American society. . . must not contain offensive language . . . must teach the true history and heritage of the United States . . . shall teach that traditional rules of grammar are a worthwhile subject for academic pursuit and are essential for effective communication . . . shall encourage loyalty to the United States . . . and emphasize the responsibilities of citizenship and the obligation to redress grievances through legal processes . . . must not encourage sedition or revolution against our government or teach or imply that an alien form of government is superior. (quoted in Moffett 23)

Mrs. Moore did not invent these guidelines; they are spelled out by Mel and Norma Gabler of Texas, who have a nationwide reputation for successful efforts to censor textbooks. Such guidelines would have comforted my father, a member of the John Birch Society, for if textbooks or writing assignments could not "intrude upon the privacy of the student's homes," then his nocturnal crimes would remain hidden from the scrutiny of public authorities.

Since colleges and universities are not as vulnerable to parental control as secondary schools, it might be assumed that professors need not be concerned with the risks of assigning personal writing. However, even graduate students, when deprived of the conventional boundaries of academic discourse, need to analyze the problems of audience they may encounter when using the personal. For example, if a student wishes to use an autobiographical essay as a writing sample for admission to graduate school, will such an essay be appropriate for a more distant, and necessarily judgmental, reader? In other words, if someone who lacks professional status writes autobiographically, will she lose the very audience she intends to persuade? Through discussions of actual audiences beyond my classroom, I try to prepare students for the politics of the academy and, at the same time, give them the freedom to write, or not to write, in this hybrid genre. Recently, for example, I directed an autobiographical-critical thesis—an analysis of Edith Wharton's *The Mother's Recompense*—written by a woman, who, like Wharton's protagonist, is herself the mother of daughters. Because she is exceptionally intelligent and mature, and because she expressed an interest in doing something different in her thesis, something more creative, I suggested that she read some models of autobiographical academic essays in *The Intimate Critique*. Afterward, we agreed, she could decide whether she would like to try writing in this mode.

Although I told Sue[4] that some professors might not approve of autobiographical criticism and, as a result, she would have to choose her thesis committee with great care, she persisted in her choice. When I pointed out, given the problem of audience, that when applying for doctoral study, she might not wish to submit an autobiographical thesis as a writing sample, still, she persisted. In fact, I was probably more anxious than she, partly because I know how competitive it has become to even be admitted to graduate schools in English. Although I explained how difficult it is to gain admission into graduate school and how finding a tenure-line position is even more difficult, Sue persisted. That spring (1993), when the Women's Caucus for the Midwest Modern Language Association issued a call for papers on the topic of the synthesis of autobiography and theory in academic writing, I suggested that Sue submit a paper on the pleasures and dangers of writing in this hybrid genre. Presented under the title, "Wagering It All in Double Jeopardy: Autobiography in a Graduate Paper," her paper provides valuable insights, from a graduate student's perspective, about the risks and rewards of synthesizing feminist autobiographical theories—from writings by Adrienne Rich, Jane Tompkins, Nancy Miller, Diane Freedman, and others—with the theories of Mikhail Bakhtin.

In her autobiographical introduction to "Wagering It All in Double Jeopardy," Sue describes a conversation at a dinner party which illustrates, in extremis, some of the audience problems she would face. After asking probing questions about her thesis, a male professor at the dinner party "picked up his fork," she writes, "pierced his artichoke heart, and exclaimed, 'Well! I knew, sooner or later, it would devolve to this! Now anyone's interpretation is correct. So much for universal truth!' " (2). Undaunted by this negative response, she persisted. One reason she decided to use autobiographical criticism, she explains, is that conventional criticism tends to "appropriate the dialogism of the novel" (4), while personal criticism, in which "the author and audience occupy the same plane . . . surmounts the distance of monological language" (4). When Bakhtin describes such moments as "border violations" (Bakhtin 33), Sue argues, he is speaking of "border crossings" similar to those identified by Diane Freedman in *An Alchemy of Genres*. To further support her synthesis of autobiography and theory, Sue calls upon bell hooks, who argues that "feminist theorists . . . need to be conscientious about not supporting monolithic notions of theory. We will need to continually assert the need for multiple theories emerging from diverse perspectives in a variety of styles" (37).

Since I had never before invited a graduate student to participate in a conference presentation, I worried that Sue might find it threatening to present a graduate student's perspective at a conference dominated by professors. However, once again, she demonstrated intelligence, self-confidence, and a sense of humor. Theory should not be used as a "power over" others, she argued, but rather as a " 'power of' reinforcing choice" (5). The dangers of using autobiography, as she sees them, are both personal and political. In using autobiography, she says, "We risk our own feelings of security" (5). "Will we be understood?" she asks, "Will we embarrass ourselves? our families? those we love?" (5). However, for graduate students the specific danger is that by "using the experiential, we all risk loss of credibility," a risk she views as "much greater for the graduate student, a voice constantly struggling for credibility, than it is for the established writer" (5). As she points out, "Many of the poet-critics who serve as role models for graduate-level experiential writing first established themselves through traditional theory" (5). Yet she argues that graduate students who can depend upon "mentoring from sensitive, feminist professors" (6) should at least attempt autobiographical criticism.

However, even with such mentoring, the risk of failure is much greater when writing in this hybrid genre because, as she explains, "exposition, which calls for directness of purpose and a straightforward thesis, often exists in conflict with narration, a style associated with slower development, an unfolding" (6). Sue found that, as a result of this tension between the two modes, she was revising much more extensively. Of course, as her major professor, I was the person requesting these major revisions and, though the trust between us was strong, I worried that she would misinterpret my criticisms. I addressed this concern by telling her how I, too, had struggled with the problem of revisions. At the same time, I recognized the validity of her cautionary remark that "the graduate student who is unfamiliar and unpracticed in combining these two styles, because of the structure of the syllabus in a particular graduate level course, may lack the time to develop this skill" (6). Only because Sue had asked me to direct her thesis very early in her graduate program did she have the time for such extensive revision. In fact, she took an incomplete in an independent study with me in order to revise the paper in which she first attempted autobiographical criticism. Part of the difficulty, as I see it, is that she was learning to write in this hybrid genre while, at the same time, she was reading the theory which enabled her to justify it. Because I had learned the theory first, it may have been easier for me to later combine it with autobiography.

Yet, in the final analysis, Sue was excited to be engaged in feminist writing that transgressed academic conventions of the "impersonal" and the "universal." Despite the dangers—her concern, for example, that "as I submit my work for publication and for consideration in doctoral programs, my concern is that, similar to its reception at the dinner party, my work will be devalued based on form before the content of the work is ever considered" (6)—she persisted in writing an autobiographical thesis. Unfortunately, the end result of Sue's experiment was mixed. Although a chapter of her thesis, "The Solace of Separation: Feminist Theory, Autobiography, Edith Wharton, and Me," was accepted for publication in this volume, her application for graduate study at the University of Iowa was not successful. However, she may have been turned down, not because she wrote an autobiographical thesis, but because Iowa took so few of the students who applied: only fifteen out of approximately six hundred. We will never know for certain how her writing sample was evaluated, nor will we know how other factors—such as where she had earned her master's degree—entered into the decision. However, having wagered it all, she had, in a certain sense, lost.

At first, after learning that Sue had not been accepted by the University of Iowa—the only school that, due to family responsibilities, she could have attended—I felt as if I had mentored her poorly, especially since her academic record is excellent in all respects. However, since I had warned her of possible consequences of writing autobiographically, not once but any number of times, I finally renounced this guilt. As always, Sue accepted, without remorse or recrimination, the consequences of her choice. Even so, despite the pleasures of mentoring a student who had the courage to write autobiographical criticism, I am not exactly eager to do so again. But news travels fast among graduate students and, recently, a young woman who had heard about Sue's experience with the genre asked me to direct an autobiographical thesis in which she analyzes depictions of rape in the fiction of Joyce Carol Oates. Since I had just completed a book on Oates, I should have welcomed this opportunity and, to some degree, I did. However, I also know how emotionally exhausting it was for me to write autobiographically about father-daughter incest in Oates's fiction, and I didn't know whether she could manage the emotional turmoil she would undoubtedly experience during the writing process. That is why I advised her, as a therapist once advised me, "Do not write about a traumatic personal experience such as rape unless you feel safe." However, since I am not a trained therapist, I wonder whether, as an English professor, I should be providing occasions for therapeutic writing.

Given the current political climate, which I perceive as a period of backlash against feminist issues, I think my caution is justified. As I write, during the spring of 1994, resistance to incest stories has intensified dramatically. At present those legal cases in which incest victims have later dropped their charges—because, they explain, their memories have been proven unreliable—are frequently in the news. For example, on "60 Minutes" (17 April 1994), Morley Safer reported on a number of legal suits which were dropped by patients who later acknowledged that they were not remembering the experience, but responding to suggestions by their therapists. One month later, NBC (10 May 1994) brought us the news that Gary Romana was suing the two therapists who had assisted his daughter in remembering paternal sexual abuse. During the same month, *The New York Times Review of Books* (15 May 1994) published a front-page review called, "The Monster in the Mists," with the subtitle: "Are long-buried memories of child abuse reliable? Three new books tackle a difficult issue" (1). Only one of the books, Lenore Terr's *Unchained Memories: True Stories of Traumatic Memories, Lost and Found*, argues, though not to the complete satisfaction of the reviewer, that repressed memories of childhood trauma may turn out to be valid. However, the April issue of *NEA Today*, the newsletter of the National Education Association, did publish an interview with Dr. Brian Abbott, an expert on sexual abuse, in which the doctor recommends that school personnel respond to stories of abuse by listening to and supporting the child. "Try not to communicate any disbelief," Abbott advised, "because what's most devastating to a child is disbelief or inaction" (13). Abbott concluded with information that a special program, "Break the Silence: Kids Against Child Abuse," would be airing on network television in May. During this same two-month period, the daytime soap, *Days of Our Lives,* was running an incest story.

Intense interest in the topic has, predictably, created resistance, not only in the media, but also in courtrooms. For example, even though Holly Romana's father was found guilty of incest, a different jury recently awarded Mr. Romana damages when he sued his daughter's therapists for malpractice, charging them with "implanting" memories of paternal sexual abuse in his daughter's mind. Even though Holly's therapists, as well as her mother and sisters, believe Holly, jurors felt that, because of the methods the psychiatrist had used, they could not determine whether Holly was remembering actual experiences of childhood sexual abuse or fantasizing them. This method of discrediting the daughter's story has a familiar ring: almost one hundred years ago, Freud reversed his own theory—his view that hysteria had been caused by sexual abuse—when he concluded that his female patients had fantasized, rather than actually experienced, paternal sexual abuse. According to Judith Lewis Herman, such a pattern—a period of "active investigation" followed by a period of "oblivion" (7)—characterizes the history of psychological investigations of trauma. "Though the field has in fact an abundant and rich tradition," she says, "it has been periodically forgotten and must be periodically reclaimed" (7).[5]

During a period of backlash, such as the present, it becomes increasingly dangerous for women to write autobiographically about experiences of sexual violence. As a female professor in a male-controlled institution, I must recognize that I cannot protect students from the negative consequences of autobiographical academic writing. To some extent, I occupy the place of a mother who, such as Mrs. Romana, cannot protect her daughter from the abuse—whether by doctors, lawyers, journalists, or therapists—that sometimes follows public disclosures of rape. Even though Holly's mother believed and supported her daughter, she could not control abuses by the legal system, which implied that Holly may have lied about the abuse, or the media, which blamed Holly for injuring the Romana family. Although Holly's mother said, angrily, that her former husband "shouldn't receive a penny for raping his daughter" (CBS News 16 May 1994), the jury had nevertheless awarded him damages. In addition, after this verdict was announced, a television report by CBS implied that Holly, not her father, was responsible for destroying her family. A young female reporter asked Holly, "Do you feel sorry that you have destroyed your family?" but since this question was not addressed to Holly's father, the report left viewers with the impression that the victim, not the perpetrator, was responsible for the family's suffering. As illustrated by the Romana case, those of us who wish to support academic daughters who write autobiographically, especially about topics such as rape, must be aware that we cannot control the reception of student texts.

Nevertheless, I believe that feminist professors must support students who choose to speak out against their abusers while, at the same time, preparing them for negative responses from different audiences. The greatest danger is, of course, that victims of sexual violence will be accused of lying. Such accusations, as I know from experience, are even more damaging than the experience of sexual abuse itself. For, if a woman's reality is denied, it becomes difficult for her to assert her point of view with self-confidence. In other words, it is not only the reality that I was sexually abused as a child, but the fact that this reality was denied by my family, as well as by society, that for many years damaged my ability to speak or write with confidence. Fortunately, the emergence of the women's movement during my lifetime provided me with the healing presence of a community willing to believe my story and share my suffering. In other words, I found a safe space in the feminist community. Knowing the importance of this space, I believe that feminist professors must resist intimidation during a hostile political climate; instead, we must heighten our resolve to bear witness. Because the feminist professor has greater security and status than her students, she must accept responsibility for providing students with a "safe space." At the same time, she must recognize that this "safe space" is not inviolable. I recommend, therefore, that autobiographical writing never be required in classrooms; instead, it should be offered as an option. As I know from my own experience, such freedom of choice is essential.

Notes

1. Though not written for an academic audience, my next autobiographical essay, "Of Bread and Shadows, Beginnings," which appeared in an anthology of Norwegian-American writings, also illustrates how dangerous autobiographical writing can be. The piece received such mixed reviews from my family—it was praised by a sister, but condemned by an aunt who refused ever to speak to me again—that my anxieties about autobiographical writing only increased. When my aunt committed suicide on Father's Day some years later, I realized that the family secrets only hinted at in this essay had threatened her shaky public persona. Only in retrospect did I understand that she viewed herself as the protector of family secrets that I was threatening to reveal.

2. Linda Alcoff and Laura Gray give numerous examples of television talk shows, from "Phil Donahue" to "Sally Jessy Raphael," which deny the power of theoretical analysis to survivors of sexual violence. Alcoff and Gray describe a formulaic pattern of presentation which opens with emotional "confessions" by survivors—"The host of the show makes sure to ask questions that are sufficiently probing to get the survivors to cry on screen"—after which "the inevitable expert shows up; almost invariably a white man or woman with a middle-class and professional appearance, who, with a sympathetic but dispassionate air, explains to the audience the nature, symptoms, and possible therapies for such crimes of violence" (277). Through the use of this pattern, "survivors are reduced to victims, represented as pathetic objects who can only recount their experiences as if these are transparent, and who offer pitiable instantiations of the universal truth the experts reveal" (277). Their numerous examples include: ABC's "The Home Show," co-hosted by Gary Collins and Dana Fleming, September 10, 1990; "Sally Jessy Raphael," January 21, 1991; "Geraldo," November 14, 1989; and "Oprah Winfrey," April 14, 1988. Geraldo Rivera, whose shows "are often organized around having survivors, rather than perpetrators explain and defend them" (277), is the worst, while Oprah Winfrey, who does not allow women "to be put in the position of having to defend the truth of their stories or their own actions" and "does not always defer to an expert but presents herself as a survivor/expert" (278), is the best.

3. For example, in a review of Harriet Lerner's *The Dance of Deception*, Judith S Antrobus, who describes Lerner's style as "self-confessional" because she uses "examples from her own experience," says, "I suppose she does this to make you feel at home; the implication is that she knows how you feel because she's been there.... Yet I felt manipulated by Lerner's confessional style. What begins as a confession often ends up as self-congratulation" (28). Antrobus objects whether Lerner attributes her success "to luck" or describes it as "fame and glory" (28). To ascribe her success to luck is "a typical female disclaimer," according to Antrobus, while calling it fame and glory "seems over-inflated . . . and belies her stated modesty" (28). At least by Antrobus, Lerner is damned if she's modest and damned if she's immodest.

4. Susan L. Woods has given me permission to use her name and cite her unpublished paper.

5. What is the reason for such "episodic amnesia" in the history of the study of trauma? Neither changes in fashion nor loss of interest can account for such a pattern, according to Herman; the answer is that traumatic events force bystanders to take sides. As Herman points out, "It is very tempting to take the side of the perpetrator. All the perpetrator asks is that the bystander do nothing. . . . The victim, on the contrary, asks the bystander to share the burden of pain. The victim demands action, engagement, and remembering" (7).

Works Cited

Alcoff, Linda, and Laura Gray. "Survivor Discourse: Transgression or Recuperation." *Signs* 18.2 (Winter 1993): 260–90.

Antrobus, Judith S. "In Praise of Honesty." *The Women's Review of Books* XI.2 (November 1993): 28–9.

Bakhtin, Mikhail M. *The Dialogic Imagination.* Austin: University of Texas Press, 1981.

Baym, Nina. "The Madwoman and Her Languages: Why I Don't Do Feminist Literary Theory." *Tulsa Studies in Women's Literature* 3.1/2 (Spring/Fall 1984): 45–59.

Bloom, Lynn Z. "Teaching College English as a Woman." *College English* 54.7 (Fall 1992): 818–25.

Brown, Lyn Mikel, and Carol Gilligan. *Meeting at the Crossroads: Women's Psychology and Girls' Development.* New York: Ballantine Books, 1992.

Daly, Brenda. " 'I VIVIDLY REMEMBER, pretty well': A Witness Against Her Self." *Hurricane Alice* 1.2 (Fall/Winter 1983): 1–4.

———. "My Father, My Censor." *Nexus.* Eds. Diane Freedman and Olivia Frey. Under consideration by a university press.

————. "My Friend Joyce Carol Oates." *The Intimate Critique*. Eds. Diane Freedman, Olivia Frey, and Frances Murphy Zauhar. Chapel Hill, NC: Duke University Press, 1992. 163–73.

————. "Of Bread and Shadows, Beginnings." *There Lies a Fair Land: An Anthology of Norwegian-American Writings*. Ed. John Solensten. St. Paul, MN: New Rivers Press, 1985. 146–53.

Elbow, Peter. "Reflections on Academic Discourse: How It Relates to Freshmen and Colleagues." *College English* 53.2 (February 1991): 135–55.

Finke, Laurie. "The Rhetoric of Marginality: Why I Do Feminist Theory." *Tulsa Studies in Women's Literature* 5.2 (Fall 1986): 251–72.

Freedman, Diane. *An Alchemy of Genres*. Charlottesville, VA: University Press of Virginia, 1992.

Frye, Joanne. *Living Stories, Telling Lives: Women and the Novel in Contemporary Experience*. Ann Arbor, MI: University of Michigan Press, 1986.

Gallop, Jane. *Reading Lacan*. Ithaca: Cornell University Press, 1985.

Greene, Gayle. *Changing the Story: Feminist Fiction and the Tradition*. Bloomington: Indiana University Press, 1991.

Herman, Judith Lewis. *Trauma and Recovery*. New York: Basic Books, 1992.

hooks, bell. *Talking Back: Thinking Feminist, Thinking Black*. Boston, MA: South End Press, 1989.

Miller, Nancy K. *Getting Personal: Feminist Occasions and Other Autobiographical Acts*. New York: Routledge University Press, 1991.

Moffett, James. *Storm in the Mountains: A Case Study of Censorship, Conflict, and Consciousness*. Carbondale, IL: Southern Illinois University Press, 1988.

Patai, Daphne. "Point of View." *The Chronicle of Higher Education* 51.25 (February 23 1994): A52.

Schlafly, Phyllis. "Parents Speak Out Against Classroom Abuse." *Phyllis Schlafly Report* 18.1 (June 1985). Alton, IL: Eagle Trust Fund.

Terr, Lenore. *Unchained Memories: True Stories of Traumatic Memories, Lost and Found*. New York: Basic Books, 1994.

Tompkins, Jane. "Me and My Shadow." *New Literary History* 19 (1987): 169–78.

Woods, Sue. "Wagering It All in Double Jeopardy: Autobiography in a Graduate Paper." Presented at the Midwest Modern Language Association, 5 November 1993, Minneapolis, MN.

The Solace of Separation: Feminist Theory, Autobiography, Edith Wharton, and Me

Susan L. Woods

The lives and experiences of women are filled with empty spaces, and the writings by and about women reflect them. Recently, feminist critics such as Nancy Chodorow, Dorothy Dinnerstein, and Marianne Hirsch have enlightened us by reexamining and redefining these spaces. But what are the spaces, the gaps, in women's lives and women's writing, that these feminist critics have identified? Just as every woman is unique, the void and unvoiced in each woman's life will also be different. For me they include the ignored maternal subjective, the complexities of the mother-daughter relationship, and the survivor's perspective of the incestuous experience. Significantly, I choose to compensate for the cultural spaces inherent in my gender socialization through the control of my physical space. I find this need to control physical space a common theme in the lives and writings of women. For example, the riveting scene for me in Edith Wharton's *The Mother's Recompense* is the moment when Kate Clephane discovers her daughter and her former lover locked in a passionate embrace. This scene resonates with the silent and silenced subjects of women's lives: incest, the maternal subjective, and spatial definition and control.

—the orgasmic, incestuous moment . . .

> The young man's arms were around [Anne], her cheek was against his. . . . [Kate] felt the same embrace, felt the very texture of her lover's cheek against her own, burned with the heat of his palm as it clasped [her daughter's] chin to press her closer. (221)

—the complexities of the maternal subjective . . .

> A dark fermentation boiled up into her brain; every thought and feeling was clogged with thick entangling memories . . . Jealous? Was she jealous of her daughter? (221)

—the female need to control/define their space . . . .

> She must put the world between them—the whole width of the
> world was not enough. (221–22)

As I began to read the extensive literature available on the silent and silenced spaces of women's lives, I reflected on the gaps in my own life, both academic and personal. Edith Wharton's novel *The Mother's Recompense* exemplifies for me the interstices of women's relationships. In this paper I will first examine M. M. Bakhtin's theory of language in order to analyze how his concept of dialogism informs and enlightens a theoretical discussion of the maternal subjective, mother–daughter narratives, and incest in terms of spatial metaphors as signifiers of intersubjective relationships. Through an autobiographical reading of *The Mother's Recompense*, I will attempt to interpret the gendered significance of space as signified in Wharton's text and as I experience it in my life and work.

An important strategy of my academic writing has been to situate myself. After Virginia Woolf's "A Room of One's Own," I thought it important (or maybe I just liked hearing it) to let you know I had my own space. Echoes of this situational writing can be found in the writings of other feminist critics as well. In "Me and My Shadow," Jane Tompkins tells us where she is—"the birds outside my window . . . just myself as a person sitting here in stockinged feet, a little bit chilly because the windows are open, and thinking about going to the bathroom. But not going yet" (169). I have now reached a point in my life, however, where it is becoming increasingly difficult to define my space. Part of my family (a husband, two daughters, and two cats) live in Grinnell, a small town in Iowa; my son lives with his father in Bondurant, another, smaller town; and I divide my time between Grinnell and Ames, where I am attending graduate school, picking up my son every other weekend on my drive home. In a society where more is better, I am living a rather malformed adaptation of Woolf's dream. I not only have a room of my own, but I have acquired two homes, with special interest in a third.

There are many adjustments to be made in such an arrangement, especially since living out of suitcases can be fragmenting. Before I continue, I should clarify that my family has been very supportive of my efforts to complete a graduate degree and that I am fortunate in that both my "spaces" are comfortable and homey. That is not to say that this division, this parceling of my time and space, does not have its stresses. It does. I could spend the rest of this paper discussing the guilt associated with raising an eighteen- and a sixteen-year-old in absentia; however, my purpose here is to discuss gaps, more specifically the gap between my family and my research, my academic self and all those other selves I am and am not.

The division I experience in my personal life, a division I have reluctantly chosen, is also present in my academic life, a division I have not questioned. My academic writing has a particular style, a style developed as an undergraduate in the search for "the grade" and refined as a graduate student in the search for the "authoritative voice." I was fortunate as an undergraduate to be able to enroll in creative writing courses as an outlet for my personal voice. So, while I was writing analyses of the complexity of Portia's character in *The Merchant of Venice,* I was simultaneously developing the character of a child molester for one of my short stories (the rewriting of a personal experience). Both of my voices, the academic/authoritative and the personal/experiential, had their outlet. But they were never integrated. Although Portia and Pecola, and Touchstone and Tea Cake, intrigued me as much as the characters I imagined for my short fiction, I would not (or could not) write about them in the same way.

The reason I am experiencing this separation of my academic and personal voice can be explained by M.M. Bakhtin's theory of language. According to Bakhtin in *The Dialogic Imagination,* all languages exist as heteroglots. With this definition, the context of an utterance is given primacy over the text itself. At any given moment, a series of conditions (social, chronological, spatial, etc.) place internal and external pressure on utterances, insuring that a word uttered in a particular place and at a particular time will have a different meaning from the same word uttered in different places and at different times. Bakhtin calls these forces centripetal and centrifugal because they simultaneously strive to centralize and decentralize language. The novel (and my own short stories), Bakhtin argues, is a centrifugal force while criticism, an attempted controlling of language, is centripetal. As a result of the presence of these forces, the incongruities, spaces and gaps, of a culture's language are illuminated. In my own life, I find myself moving between these two forces, reading the decentralized word then writing about that word in an academic, centralized language. My language is further divided between my academic and my personal spaces.

My answer to this problem of division is to attempt what Bakhtin calls dialogism—in this instance, an attempt to fill the space between my theoretical/critical and personal/creative voices, to write myself a new place. In dialogic language "everything means, is understood, as a part of a greater whole—there is a constant interaction between meanings," and no one stratification of language is privileged over another (Bakhtin 426). The result of dialogism is the reflection of the incongruities between languages. Perhaps this form of writing, then, is simply another attempt at controlling space, at creating a space of my own.

I turn my attention now to an analysis of spatial signifiers in Edith Wharton's *The Mother's Recompense,* specifically to the critical dissatisfaction with the ending of the novel. While others interpret the heroine as a martyr, I read her character as a maturing woman who achieves independence through the controlling of her personal space. I empathize with her choice to live apart from her daughter and former lover. Such empathy probably stems from the fact that I currently choose to live apart from my family. Perhaps a dialogic discussion of the various interpretations of the novel would, as Bakhtin predicts, open up a new space for understanding, a re-thinking of the text and a re-visioning, not only of Kate Clephane, but of all women who struggle, as I do, to move from victim to survivor.[1] Because Bakhtin's understanding of language is so closely aligned with feminist theory, as in the concepts of otherness, hierarchies, and power/victimization, the act of placing the devalued personal voice alongside the powerful academic voice may reveal strengths in both. I intend, therefore, to discuss the struggle for voice/space in the novel, especially as that struggle exists for women (mothers and daughters) who are incest survivors, a theme present in the novel (and most of Wharton's other works), as well as in Wharton's and my own life. I propose that Wharton, in an attempt to imagine an alternative to the Freudian concept of the phallus, employs what Jessica Benjamin in *The Bonds of Love* calls a spatial metaphor, liberating the oppressed otherness of language and gender. Wharton's heroine comes finally to exist *as* Bakhtin's dialogic, free from the centrifugal forces of patriarchal language and space.

But what am I to do with those who say I cannot (must not) do this? With those who believe there is no place for the personal in academic criticism? Again, Tompkins' essay helped me find an answer. Throughout her essay, Tompkins develops tension in the text with the interjections that she is thinking about going to the bathroom but "not going yet." It is this tension that prompts readers like Nancy K. Miller to ask what this essay is about. "Is it about going to the bathroom? Or is it about the conditions of critical authority? Or are they the same question?" (Miller 7). For me, this confusion about authority and bodily functions began at an early age. I was nearly six years old when the neighbor boy told me that I couldn't go to the bathroom standing up and he could. This made no sense to me. Of course I could, if I wanted to. And at that moment, with little Johnny staring down at me from the other side of my own teeter-totter, I really wanted to. So, I did. I jumped off the teeter-totter, sending Johnny crashing to the ground, spread my legs and let go. Johnny told me it didn't count. I had been too messy. But I was determined that, with practice, someday I would be as good at it as he was. Well, now Johnny owns one of the largest florist businesses in Des Moines and I search for authority in academia instead of on the playground. (Or are they the same thing?) So, for those who would tell me I can't write in this genre and be taken seriously, my response is, of course I can. Things may get a little messy, though—at least until I have some practice.

I: A Personal Reading

Coming home is always hectic. I suffer from mothering withdrawal. Like Kate Clephane, I have this schizophrenic fear that, because of my absence, either the family will have fallen into complete chaos or they will have gotten along just fine without me, thank you very much. I'm still not sure which would be harder for me to accept. The sun is shining today, and the bedroom has windows on two walls which let in the pasture. It's the middle of April and too cold to open up the house. But the sun is warm, and I fight off sleep. Wharton criticism is spread out on the peach coverlet. As I reread the ending of The Mother's Recompense *for the fourth time, I suddenly think of Grandfather.*

Grandpa was a crusty old man. He married Grandma when she was sixteen. He lost his right hand in a hunting accident. He took me skeet shooting. He was diabetic and bald. I loved him. One night my mother turned to my sister and me and told us that Grandpa was getting old. Sometimes, she explained, old men do things they shouldn't with little girls. If Grandpa ever did anything like that with either one of us, we were to tell her. My first thought was—How did she find out? Grandpa loved me in a special way, holding me on his lap on the front porch swing, his hand slipping under my blouse and rubbing the training bra I was so proud of. Somehow my mother had found out, and now he was going to get into trouble. Like the heroine of the novel, I waffled between the need for others to know and resolve this tension and my need to avoid "sterile pain." I had to be very careful. This was wrong and I couldn't imagine what would happen if anyone found out. I had to protect Grandpa from my mother, from that all powerful mother who knew things instinctually.

But why this reading? What in the text has stirred such powerful memories? How is my response to the novel affected by personal experience? Bear with me as I explore the questions raised by my reading of the novel, questions this paper attempts to answer. In part, I have a strong affinity with Kate Clephane because I choose to exist separate from my daughters. I have come to realize that the process of my own individuation requires a bending, if not breaking, of the maternal bond. Similarly, I respond strongly to the novel's incest motif. True, one could argue that the ambiguous nature of incest in the novel hardly compares with the violation of grandfather-granddaughter incest.[2] And yet, the very violation of the limits of the incest taboo are so overpowering that, as a survivor, incest motifs raise internalized fears of re-engulfment by the perpetrator. Therefore, in reading this novel, I find myself pulled between insatiable desires—to either abandon or be subsumed by motherhood—to respond to incest with either the red eyes of Beatrice Cenci or the loving eyes of Anne Clephane.

Finally, I respond strongly to the novel's resolution, to Kate's decision to return to Europe. You see, I also resolved the problem with my grandfather, but at a great cost. Never again did I sit with Grandpa on the front porch swing. Instead, I took frequent walks to the drugstore uptown for a cherry coke and explored the railroad tracks that ran alongside the house. In the winter, I sat in the parlor with Grandma and mother

*where I learned to knit and crochet. More than once I heard Grandma comment on how
ladylike I was becoming. I would never have traded my relationship with Grandpa for
my skills at needlework. But knowing Grandpa was safe, knowing I was safe, knowing
my mother was safe was recompense enough for all that separation. The crafts of women
hold such sorrow for me.*

II: Intervals/Interstices/Incest

(The place I am is my home in Ames. The house, which I share with an
English professor, sits at the edge of a small woods; windows line the northwest
wall. The property has a steep slope down to a creek, and the windows set the
living room right in the treetops. But, unlike Tompkins, I'm not faced with "a
floor to ceiling rectangle filled with green, with one red leaf" ("Me and My
Shadow" 30). The winter has been unusually long. This is the last day of
March, and it has been raining for three days. The weather channel predicts
snow tomorrow. But, as I sit here thinking about Edith Wharton's *The Mother's
Recompense*, I find I'm glad that the sky is overcast today. Maybe I feel a little
like Kate Clephane. The sun would be a distraction.)

The opening of *The Mother's Recompense* finds Kate Clephane distracted
"by the slant of the Riviera sun across her bed" (3). Kate has taken up
residence with a band of social outcasts, a group of gamblers, alcoholics, and
people, mostly women, with something to hide. Kate's secret is the abandonment of her husband and infant daughter nearly twenty years before the start
of the novel. Fleeing from what she considers an impossible situation, a controlling husband and an oppressive Victorian society, a society that conceals,
Kate leaves New York with Hylton Davies. After their short, two-year affair,
Kate remains in Europe. Her attempts to re-establish her relationship with her
daughter are thwarted by her in-laws, her letters returned unopened.

Following the death of Kate's ex-husband and mother-in-law, Kate's now
wealthy daughter, Anne, invites her mother to return to New York and live with
her in the family home. The reunion is everything Kate could have hoped for.
She not only re-experiences the joy of her daughter, but polite New York
society avoids any reference to her sordid past. The mother-daughter reunion,
however, is also complicated by many factors: living in the patriarchal house of
her ex-husband, a house that recalls many painful memories; the unforeseen
independence of Anne as a result of Kate's absence during her childhood; and,
most importantly, Anne's engagement to her mother's former lover. Kate's first
response to Anne's engagement is to attempt to stop the wedding, a union Kate
views as incestuous. Failing this, Kate accepts their marriage, refuses a marriage
proposal of her own from the stuffy Fred Landers, and returns to the Riviera,
maintaining contact with Anne and Fred through frequent letters.

It is this ending, this returning to France, that critics have made problematic for me. Unlike many who critique the novel, I find the ending satisfying, my satisfaction rooted in the need to control my space and my identity. (I am unsure where this need comes from—the pressures of the maternal role?—the result of an incestuous experience?) However, in his 1986 introduction to the republication of *The Mother's Recompense*, Louis Auchincloss finds fault with the novel's accessibility to the reader of today:

> Kate is making too much of the circumstance. Her horror approaches the horror of Oedipus when he learns that he has married his mother. Kate, like Hamlet in T.S. Eliot's essay, "is dominated by an emotion which is inexpressible because it is in excess of the facts as they appear." (ix)

Similarly, Marianne Hirsch, in *The Mother/Daughter Plot: Narrative, Psychoanalysis, Feminism*, criticizes Wharton for "fail[ing] to redefine the terms of the daughterly. . . text" (121). Hirsch interprets Kate's actions as "underscor[ing] the compulsory heterosexuality and triangularity" of mother-daughter plots (121). As a "reader of today," I dismiss Auchincloss' criticism based on the fact that I did not struggle with Kate's reaction. Although I agree with Hirsch that Wharton fails to redefine the daughterly text, I understand Wharton to be foregrounding the maternal subjective, a move that Hirsch calls for. Cynthia Griffin Wolff believes that the ending *punishes* Kate by permanently exiling her for refusing Fred Lander's marriage proposal and a return to New York society. This interpretation, however, strips Kate of the power of choice. It is the ability finally to choose her own destiny that offers Kate, and me, comfort at the novel's conclusion.

Lev Raphael takes a different approach in *Edith Wharton's Prisoners of Shame*. For Raphael, Kate's actions are determined by shame, a crippling emotion that leaves the mother with no alternatives. While Raphael does understand the ending to be a happy one, he finds little recompense of his own in that fact. "Wharton's happy ending does little to counteract the negative arc of the book" (52). While I agree that Kate's earlier actions were motivated by shame, I believe a marriage to Fred Landers, a man she did not truly love, to be a far more shameful choice. By contrast, my own interpretation finds a measure of agreement in Katherine Joslin's *Edith Wharton*. Joslin understands the ending as I do:

> Kate Clephane's 'recompense' is an understanding of her 'desolation,' her place in society as a woman outside the traditional roles. . . . She is not Mrs. John Clephane nor is she Mrs. Fred Landers; she is Kate Clephane. In her return to Europe, she reembraces her expatriate self. Wharton draws for us

> a portrait, not of a young lady, but of an aging woman, who comes to
> recognize and accept the delicate nature of her life in middle age. (127)

I view Kate's decision to live apart from the oppressive New York society, apart
from her ex-lover, even apart from her potentially controlling daughter, as
representative of her first completely independent action, her understanding of
the complexity of the mother/daughter relationship, and her need to control
her physical space. Perhaps my understanding of the novel requires the reader
to be "older," a reader facing the delicate nature of her own middle age.
Perhaps it harkens back to my own struggle with defining my space.

A spatial alternative, as mentioned above, to the "hegemony of the phallus
as the sole embodiment of desire" is offered by Jessica Benjamin in *The Bonds
of Love* (86). According to the traditional Freudian proposition, femininity is
defined as not masculine, by what a woman lacks—the phallus. In this interpretation of gender identity, the penis symbolizes power and individuation, the
only way to find subjectivity. However, Freud was unable to imagine an
alternative female symbol of subjectivity. The feminine, instead, is represented
by sacrificial motherhood. This emphasis on motherhood as sacrificial and
passive results in the female loss of subjectivity.

While Freud failed to recognize the influence of culture on the development of gender roles, Benjamin proposes a cultural analysis of the phallus.
In a society where mothers are the primary caretakers of children, the phallus
comes to represent, to both sexes, the powerful outside world as well as a
weapon against the powerful, idolized mother. Penis envy then becomes the
desire of the woman to exist spatially in a public place, to be granted recognition and subjectivity. Benjamin's female alternative to the phallus is the
"intersubjective model."[3] She explains that the phallus, the "intrapsychic model,"
establishes difference between *I* and *you*, while the intersubjective model establishes recognition *between* and *within*. Benjamin's model, based on mutuality
and recognition, is a spatial metaphor that counters Freud's symbol of the
phallus, based on separateness and power:

> The significance of the spatial metaphor for a woman is likely to be in just this
> discovery of her *own*, *inner* desire, without fear of impingement, intrusion, or
> violation. . . . Certainly, woman's desire to be known and to find her own inner
> [as well as public] space can be, and often is, symbolically apprehended in terms
> of penetration. But it can also be expressed as the wish for an open space into
> which the interior self may emerge, like Venus from the sea. (128–9)

Slowly, Kate, unlike thousands of traditional male heroes, comes to
recognize the otherness of her daughter and, therefore, the need of each
woman to determine her own space. Initially, the differentiation between

mother and daughter is obscured. The mother in Kate admits to the fact that she still likes being "mothered." She envisions Anne as part of herself, "that other half of her life, the half she had dreamed of and never lived" (60). Kate is even willing to sacrifice her own existence for her relationship with her daughter. "To see Anne living [her life] would be almost the same as if it were her own" (60).

> To be with Anne, to play the part of Anne's mother—the one part, she now saw, that fate had meant her for—that was what she wanted with all her starved and world-worn soul. To be the *background*, the *atmosphere*, of her daughter's life; to depend on Anne, to feel that Anne depended on her; it was the one perfect companionship she had ever known. . . . (emphasis mine 69)

The result of such a concept of motherhood is the denial of subjectivity, reducing Kate to a metaphysical state in which she is subsumed. When Kate finally accepts her daughter's and her own individuality, each woman can exist outside their relationship to each other, in a separate space. Where, previously, Kate's world revolved around the men in her life (John Clephane, Hylton Davies, Chris Fenno, Fred Landers) she now begins to desire her own place in that public world. No longer in a psychological place where she is defined by her role as wife or mother, as Joslin says, Kate comes to live fully in her individuality.

The moment of her liberation comes when Kate recognizes and rejects the monologic language/space, with all its repressive forces, of the father/husband. This repression is represented by the monologic language of the law and enacted through the return of Kate's letters, in which she pleads to see her daughter, by her husband's law firm. It is this monologic language that Kate is forced to appropriate by a daughter who places her in the father's role at her wedding:

> "Your mother seems to think it's your uncle who ought to give you away."
> "Not you, mother?" . . .
> "I want what you want." Their thin-edged smiles seemed to cross like blades. (235)

Kate's discomfort with this role—the role of the father—and the language it represents is related to her subsequent choice to live in Europe, among various peoples of various languages, a choice exemplifying her rejection of patriarchal language.[4] Finally, in this dialogic space, Kate exists for her daughter, Fred Landers, and others, *as* language, her only representation being in the form of letters. Having declared her separateness from her daughter, her former lover, her potential lover, and the monologic language system they all employ, Kate creates her own distinct space, her own world, and, through epistolary language, encourages others to relate to her dialogically. Unlike the monologic language of the law, dialogic language, based on the recognition of otherness, always anticipates a response. Kate's letters, a representation of dialogism, expect and receive responses.

The incest motif in the novel, a theme closely tied to the mother-daughter relationship, is also represented through spatial metaphor. Benjamin states that the spatial metaphor is frequently used when women "try to attain a sense of their sexual subjectivity":

> For example, a woman who was beginning to detach herself from her enthrallment to a seductive father began to dream of rooms. She began to look forward to traveling alone, to the feeling of containment and freedom as she flew in an airplane, to being alone and anonymous in her hotel room. Here, she imagined, she would find a kind of aloneness that would allow her to look into herself. (128)

Obviously, the attainment of sexual subjectivity is further complicated, if not completely compromised, by an incestuous experience. Here, then, is another connection between Edith Wharton, Kate Clephane, and myself. All of us experienced the spatial violation of incest, whether actual or fantasized, and, in an attempt to "detach" ourselves from that experience and those memories, we anticipate and enjoy our moments alone: Edith Wharton in Ste. Claire-le-Chateau, a converted monastery on the Riviera; Kate Clephane in the Petit Palais; and me in my Grandmother's parlor, or walking uptown, or in Ames, Iowa, anywhere except the front porch swing. For it is in these open spaces that women discover their "own, inner desire, without fear of impingement, intrusion, or violation" (Benjamin 128).

An acquaintance with a breadth of Wharton's work will most assuredly reveal the author's preoccupation with the incest theme.[5] Perhaps the most famous of Wharton's incestuous writings is the "Beatrice Palmato" plot summary and "Unpublished Fragment." "Beatrice Palmato" outlines a story in which the father, left in charge of his young daughter because of the mother's mental instability, educates her, during which time a deep intimacy develops. At age eighteen, the daughter marries a man who is obviously her intellectual inferior. The father dies when Beatrice is twenty. After the birth of their own daughter, Beatrice displays an abnormal jealousy of her husband and daughter's relationship. During a moment of epiphany, the husband comes to understand the incestuous relationship between Beatrice and her father. The story ends with Beatrice's suicide, followed by an intimate discussion between Beatrice's husband and the brother of Mr. Palmato.

Interestingly, there are several similarities between the "Beatrice Palmato" outline and Wharton's personal life. Like Beatrice, Wharton's father was instrumental in her education. Her father not only taught her to read and introduced her to literature, but Wharton began to look on him as the source of her own literary inspiration. Her father's library was open to her and, though her mother did not allow her the raciness of novels, she took advantage of the library's store of Elizabethan and classical literature. Her romanticized view of the patriarchal library occasioned her to write, "Whenever I try to recall my childhood it is in my father's library that it comes to life. I am squatting on the thick Turkey rug . . . dragging out book after book in a secret ecstasy of communion. . . . There was in me a secret retreat where I wished no one to intrude" ("Life and I" 69–70). Wharton, like Beatrice, is twenty when her father dies. A second similarity is that both Wharton and Beatrice Palmato marry inferior men. It is well known that Wharton's friends were surprised by her union with Teddy. After a rocky start in which consummation of the marriage was delayed for several weeks, Edith and Teddy lived virtually celibate lives. Further, the name Beatrice Palmato is most probably an allusion to Beatrice Cenci, a sixteenth-century Roman woman involved in a plot to murder her incestuous father.[6] Red-eyed Beatrice Cenci, in fact, makes an appearance in *The Mother's Recompense* in the form of a classical portrait hanging above the double bed of Kate Clephane when she returns to New York.

While the "Beatrice Palmato" revolves around the incest theme, complicated by the similarities to both the Beatrice Cenci story and Wharton's own life, the "Unpublished Fragment" is an explicitly erotic depiction of father-daughter incest, a depiction that portrays the daughter as fully sexualized and excited by the culmination of father-daughter intimacy.

> But she hardly heard him, for the old swooning sweetness was creeping over her. As his hand stole higher she felt the secret bud of her body swelling, yearning, quivering hotly to burst into bloom. . . . The sensation was so exquisite that she could have asked to have it indefinitely prolonged. . . . (Erlich 175)

Cynthia Griffin Wolff, who first discovered the "Beatrice Palmato" and "Unpublished Fragment" at the Bernicke Library at Yale University, dates these writings at 1919–20, just prior to the publication of *The Mother's Recompense*. Wolff goes on to maintain that both pieces should be interpreted as fiction. It would be useless to speculate whether or not Wharton herself was a victim of incest, an accusation that, at this point, could be neither proved nor disproved. Some critics read Wharton's incest themes, present in not only *The Mother's Recompense* but a variety of Wharton novels, as a demonstration of the author's own victimization. However, whether Wharton's incest motifs are a result of her being a victim of actual incest or of the Victorian social constraints to repress sexuality, both her life and her work are emblazoned with what is today understood to be a pattern of behavior common to present-day incest survivors.[7]

Several of the eccentricities of Wharton's life including the repression of all sexual knowledge, her subsequent sexual abstinence, and a variety of psychosomatic illnesses can be explained by presuming the hypothesis that Edith, as a young girl, was the victim of an incestuous relationship. Wharton suffered from a pattern of illnesses common to incest survivors: phobias, mood swings, severe reactions to temperature changes, nausea, asthma, and anorexia. Wharton writes, in 1908, to her friend Sara Norton:

> For twelve years I seldom knew what it was to be, for more than an hour or two of the twenty-four, without an intense feeling of nausea, and such unutterable fatigue that when I got up I was always more tired than when I lay down. This form of neurasthenia consumed the best years of my youth, and left, in some sort, an irreparable shade on my life. (Lewis 139)

Neurasthenia, a popular diagnosis for upper-class Victorian women, was thought to be the result of an overexertion of energy, perhaps brought on by the sexual repressiveness of Victorian codes of conduct. It should be mentioned that neurasthenia was often cured by a profession. For example, Jane Addams suffered from this disease for eight years until she founded Hull House. Whether or not Wharton's disease was the direct result of an incestuous experience, as a highly intelligent and ambitious woman she would naturally suffer from the confusion presented by the juxtaposition of her literary self against the ideal of the refined Victorian woman.

While much of this discussion has focused on Wharton and her relationship with her father (a discussion that exemplifies Benjamin's interpretation of the phallus as symbolic of the outside world and penis envy as the daughter's desire of a place in that world), it is important to understand the complexities of the mother's role as well.[8] Erlich addresses Wharton's complicated relationship with her mother. In her book, Erlich discusses the employment of nannies and their effects upon children in upper class New York society. While Erlich describes in detail the animosity between Wharton and her mother, she cannot be certain of its origin:

> This exaggerated sense of guilt must have derived from the idea that she deserved punishment for some injury to her mother—perhaps by regarding Nanny Doyley as her psychological mother, perhaps by trying to become her

father's sweetheart. The denial and sacrifice of her own sexuality for so many years suggest atonement for a strong oedipal rivalry with her mother. (125)

Erlich goes on to say that the presence (intrusion) of the nanny could have resulted in an unresolved oedipal phase, "making space in the child's psyche for unusually florid incestuous fantasies" (31). While I find theorizing about the importance and consequence of the nanny in Wharton's life fascinating, I find this type of conjecturing no less 'reaching' than to entertain the possibility of father-daughter incest. In fact, Erlich goes on to imagine just this possibility.

Erlich raises the possibility of father-daughter incest to explain Wharton's peculiar habit as a child to "make up." Wharton wrote, in "Life and I," about her attempts to behave as other children. Bearing the mundane play of childhood for as long as she could, Wharton would find it necessary to retire to her mother's bedroom where, with selected books from her father's library, she would pace the floor, making up stories even before she could read.

> And in another instant I would be shut up in her bedroom, & measuring the floor with rapid strides, while I poured out . . . the accumulated floods of my pent-up eloquence. Oh, the exquisite relief of those moments of escape. (12–13)

This need to have the mother witness, and perhaps resolve, the tension brought from the library strongly suggests an incestuous experience. It is also representative of the dialogic act. For Wharton, in an attempt to liberate herself from the controlling language of patriarchy, of the father's library, enacted these scenes of "making up" before she was able to read. She was able to juxtapose the hegemonic language of the father, represented in the books she carried, alongside the suppressed voice of the Victorian female child. (Similarly, in an attempt to liberate myself from the controlling language of patriarchy, I juxtapose the hegemonic language of criticism alongside the suppressed voice of personal experience.)

And so I am left with a montage, bits of Wharton's life—an intelligent, frustrated child, an erotic and aging author. I am left also with my frustration with the criticism of the ending of *The Mother's Recompense* in which Kate chooses to live in a separate place from her daughter. I admire Kate's choice of the solace of separation. But is mine a misreading? What have I missed? I gain some comfort from the fact that Wharton herself was frustrated by these same questions. Louis Auchincloss, in *Edith Wharton: A Woman in Her Time,* states that, with her later fiction, critics began to write about a "drop in quality of Edith's fiction" (171). Wharton, concerned about their remarks, responds in a letter:

Thank you ever so fondly for taking the trouble to tell me why you like my book. Your liking it would be a great joy, but to know why is a subtle consolation for densities of incomprehension which were really beginning to discourage me. No one else has noticed "Desolation is a delicate thing" [the quotation on the title page] or understood that the key is there. The title causes great perplexity. . . . You will wonder that the priestess of the life of reason should take such things to heart, and I wonder too. I never have minded before, but as my work reaches its close, I feel so sure that it is either nothing or far more than they know. And I wonder a little desolately which. (Lewis 483)

And so it is with my own reading. It is either nothing or far more. While others tell me I *Ought to!* live and read in the spaces society has assigned for me, I find solace in the fact that separation, whether from my family or from other critics, is recompensed by the growth of reason in my own life. Up to this point, I feel neither the desolation nor the doubt that Wharton expresses, but I anticipate that, someday, I might.

III: Interstate 80, Near Newton, Iowa: A Journey Toward the Integrated Voice

It's seventy minutes from Grinnell to Ames and I enjoy the time alone. My car is equipped with a tape deck, and I once listened to all of *Winesburg, Ohio* en commute. Sometimes I tune into Rush Limbaugh. (I teach a composition class on argumentative writing and it's good for me to listen to the opposing viewpoint.) The drive in December is especially long due to the cold weather and the early sunsets. I blame December for my passing interest in country music and the fact that I know all the lyrics to several Randy Travis songs. The car speeds along at 68 miles per hour, and sometimes I pass Colfax or Mitchellville without even realizing it. It wasn't always this easy. The first time I left I cried. Commuting is easier now, and, because it is, I don't get letters anymore. But, like Kate Clephane, I do miss the letters. Being so self-sufficient is lonely.

May is a lovely month. The sogginess of spring is over. The land is drier and a deeper green. I roll the car window down an inch or two and let the wind blow on my hair. On this particular drive I think about *The Mother's Recompense* and my Grandpa, about Kate Clephane and myself. I understand my reading now, my comfort in Kate's "desolation." This is the novel as I, too, would have written it, as I did write it in my own experience with my Grandfather, as I rewrite it now in my continuing re-examination of that and other relationships.

The concept of rewriting is present in the ending of *The Mother's Recompense* when Kate feels as though "she had . . . simply turned back a chapter, and begun again at the top of the same dull page" (261). Aline, Kate's maid, then poses a relevant question—"What was the good of all the fuss if it was to end in *this*?" (261). The good of it is not the ending. The recompense is in the writing and the rewriting of it, in the control of space and language. As Kate considers it philosophically, the good of it is that "To begin with, it had been her own *choice* . . . and that in itself was a help" (emphasis mine 262). *Desolation* by choice, a privilege not often given to the incest victim, *is a delicate thing*. As delicate as the afghans and doilies in my hope chest.

The incest theme in *The Mother's Recompense* is, as Erlich defines it, oblique, "incest at one remove from technical actuality" (146). This helps to explain Auchincloss' remark that "Kate is making too much of the circumstance. . . . the prospect of a sexual union between Anne and Chris Fenno [is not] sufficiently revolting to cause Kate such trauma" (ix). Yet, I realize now that the incest theme does not simply lie in the relationship of these two characters. Kate and Anne both have desires for the other that border on the sexual. Further, the definition of the characters with whom Kate is involved is often vague—"Why, in the very act of thinking of her daughter had she suddenly strayed away into thinking of Chris?" (73). Anne and Chris are reciprocal characters in Kate's incest motif. The story opens on Kate's anticipation of a telegram from Chris Fenno begging her to "*Take me back*" (7). A telegram does arrive with a message offering reunion; however, instead of coming from the former lover, it comes from Anne. "*I want you* to come home at once"—and again—"*I want you* to come and live with me" (emphasis mine 10).

At the moment of reunion, Kate experiences her now adult daughter in a physical and sensual way:

> She thirsted to have the girl to herself, where she could touch her hair, stroke her face, draw the gloves from her hands, kiss her over and over again, and little by little, from that tall black-swathed figure, disengage the round child's body she had so long continued to feel against her own. (30)

Later, after Anne's engagement to Chris Fenno, Kate walks in on the two young lovers embracing each other and responds with jealousy. I would suggest Kate's jealousy is as much for the (physical) love of her daughter as it is for her lost lover. Anne is attracted to her mother, as well. Falling easily into the role of lover, Anne usurps the father's character by (re)giving her mother the family jewels for her coming out into New York society. With echoes of the father's manipulative love, Anne attaches a note instructing "Darling, these belong to you. Please wear some of them tonight . . ." (63).

Given the oedipal twist Wharton places on these characters, separation is the only option open to Kate Clephane, an option that Wharton also chose, and the only option I could imagine in my own life. After Wharton's divorce, the author developed a circle of friends not unlike the outcasts Kate Clephane befriended. Among these were Gaillard Lapsley, Howard Sturgis, Robert Norton, and Percy Lubbock. All far younger than Wharton, the group revolved around her, and she spent her later years in Europe, fiercely independent yet flirting and being fussed over.

Perhaps Wharton, like Kate and myself, found solace in separation, in the control of her space. Kate Clephane had previously sought her identity by establishing relationships with men (husband, lovers, boyfriend) and, thereby, with what she believed she lacked (power, penis, personhood). Through separation and the establishment of her own space, Kate chooses to find her subjectivity not in what she lacks but, rather, in what she is. *The Mother's Recompense* is, perhaps, also a rewriting of Wharton's own incestuous experience (perceived or actual), an attempt to re-imagine her family relationships. In this way, Wharton writes a story where everyone wins. Anne gets to have the lover-father, a desire directly expressed in the "Unpublished Fragment," in Wharton's feelings for her father, and in my own love for my Grandfather. Rewriting her life experience resolves Wharton's dilemma with incest, filling the gap between the "Beatrice Palmato" story line, the suicidal horror of the incest victim, and the "Unpublished Fragment," "the daughter's pleasure in bringing to climax a lifetime of paternal seduction" (Erlich 37). Kate is recompensed by the control of her life, her space, and her language, a control that is vital to the incest survivor (I imagine her walking uptown for a cherry coke), while Anne's recompense is the continued relationship with the incestuous parent (sitting on a front porch swing talking about skeet shooting). It also occurs to me, as I (re)write my own incest experience, the recompense for the separation from my grandfather was my knowledge of our safety. Similarly, Kate is recompensed with the knowledge of Anne's safety from "sterile pain."

IV: Shutting away in a little space of peace and light is the best thing that had ever happened . . . . (*The Mother's Recompense* 272)

Twice during my many journeys between my two homes, my two spaces, I have been surprised. At mile marker 153 of I-80, the ditch along the south side of the interstate slopes up, reaching toward the cornfield on the other side of the fence. The ditch is blanketed with prairie grass native to Iowa, which revolves around the color wheel of nature's seasons. In the spring the slope is chartreuse, the color of Easter grass.

By the fourth of July, it has darkened to an emerald green. August turns the ditch to a burnished red, and, by November, it is the color of wheat. The first surprise was in December. The snow-covered slope was white but not without color for, in the middle of this grassy embankment, there stands a solitary pine tree exquisitely shaped. It was a week before Christmas, and the tree stood fully decorated for the holiday. Complete with red and silver garlands, ornate bulbs, and wrapped gifts nestled beneath its lowest branches, the tree rose above the traffic. There are no structures built close to this spot, no houses or businesses, and I am convinced that the tree was decorated just for me. The hair rose on the back of my neck as I thought, perhaps, I was the only one who saw it.

The second surprise came this spring as I first began writing this paper. Easter was a week away, and, as I drove the seventy miles between Grinnell and Ames, I again noticed the tree. This time it was covered with brightly colored Easter eggs hanging from silver threads. Did anyone else see it? If, as I imagine, I am the only person to notice this solitary tree growing on this strip of pasture, the surprise comes from such a private revelation in such a public space—the same surprise I feel in the autobiographical moment of an academic essay. Therefore, if I am not completely comfortable in the restrictions of my respective spaces and voices, I find solace in the fact that, sometimes, when travelling between them, there is joy in the open spaces of the journey.

Notes

1. I make a distinction here between dialogic and revisionary, between Bakhtin and Adrienne Rich. According to Rich, revision involves entering the text from a new perspective with an understanding of the cultural assumptions that both inform and limit us. Bakhtin's dialogism requires entering the text in search of conflicting cultural codes clothed in language. As a feminist, I would adopt Rich's revisionary stance in all critical reading whether or not I am employed in dialogic criticism.

2. Others, including some who have read this essay, might minimize the sexual abuse I describe by stating that my grandfather's preoccupation with my bra is innocent of incestuous intent. In response, I use Ellen Bass and Laura Davis' definition of incest which does not require penile penetration for victimization to occur. In the words of the authors, "the severity of abuse should not be defined in terms of male genitals. Violation is determined by [the victim's] experience as a child. . . . The precise physical acts are not always the most damaging aspects of abuse. Although forcible rape is physically excruciating to a small child, many kinds of sexual abuse are not physically painful. They do not leave visible scars" (21).

3. Benjamin's intersubjective model is similar to Bakhtin's dialogism in that both recognize the influence of culture and depend on a recognition of other. As Benjamin states, "intersubjective theory describes capacities that emerge in the interaction between self and others. [The self] sees its aloneness as a particular point in the spectrum of relationships rather than as the original 'natural' state of the individual" (*Bonds of Love* 20).

4. An argument could be made here that Kate's associations in Europe represent the carnivalesque as defined by Bakhtin. Mrs. Plush, Mrs. Minity and Lord Charles, because of the various roles they play and secrets they keep, are representative of Bakhtin's mask of carnival.

5. Incest motifs can be found in *The House of Mirth, Hudson River Bracketed, Summer, The Gods Arrive,* and *The Mother's Recompense.* For a full discussion of the presence of this motif in these works see Gloria Erlich's *The Sexual Education of Edith Wharton.* Other critics who have also recognized and addressed this theme include Cynthia Griffin Wolff in *Feast of Words* and Adeline R. Tintner in *Mothers, Daughters and Incest in the Late Novels of Edith Wharton.*

6. In a fascinating side note, Beatrice Cenci and Edith Wharton's mothers were both named Lucretia.

7. For a full discussion of the pattern of behavior common to present-day incest survivors, especially as it pertains to the survivors' tendency to establish controlling relationships with men, see Ellen Bass and Laura Davis' *The Courage to Heal: A Guide for Women Survivors of Child Sexual Abuse.*

8. Marianne Hirsch also discusses how the maternal role in *The Mother's Recompense* underscores the compulsory heterosexual paradigm, in *The Mother/Daughter Plot: Narrative, Psychoanalysis, Feminism.*

Works Cited

Auchincloss, Louis. *Edith Wharton: A Woman in Her Time.* New York: Viking Press, 1971.

Bakhtin, M.M. *The Dialogic Imagination.* Trans. Caryl Emerson and Michael Holquist. Austin: University of Texas Press, 1981.

Bass, Ellen, and Laura Davis. *The Courage to Heal: A Guide for Women Survivors of Child Sexual Abuse.* New York: Harper and Row, 1988.

Baym, Nina. "Melodramas of Beset Manhood." *Feminism and American Literary History.* New Brunswick: Rutgers University Press, 1992. 3–18.

———. "The Madwoman and Her Languages." *Feminism and American Literary History.* New Brunswick: Rutgers University Press, 1992. 199–213.

Benjamin, Jessica. *The Bonds of Love: Psychoanalysis, Feminism, and the Problem of Domination.* New York: Pantheon, 1988.

Daly, Brenda O. "I Stand Here Naked, and Best Dressed in Theory: On Feminist Re-Fashionings of Academic Discourse." This volume.

Daly, Brenda O., and Maureen T. Reddy, eds. *Narrating Mothers: Theorizing Maternal Subjectivities.* Knoxville: University of Tennessee Press, 1991.

Duggan, Lisa. "The Social Enforcement of Heterosexuality and Lesbian Resistance in the 1920." *Class, Race, and Sex: The Dynamics of Control.* Eds. Amy Swerdlow and Hanna Lessinger. Boston: G.K. Hall & Co., 1983.

Erlich, Gloria C. *The Sexual Education of Edith Wharton.* Berkeley: University of California Press, 1992.

Freedman, Diane P. *An Alchemy of Genres: Cross-Genre Writing by American Feminist Poet Critics.* Charlottesville: University Press of Virginia, 1992.

Green, Kathleen, and Laura Roskos. "Packaging the Personal: An Interview with Nancy K. Miller." *Discourse: Theoretical Studies in Media and Culture* 15.2 (Winter 1992–93):51–63.

Herndl, Diane Price. "The Dilemmas of a Feminine Dialogic." *Feminism, Bakhtin and the Dialogic.* Eds. Dale M. Bauer and Susan Jaret McKinstry. Albany: SUNY Press, 1991. 7–24.

Hirsch, Marianne. *The Mother/Daughter Plot: Narrative, Psychoanalysis, Feminism.* Bloomington and Indianapolis: Indiana University Press, 1989.

hooks, bell. *Talking Back: Thinking Feminist, Thinking Black.* Boston: South End Press, 1989.

Joslin, Katherine. *Women Writers: Edith Wharton.* New York: St. Martin's Press, 1991.

Leitch, Vincent B. *American Literary Criticism from the 30s to the 80s.* New York: Columbia University Press, 1988.

Lewis, R.W.B., and Nancy Lewis, eds. *The Letters of Edith Wharton.* New York: Charles Scribner's Sons, 1988.

Lutz, Tom. *American Nervousness: An Anecdotal History.* Ithaca: Cornell University Press, 1991.

Miller, Nancy K. *Getting Personal: Feminist Occasions and Other Autobiographical Acts.* New York: Routledge, 1991.

Raphael, Lev. *Edith Wharton's Prisoners of Shame: A New Perspective on Her Neglected Fiction.* New York: St. Martin's Press, 1991.

Rich, Adrienne. *Of Woman Born: Motherhood as Experience and Institution.* 10th ed. New York: W.W. Norton, 1986.

Smith-Rosenberg, Carroll. *Disorderly Conduct: Visions of Gender in Victorian America.* New York: Oxford University Press, 1985.

Tintner, Adeline. "Mothers, Daughters, and Incest in the Late Novels of Edith Wharton." *The Lost Tradition: Mothers and Daughters in Literature.* Eds. Cathy N. Davidson and E. M. Broner. New York: Ungar, 1980. 146–156.

Tompkins, Jane. "Me and My Shadow." *New Literary History* 19 (Autumn 1987): 169–178.

Tuttleton, James, Kristin O. Lauer, and Margaret P. Murray, eds. *Edith Wharton: The Contemporary Reviews*. Cambridge: Cambridge University Press, 1992.

Wharton, Edith. *The Gods Arrive*. New York: Appleton, 1932.

———. *The House of Mirth*. New York: Scribner's, 1905.

———. *Hudson River Bracketed*. New York: Appleton, 1929.

———. *The Mother's Recompense*. (1925) New York: Charles Scribner's Sons, 1986.

———. "Life and I." Wharton Archives, Beinecke Library, Yale University, New Haven, Conn.

———. *Summer*. New York: Appleton, 1917.

White, Barbara A. "Neglected Areas: Wharton's Short Stories and Incest." *Edith Wharton Review* 8.1 (Spring 1991): 2–12.

Wolff, Cynthia Griffin. *Feast of Words: The Triumph of Edith Wharton*. New York: Oxford University Press, 1977.

Fighting Back on Paper and in Real Life:
Sexual Abuse Narratives and the Creation of Safe Space

Sonia C. Apgar

With the increased awareness of sexual abuse in the past decade has come a growing number of texts on the subject, including psychological treatises and sociological studies, popular press and self-help books, autobiographies and anthologies of first-person narratives in which survivors tell their own stories. On a large scale, each of these genres is both a product of (and integral to) the ongoing process of cultural work. On a smaller scale, while each personal narrative is a product of a survivor's recovery process, the construction of these narratives is also an important part of the process itself, providing each writer with a safe space in which to both come to terms with her experience and to (re)establish her sense of "self."

Acts of violence inflicted by one human being on another carry the inherent message that the recipient is not an equal, not worthy of basic human respect. According to Judith Lewis Herman, Director of Training at the Victims of Violence Program at Cambridge Hospital, this results in damage to the sense of self-identity and self-worth and, for survivors of sexual abuse, generates subsequent and chronic feelings of shame, doubt, guilt, and inferiority (53–54). Louise DeSalvo, writing about the effects of incest in her introduction to *Virginia Woolf*, notes that such abuse

> forces the survivor into abandoning the belief in her own personal worth, the possibility of her own personal safety, the belief that the world is a meaningful and comprehensible place. To have been incestuously abused means that someone who should have given you care, and should have protected you, saw you as being fit for abuse. (11)

If a survivor blames herself for being abused, or represses the memories, she can retain the myth that "the world is [otherwise] a meaningful and comprehensible place" and maintain the standard cultural illusion that if she acts properly, she will be safe (Herman 53–54). This psychological sleight of hand, however, creates an enormous amount of psychological tension, manifesting itself in a wide range of self-destructive and anti-social behaviors, physical ailments, and psychological disorders (Herman and Hirshfield 12, 139–140). Often, it is in seeking help in dealing with these symptoms that women begin to recall repressed memories and thereby begin the recovery process. Recovering a positive sense of identity and feeling of self-worth is a long and terrible struggle (for many, a lifelong task), but according to the work of Herman and others, survivors can and do succeed in reversing much of the psychological damage (123–154).

One of the major components of the recovery process is the establishment of a coherent personal narrative that not only fits *with* the survivor's memories and perceptions, but also fits *into* the social constructions or cultural norms available to her. This task is often facilitated by writing about the abuse and the feelings, people, places, and events associated with it. Writing provides the survivor with a psychological distance that allows her the possibility of analyzing her past. As Toni A.H. McNaron and Yarrow Morgan note in their preface to *Voices in the Night*, "Writing shapes, focuses, limits, and establishes minimal distance." They also suggest that working through memories in writing contributes to a sense of empowerment:

> Bringing [our worst feelings and fantasies] out of the shadows began to get them to manageable size. If a poem or scene could be shaped from the garbage heap of our memories, our bodies and psyches could begin to heal themselves. If letters could be written and actually sent to the victimizers and family members who supported them, we could begin to give some of the hatred and anger back to the appropriate sources and stop shouldering all the shame and blocking the reality entirely from our consciousness. (17)

In projecting her thoughts and feelings onto paper, the survivor begins to make connections, to see patterns. In constructing narratives from her constellations of memories, she is able to "put form around what has seemed so chaotic" (19), and hence make sense of her experience.

Sociolinguist Charlotte Linde has recently examined the personal and cultural importance of personal narratives, specifically those that fit into what she calls "the life story." Linde asserts that "all the stories and associated discourse units [that make up the life story], told by an individual during the course of his/her lifetime . . . have as their primary evaluation a point about the speaker" and provide a highly important social opportunity for establishing self-identity (21). She further maintains that they are "significant resource[s] for creating [one's] internal, private sense of self," and perhaps even more crucially that they are "major resource[s] for conveying that self to and negotiating that self with others" (98). Linde has examined three characteristics of the self that are "maintained and exchanged through language"—continuity of the self through time, the reflexivity of the self, and the relation of the self to others (100). Each is significant to both the personal narratives of sexual abuse survivors and to the recovery process.

Regarding the first characteristic, Linde notes that a person's sense of self "should be continuous—legato rather than staccato. A proper self is *not* a pointillist self, consisting of isolated moments of experience that may be remembered but do not touch or influence one another" (100–101). She draws on the work of psychologist Daniel Stern who has noted that without the sense of continuity, there can be "temporal disassociation, fugue states, amnesias, [a sense of] not 'going on being'" (99)—symptoms often reported in survivors of sexual abuse (Herman 86–87, 184–185). This lack of continuity is due to the repression of traumatic memories, a protective psychological mechanism present in most survivors that prevents access not only to memories of the abuse itself, but also to those of associated events and feelings (some of which may be years apart). (Re)establishing this sense of continuity is a crucial factor in the recovery process, and constructing personal narratives of traumatic experience facilitates the process of breaking down repressive blocking in two important ways: 1) writing offers a sense of control through psychological distancing and therefore gives a survivor a sense of safety, and 2) narration adheres to this culture's sociolinguistic requirement of temporal sequencing, thereby pushing a survivor to "fill in the gaps." According to Linde, the "narrative presupposition," which is tacitly held by speakers of English and most other western languages, causes interlocutors to assume "that the order of clauses in the narrative can be taken to mirror the order of events in [the] real world" (68). For instance, on hearing the sentence, *I got upset and I left my papers at the office,* speakers of English assume that the first event (getting upset) caused the second (leaving the papers), whereas *I left my papers at the office and I got upset* is assumed to mean that the forgotten papers caused the speaker's perturbation (111). Because the logic of English is *post hoc ergo propter hoc,* a survivor, in the process of "getting the sequence right," not only recaptures her memories, but also builds temporal self-continuity into the fabric of the narrative itself.

Further, in writing about the past, a survivor is able to establish the second characteristic Linde refers to, the "reflexivity of the self" (Herman 122). This is the ability to treat the self as "other" to gain distance and perspective (100). Without this reflexivity, she quotes Stern as saying, "there can be paralysis, the sense of non-ownership of self-action, the experience of loss of control to external agents" (99)—again symptoms reported by many survivors. The narrative process, because it entails the self-in-the-present-as-writer relating an incident about the self-in-the-past-as-subject, creates a distinction between the narrator and protagonist and thus interposes distance between them. Because narrative is by definition past tense, it provides the survivor both the distance and perspective from which to examine, reflect on, and adjust the presentation of the self she is inscribing. This "ability to relate to oneself externally, as an object or as an other," Linde notes, "pertain[s] particularly to narrative," because the act of personal narration requires self-observation and the presentation of a self-identity (120–121). Moreover, personal narratives are fundamentally involved with the social evaluation of the participants and their actions and always involve the question of whether or not an action (and therefore the actor) is expected or proper. This evaluation is primarily internal and, in writing about the past, the writer is forced to reflect on and judge herself and others involved in the story—obviously at a "removed standpoint" (121). As Linde observes, "All questions of 'How am I doing?' require the evaluations of an observer and narrator who are related but not identical" (121).

Although self-reflexivity is to some extent supported by every speech act, it is perhaps most firmly established in narration, where it allows for the presentation of the moral value of the self—which, Linde suggests, is one of the most important functions of personal narratives. Significantly, she asserts, "People do not want just any objectifiable self; they want a good self, and a self that is perceived as good by others" (122). This is certainly no less true for survivors of sexual abuse than for the general population. It is in fact arguable that for survivors the establishment of a "good" or moral self is of mortal significance: Those who have been sexually abused are more likely than their peers to disfigure themselves, severely abuse drugs or alcohol, be raped (again), become involved in other abusive relationships, and experience suicidal tendencies—on which they often act (DeSalvo 11). Unsurprising, then, is Herman's observation that "many or even most psychiatric patients are [sexual abuse] survivors" (122).

Related to the reflexive function of establishing a moral self is the ability to see the self as related to but separate from others, another characteristic which Linde suggests is "maintained and exchanged through language." For example, reflexivity is established linguistically in a number of ways most basically by linguistic markers that formally distinguish between persons (e.g., pronouns). More importantly for this discussion, however, the social and interactive nature of narrative itself establishes this property of distinguishability in two ways. First, narration is a relational act which necessarily implicates an addressee (even if the addressee is the writer herself). Second, the narrator indicates her relation to the protagonist and to other characters in her narrative, either implicitly or explicitly (102). Thus, narrative is, as Linde points out, "an extremely powerful tool for creating, negotiating, and displaying the moral standing of the self." For while narratives may be created for a variety of reasons and with many points in mind, "part of the hidden point of narrative is to show that the narrator knows what the norms are and agrees with them" (123). By establishing herself as a moral and therefore worthy member of society, the survivor necessarily distinguishes herself as separate from but related to others. The act of constructing personal narratives of traumatic experience facilitates the process of breaking down repressive blocking.

Often, while working to re-establish her sense of self-worth and independence, a survivor will break off her ties and identifications with her abuser(s) and any friends and family members who refuse to acknowledge and support her in her recovery. This is usually when she begins to listen to what Belenky, Clinchy, Goldberger, and Tarule, in their work on women's development have called "the 'still small voice' within" (McNaron and Morgan 40–46). At this point, they note, she generally finds "an inner source of strength," and a fundamental transition follows that has "repercussions in her relationships, self-concept and self-esteem, morality, and behavior" (54). One of the frequently reported repercussions is seeking out other survivors with whom to identify. This allows for support of her "new self," her remembering, and her recovery. Crucial to this transition is the sharing of personal narratives (Herman 205–213). As McNaron and Morgan reported, "The sharing of undiscussable, taboo information left millions of women no longer believing that we were the only ones not to fit society's ideals. Millions of women began to view our own lives and the lives of other women as more accurate than literature, social prescriptions, statistics" (16). A survivor needs a community that validates her experience and sense of self. Personal narratives in both spoken and written form provide the vehicle for communal exchange and growth because, in their constructions of coherence, they necessarily make (at least) tacit reference to both personal beliefs and social norms and expectations and allow for an examination and potential reformulation of the available subject positions and cultural constructions that endanger women.

A woman can use her writing to empower both herself and others by confronting denial, sorting out the cultural narratives that cast women as victims, and reinscribing herself as self-empowered and resistant to attack. Herman, pointing to the importance of reconstructing life stories in the recovery process, notes, "remembering and telling the truth about terrible events are prerequisites both for the restoration of the social order and for the healing of individual victims" (1). In her work with Cambridge Hospital's Victims of Violence Program, she has identified three stages in the recovery process that are entailed in (re)constructing the survivor's life story and coherent self-concept: remembrance and mourning, re-establishing a coherent self, and re-establishing connections with others. At each of these stages, personal narratives in which a survivor explores sexual abuse can be of great value, because the reality of what happened (sexual abuse) and society's need for denial conflict head-on and thwart attempts to make sense of, let alone grow beyond, these experiences.

According to Herman, reconstructing a survivor's life story begins with a review of her life before the trauma and the circumstances that led up to the event (175). Many of the first person narratives in anthologies such as *Voices in the Night, The Courage to Heal,* and *I Never Told Anyone* are representative of the writing done during the first stage of the recovery process, that of remembering and mourning. Reclamation of the survivor's earlier history is crucial "in order to 'recreate the flow' of [her] life and restore the continuity with the past," Herman asserts, adding that the survivor should be encouraged to relate all "her important relationships, her ideals and dreams, and her struggles and conflicts prior to the traumatic event" (McNaron and Morgan 41–42). This exploration, she explains, provides a context within which the trauma can be understood and integrated (176).

Gudrun Fonda, a contributor to *Voices in the Night,* in writing about her experiences with her sexually abusive father provides an excellent example of this process of reconstruction. Her narrative "Daddy's Girl" begins with the explanation that her father had gone "overseas in the army" just before she was born and returned approximately five years later. Gudrun's mother and her mother's best friend (and apparently her lover) Meg had raised Gudrun up until this point, and she notes that they were very happy. However, when her father returns he realizes "the change in circumstances," and, as Gudrun tells it,

> He was outraged, and he had a gun. My mother and Meg were pretty young, around twenty-two at the time. They moved out, and took me with them to a one room apartment. My father stayed in the house, and kept everything. . . . We were hiding.
>
> Then there was the divorce. My father got custody of me. Some adult, I guess a social worker, explained what had happened in the courtroom. The social worker told me what a divorce was and that my parents were parting for good. I didn't believe her. Meg and Mom were my parents and I knew they loved each other, so I didn't believe they were getting divorced. The social worker looked at me as though I were incurably thick, and explained who my parents were. She told me how lucky I was that my father had returned to give me a normal home. (40)

The second step Herman reports is the reconstruction of the traumatic event as a recitation of fact. She reports that an "organized, detailed, verbal account, oriented in time and historical context," can then be assembled "out of the fragmented components of frozen imagery and sensation" (177). The narrative must also include an account of the event, of course, as does Gudrun's, because, as Herman asserts, "A narrative that does not include the traumatic imagery and bodily sensations" does not provide the catharsis necessary to recovery (177):

The first night I lived with him, he came into my bedroom. I pretended I was asleep. It was almost summer. I was sleeping in just my underpants with a sheet over me. He pulled down my underpants and said, "You won't grow up to be like your mother, I'll see to that." I did not open my eyes or make a sound. I thought he would leave. Instead he started to rub what felt like a mushy finger between my thighs. I started to cry. . . . He said, "You will like this, you will learn to like this, you'll be glad I'm doing this." Every night that week he came into my room. I hated going to sleep. (40–41)

Herman explains that the narrative must also include the survivor's response to the event and the responses of important people in her life (177), as does Gudrun's. After her father manipulates the court into denying her mother visitation rights, Gudrun is not able to talk to her until some time later when, after noticing her mother surreptitiously watching her father drop her off at school, she takes her chances and sneaks out to her. At first, Gudrun's mother is "very surprised and frightened" and wants her to go back into the school, but when Gudrun begins to cry and tells her about her father's abuse, her mother picks her up and runs with her to the car:

Once she was inside, I think she felt safer. I had stopped crying. She was looking wild eyed. She asked me questions. I told her details. She cried and cried, "My baby, my baby, my poor baby," gasping and choking until I became frightened. Then she tried to stop crying to comfort me. She said I never had to go back there again. It was a promise. (41–42)

Gudrun relates that although her mother and Meg take her "that day in the car and [drive] very far," they are apprehended by the police the next day; a subsequent attempt also proves futile, Gudrun's mother is incarcerated, and her father moves them to another state (42–43). What Gudrun learns through all this is that while her mother and Meg love and believe her, her father cannot be trusted and the law has no interest in her story. The little self-esteem and strength she retains during the course of her childhood, despite the abuse, are based on her firm belief that while some (her father and, apparently, the courts) see her as "fit for abuse," she is loved and valued by others.

"At each point in the narrative," Herman remarks, "the survivor must reconstruct not only what happened but also what she felt. The description of emotional states must be as detailed as the description of the facts" (177). Accordingly, Gudrun notes that because her father "had a gruff kindness, actually an extravagant side, that made me love him. [But] loving him made me so confused that I hated him for confusing me" (43). When Gudrun is not yet eight her father begins raping her. When this happens, she tries to kill herself and, when unsuccessful, tells her new stepmother about the assaults.

Her stepmother, however, "washed my mouth out with soap. She said I was a crazy liar. She said God would punish me for trying to break up her marriage [and] told my father and he beat me and kicked me. All my baby teeth that were left got knocked out. He said that no one would believe me" (44). Again, she becomes suicidal: "I wanted to die. . . . I knew he would win against me. I would run out into the field and dig a deep hole and bury my face in it and scream" (44). Once again, she learns most people will not believe her, that she is not valued, that telling makes it worse. The emotional burden is nearly untenable.

In telling her story, however, a survivor begins her recovery. When it is recounted, Herman maintains, "the trauma story becomes a testimony," a story which is no longer about humiliation and shame, but about virtue and dignity. It is a process by which a survivor regains what she had lost (181). Again, Gudrun's narrative provides an excellent example: After enduring another six years' abuse, Gudrun summons the courage to leave her abusive father and stepmother. Having escaped, she now believes in herself and has confidence in her ability to survive, reporting, "I don't think they can find me here in New York City. I'm going to find a job. . . . I plan to save some money and then I'm going to try to find my mother and Meg" (46). Herman refers to the survival narrative as "testimony" because it has both a "private dimension" and a "public aspect," is both "confessional and spiritual" as well as "political and judicial." "Testimony," she notes, "links these meanings" and gives a "new and larger dimension to the [survivor's] individual experience" (181). When kept private, personal narratives such as Gudrun's offer their authors a safe place to work through the aftermath of trauma and, when published, give others permission to remember, identify with, and make sense of the abuse they suffered.

Once a survivor has gotten out her story, and thereby integrated the traumatic memories into her consciousness, she has reached the second stage of recovery, that of re-establishing a strong and coherent sense of self. Herman writes, "Having come to terms with the traumatic past, the survivor faces the task of creating a future. She has mourned the old self that the trauma destroyed; now she must develop a new self. . . . In accomplishing this work, the survivor reclaims her world" (196). At this point she can begin to take steps to "increase her sense of power and control [and] protect herself against future danger" (197). Personal narratives of successful self-defense such as those included in *Her Wits About Her: Self- Defense Success Stories by Women* are representative of the survivor narratives told at this stage. In (re)writing themselves as strong and resourceful, unwilling to yield their right to safety, survivors "can begin to reconstruct the normal physiological response to danger," Herman explains, and in doing so "rebuild the 'action system' that was shattered and fragmented by the trauma" (198).

In order to (re)inscribe herself as strong and resourceful, a survivor must have alternative models to the cultural narratives offering only passivity and victimization to women. Many of the contributors to *Her Wits About Her* reported being extremely passive by social training or pacifists by political commitment, but they also knew of women who had fought back, women they were able to pattern their defensive actions after when it became necessary. One of these women, Rashida, observes, "I have always been a passive person, taught to compromise instead of [using] force—an unusual attitude in my rough neighborhood" (182). However, things changed for her when she was grabbed and pulled into a car while walking home one evening. She reports, "I began to get angry. These [five] men had placed me in a situation where I felt there was no compromise. I had to either fight and get away, or submit to being raped repeatedly" (182). A high school student at the time of her abduction, Rashida tells of how she "sat quietly while we rode to an old cemetery," but notes that when the men stopped the car she was ready:

> Most of the guys got out of the car, except for the one on my right. He had put his arm around my neck to keep me in place. The others were outside of the car taking their pants down. When one of them climbed into the backseat and moved towards me, I snapped. I bit the arm that held me, hit the guy behind me in the gut with my right elbow, and kicked the guy coming toward me, all at the same time. The one holding me let go, and the one facing me got out of the car, hurt. I got out of the car quickly and ran. The other men were so surprised, they didn't move fast enough to stop me. (183)

Physically and emotionally bruised, but alive, she learns from the police the next morning that "a young man had come to the emergency room with a severe human bite that required stitches on his right arm" (184). Empowered by her sense of herself as strong and resourceful, she asserts, "I would never allow anyone to take my dignity and my control away from me now" (184). In fighting back, she has empowered herself by rejecting the role of victim; in telling her story, she has (re)inscribed a strong and coherent self.

While these personal narratives are important to the recovery process of their authors, they also serve an important role in the recovery of other survivors who read them, serving not only as triggers for repressed memories, but also as patterns for further (re)inscriptions. Denise Caignon, who along with Gail Groves founded *Women Who Resist: The Success Stories Project* and edited the subsequent anthology, *Her Wits About Her*, observes that women are hungry to hear and tell tales of successful self-defense: "When I would mention to a woman that I was collecting stories about women who fight back, a common response was a delighted smile and 'Oh, I've got one!' or 'I have this friend who. . . . ,' as if she had just been waiting for the chance to tell her story" (xxxii). Included in this anthology is the inspiring "Asian, Female and Fierce," written by a young Japanese-American woman who uses the pseudonym Cindy Nakazawa. Her story occurred while she was "working graveyard shift as an X-ray technician in a large hospital," in an area that was completely isolated:

> [I] was sitting on a chair with other chairs right next to it. The guy, who must have been waiting in the file room, dropped a blanket on my head, grabbed my throat, and pushed me down on the chairs. . . . [He said], "Put your hands down by your sides." . . . So I said, "Fuck you, I'm not going to do that." I just grabbed his little finger and bent it all the way back to get him to let go. And I knew that I couldn't come up, because of the pressure coming down on my throat, so I'd have to go down. I kicked the chairs out from under me, fell onto the floor and rolled up in a ball. I was right in front of his groin, so I figured, I'm going for it. I punched him right in the balls, and he flew back about four feet. . . . I went after him and . . . he made a beeline out of the file room and I ran after him . . . all the way through the emergency room and out. (178–179)

Cindy's story clashes with stereotypical ideological patterns. After the attack, the police told her that, being "small, Asian, and female," she was in a high-risk category. "People kind of feed on that," she notes, "because they associate Oriental with being submissive, and they look at small, that's another check, and they look at female, that's another check. So they automatically think, Easy" (180). But being prepared physically and psychologically for self-defense pays off:

> The police told me I probably have never been hurt because I've been very aggressive in my actions. When the attacker came in, all of a sudden he was faced with somebody who wasn't going to give in. Attackers would much rather go for an easier mark, so they'll just give up on you. (179)

Women like Cindy refuse the "victim" subject position and reclaim their power by (re)writing the cultural expectations of who women are and how they conduct themselves. In doing so, they provide themselves and others new ways to imagine being in this culture. When these life writings are kept private, they empower the survivor; when they are shared, they offer strength and new possibilities to others as well.

Herman reports that by working through the first two stages (those of remembrance and mourning and of rebuilding a self-image), the survivor gradually gains the ability to enter the third stage—reconnecting with a community; for while "helplessness and isolation are the core experiences of psychological trauma, empowerment and reconnection are the core experiences of recovery" (197). As Groves, speaking of what were once her "private nightmares," reports, "Now I see them as common to the everyday terror of having been born female" (xviii). Caignon echoes this realization with her report of her recurring nightmare in which gangs of men chased her, "threatening me with death or worse. Fleeing their leering faces, I [made] my way, alone, down the well-worn labyrinths, across those underground rivers polluted with women's fears" (xxix). After collecting the success stories, however, she realized she was "not alone at all, but running stride for stride with all the other dreaming women who explore their fear, and their response to it while their bodies sleep" (xxix). In moving through the stages of the recovery process, a survivor learns to trust and depend on herself for her own safety. Once she is secure in this independence, she can build alliances with others, for only when she knows she can depend on herself can she comfortably enter into relationships of interdependence.

A woman's sense of who she is determines how she responds to the world, what possibilities she allows herself, either the actions she takes or the subject positions by which she defines her life. Her self-concept and sense of self-worth determine what she expects of and accepts from both herself and others. If she sees herself as unworthy, she will more than likely end up a victim. If she sees herself as strong and empowered, she is more likely to take whatever steps necessary to protect herself. Crucial to a woman's self-concept in the present is her understanding of her past: what she is today is a direct consequence of that understanding, an understanding that a survivor can modify through the recovery process. For, while traumatic events shatter a victim's sense of self, personal narratives offer a safe space in which to make sense of, and subsequently diminish, the psychological damage. By (re)inscribing a positive sense of self-identity and (re)constructing her subject position through writing, a survivor empowers herself; by sharing these texts, communities of survivors can empower themselves; and by (re)formulating the metanarratives they can gradually transform the culture.

Works Cited

Bass, Ellen, and Louise Thornton, eds. *I Never Told Anyone.* New York: HarperCollins Publishers, 1983.

Bass, Ellen, and Laura Davis. *The Courage to Heal.* New York: Harper & Row, 1988.

Belenky, Mary Field, Blythe McVicker Clinchy, Nancy Rule Goldberger, and Jill Mattuck Tarule. *Women's Ways of Knowing: The Development of Self, Voice, and Mind.* New York: Basic Books, 1986.

Caignon, Denise, and Gail Groves, eds. *Her Wits About Her: Self-Defense Success Stories by Women.* New York: Harper & Row, 1990.

DeSalvo, Louise. *Virginia Woolf: The Impact of Childhood Sexual Abuse on Her Life and Work.* New York: Ballantine, 1989.

Herman, Judith Lewis. *Trauma and Recovery.* New York: Basic Books, 1992.

Herman, Judith Lewis, with Lisa Hirschman. *Father-Daughter Incest.* Cambridge, Mass: Harvard University Press, 1981.

Linde, Charlotte. *Life Stories: The Creation of Coherence.* New York and Oxford: Oxford University Press, 1993.

McNaron, Toni A.H., and Yarrow Morgan, eds. *Voices in the Night: Women Speaking About Incest.* Pittsburgh and San Francisco: Cleis, 1982.

Stern, Daniel N. *The Interpersonal World of the Infant: A View from Psychoanalysis and Developmental Psychology.* New York: Basic Books, 1985.

Surviving

Historically, societal norms dictated that what happened in the home was private and should remain unspoken even there. The silence imposed on the topic of domestic violence has made it difficult to understand fully what women experienced. Women did find ways in which to write about their lives and the lives of women around them, but frequently those ways were privatized, as in the copious diaries of Virginia Woolf or the trail diaries of American frontier women, or secretive, as in the hidden poems of Emily Dickinson or the minute novelettes of the young Charlotte Brontë. More public writing, like Cather's and Woolf's fiction as well as captivity narratives and other expressly autobiographical writing (slave narratives for instance), was often motivated by specific goals, both practical and artistic, of making life tolerable for the writers, of exercising their considerable gifts, of making a place for themselves within a community which recognized and honored their presence. Of course there are great risks involved in revealing one's innermost needs for affirmation and healing. Those risks certainly account for a great deal of women writers' ambivalence about the practice as well as for the choice to keep one's writing secret, protected from outside eyes.

The essays in this section all explore the various methods of surviving—through writing—the mental, emotional, and physical consequences of a culture and/or family which tolerates the oppression of women. Historically, the essays range from mid-nineteenth century with Brontë's juvenilia to mid-twentieth century with Cather's and Woolf's later work. All of the writing predates what we might think of as the un-silencing of women's voices that commenced with the current women's movement. Indeed, to write at all, a woman would have been opposing the status quo. Within that contested space, women writers made choices about style, content, and rhetorical strategies that provide evidence of both anger over the past and hope for the future.

59

Incest and Rage in Charlotte Brontë's Novelettes

Susan Anne Carlson

Charlotte Brontë, between the ages of thirteen and twenty-three, created a secret fantasy world called Angria, a world that she constructed in hundreds of pages of tiny manuscripts that make up her juvenilia (Alexander, *Early Writings* 3). Brontë did not write these alone; until 1833 the stories were a joint venture with her two sisters, Anne and Emily, and her brother Branwell (Alexander, *Early Writings* 62), and the later works, including her novelettes, were written in an eleven-year collaboration with her brother (Alexander, *Early Writings* 161). But the stories themselves were kept a secret from the outside world; Brontë's father and aunt never read the juvenilia, though they knew it was being written, and none of Charlotte's school friends were ever permitted to see her writing (Gerin, *Evolution* 73).

Brontë uses this secret writing, this safe space, as an outlet for her erotic, forbidden fantasies, most importantly her oedipal fantasies of father-daughter seduction and female masochism. She was probably not aware of the disturbing content of her writing, since she wrote these texts with her eyes closed in a half-conscious, trancelike state (Gerin, *Novelettes* 16). But since an underlying masochistic theme is apparent in all of Brontë's novels, these overt, disturbing stories force us to question Brontë's handling of romance in her mature novels: *Jane Eyre* and *Villette*. Could the same fantasies of father-daughter love appear in those novels as well, only in a more covert and sophisticated form?

These issues have been debated before; the transcriber of much of Brontë's juvenilia, Christine Alexander, has suggested a father-daughter seduction theme (*Early Writings* 215), and Diane Sadoff, in her book *Monsters of Affection: Dickens, Eliot & Brontë on Fatherhood* (1982), argues that Brontë's "repeated subject matter" is "a woman's desire and its object, the figurative father" (129), suggesting that this theme continues in *Jane Eyre* and *Villette*. Though all these critics mention the themes of seduction and masochism in the juvenilia, they don't spend much time studying those themes in the texts. This chapter, therefore, will offer one of the few close readings of Brontë's juvenilia, primarily her novelettes, written between 1836 and 1839.

Though there is a large body of criticism on Brontë's novels, there are very few interpretations of the juvenilia, mainly because many of these texts were unknown to literary critics until quite recently; complete transcriptions were just finished in 1991. In 1856, Mrs. Gaskell received a packet of tiny papers written in microscopic print from Charlotte Brontë's widower, Arthur Bell Nicholls. The papers contained all the juvenilia written by the four Brontë children, including the stories and poetry Charlotte Brontë wrote between the ages of thirteen and twenty-three (Alexander, *Early Writings* 3). In 1895, the juvenilia were put up for auction, and separate pages of the original manuscripts were scattered all over England and America (Alexander, *Early Writings* 4). It has been only in the last fifty years, with Fannie Ratchford's groundbreaking study in 1941, and transcriptions by Winifred Gerin in the 1970s and Christine Alexander in the 1980s, that much of the juvenilia has been published. The long process of piecing the manuscripts back together began with Ratchford in 1921 and was just completed in 1991 (with most of the original manuscripts collected in the Brontë Parsonage in Haworth, England). Even with the collections together, transcription has been slow: the manuscripts are tiny (averaging one inch in length), and the writing is minuscule and cramped, almost impossible to read without the use of a magnifying glass (Alexander, *Edition Volume II* xxiii). Problems in locating and transcribing the documents have meant that much of Charlotte Brontë's childhood writing has only become available to scholars within the last three years.

The body of juvenilia is divided into three parts: The Glasstown Saga (1829–1832), which establishes a fairy tale-like empire in Africa, run first by the Brontë children (as the four "geniis") and later by the Duke of Wellington; The Rise of Angria (1834–1836), in which the Duke's eldest son wins a parcel of land "east of Glasstown," and becomes the Duke of Zamorna, ruling this new territory called Angria; and The Angrian Legend (1836–1839), in which Angrian characters and politics are developed in a series of five romances, called the "novelettes." Except for the Glasstown Saga, which seems to be a collaboration among all four Brontë children, the formation and development of Angria is written by Charlotte and Branwell Brontë (Alexander, *Early Writings* 62).

This chapter focuses on Brontë's novelettes, written between 1836 and 1839 and considered the most sophisticated writing in her juvenilia. Though the novelettes are not technically considered juvenilia, having been written in Brontë's early twenties, they are linked to earlier childhood writing because they cover the same ground: the Angria of the novelettes is an extension of the same fantasy world that Charlotte Brontë had developed since the age of thirteen, and the two Byronic heroes, the Duke of Zamorna and the Earl of Northangerland, are the adult versions of Arthur Wellesley and "Rogue," who both appear by 1830 in the juvenilia (Alexander, *Early Writings* 80). The five novelettes are extended romances with recurring characters: *Passing Events*, a series of disconnected scenes in which Mina Laury is introduced; *Julia*, scenes of Angria in which Caroline Vernon and her mother, Louisa Dance, are introduced; *Mina Laury*, the story of Zamorna's faithful, masochistic mistress, who rejects the proposal of another man; *Captain Henry Hastings*, a story in which Henry—a young man patterned after Branwell Brontë—is punished for murder, while his sister tries valiantly to save him; and finally *Caroline Vernon*, in which fifteen-year-old Caroline is seduced by her guardian, the Duke of Zamorna.

The transciber of most of Brontë's juvenilia, Christine Alexander, would argue that in fact the juvenilia is Charlotte Brontë's literary apprenticeship, her experimentation with fantasy and gothic styles, before she moves on to novels grounded in realism, most notably *The Professor* and *Jane Eyre* (Alexander, "Kingdom" 426). This private "game," which lasted most of Brontë's childhood and all of her adolescence, was a way for the young Brontës to amuse themselves in the isolation of Haworth, and to experiment with all the literary styles and language they were picking up from their voracious reading. As Alexander says, "Writing was a game for the young Brontës: a maze constructed chiefly from literary and visual models—from the *Annuals* and the works of Scott, Byron, Hogg, and Martin, among others—a maze (or web, as Brontë herself called it) constructed to confuse and amuse not only her siblings but her imagined audience" (Alexander, "Kingdom" 436).

Certainly the juvenilia are predominantly play, which accounts for the disjointedness of the texts, and the often humorous, satiric tone of the stories. But as Brontë begins writing her adolescent romances (1833–1839), her interest in her characters becomes an obsession—she writes in a "trancelike" state, and the characters appear to her as if they had a life of their own (Alexander, *Early Writings* 243). When the twenty-year-old Brontë is teaching at Roe Head School, and is immersed in the world of her novelettes, the stories become an alternative (and much preferred) reality; the characters would appear in her classroom in "dreamlike" visions, and the complex fantasy world "threatened," as Alexander says, "to blur different levels of reality in her mind" (*Early Writings* 225). Her style reflects this state of what Winifred Gerin calls "suspended consciousness" (*Novelettes* 16): hurried writing full of dashes and purple prose, resulting in an erotic, unprocessed text (Sadoff 120). It is this text in which the desires of her unconscious are apparent and disturbing: female masochism, father-daughter romance, and female rage, the same themes that reverberate in *Jane Eyre* and *Villette*, only in much cruder form.

The novelettes are often dismissed by Brontë scholars as immature attempts at Byronic Romance, a stage in literary apprenticeship that occurs before Brontë changes from romanticism to realism (with *Ashworth* and *The Professor*) (Alexander, "Kingdom" 436). Certainly these novelettes are in major part a form of imitation; Charlotte is molding her heroes from the collected works of Byron on her father's shelves; she quotes freely from *Cain, Manfred,* and *Childe Harold* throughout her juvenilia, and is familiar with other Romantic poetry as well. Brontë's early romances also reflect her fascination with the gothic; by the 1820s the gothic form had been so overused it was being parodied (Alexander, "Kingdom" 410), but was a staple in second-rate literature, especially the ladies' magazines brought into the Brontë home by Charlotte's Aunt Branwell (Alexander, "Kingdom" 411). By the time Charlotte begins to write her own romances, she has been heavily influenced by the gothic stories in *Lady's Magazine, Fraser's* and *Blackwood's Magazine,* and the conventional romances she has studied in the popular Victorian gift-books, the *Annuals,* three of which were in the Brontë home (Alexander "Kingdom" 414).

With all this "background" in mind, Charlotte Brontë writes a series of novelettes between the ages of twenty and twenty-three along with her brother, Branwell. Although it is impossible to know exactly how the two collaborated, it seems that the novelettes were written by Charlotte (Branwell provided the long-term plotlines for Angria, and Charlotte used them loosely for the extensive character descriptions and storylines). As Branwell sunk even deeper into drink in 1837, Brontë used his plotlines even less, and turned him from collaborator into character, the brother in *Captain Henry Hastings.* By 1838 (when Branwell had become addicted to alcohol and opium), the collaboration had ended (Alexander, *Early Writings* 161), and Brontë was writing the last novelettes, including *Caroline Vernon,* independently (*Early Writings* 192).

This would mean that by 1838 Brontë was in control of her own secret world, a world she had placed more value in than her daily life. It would seem at this point that Brontë could use the freedom to change the traditional role of women in the gothic, to create women who would be able to protect themselves or at least be aware of their victimization by men. For if this is writing for the most part under her control, and writing that is in secret, why isn't it different from the traditional male romance? Why doesn't she change theme, form, content, so women aren't the masochistic victims, and men their vile abusers? The women writers a generation before Brontë, Jane Austen, Anne Radcliffe, and Mary Wollstonecraft, had created a new type of Romantic writing, what Anne Mellor calls the "feminine Romantic ideology" (33), in which women establish friendly relationships with each other and with men, and avoid relationships based on possession (33–39). Their novels celebrate an "ethic of care," in which the writers espouse a character's loyalty to family and community, ties that bind him or her to a larger society (77).

But Brontë rejects this more positive vision of romance; instead, her characters are motivated by selfishness, and there is no real community or family loyalty; for all its trappings, Angria is an amoral, savage society (Chase 11). Though her narrative voice shifts constantly from satire to affection, she revels in the most brutish aspects of male romance: women's abandonment to men who abuse and neglect them. Most disturbing is the fascination these stories have with father-daughter romances, romances which culminate in *Caroline Vernon,* in which the fifteen-year-old Caroline is quite happily seduced by her father-surrogate. The disturbing thematic elements of these stories may provide the point of origin for the female masochism that reverberates through all of Charlotte Brontë's later, great heroines: Jane Eyre, Caroline Helstone, and Lucy Snowe.

In the symbolic world represented in these novelettes, the house is a male preserve and a prison for women. Women characters are rarely seen outside their homes: Louisa Dance is under house arrest in Hawkscliffe, Mina Laury rarely leaves the Cross of Rivaulx (Zamorna's military headquarters), and Zenobia Ellrington, the Bertha-like character in Angria, stays in self-imposed exile at her husband's estate. If we accept the convention that a woman's house can be a metaphor for her body (Sadoff 126), an analysis of woman's space in the novels is both revealing and disturbing. No woman in Angria has private space; every room, including her bedroom, can be intruded upon, and often a woman is threatened after a man appears suddenly in her bedroom (*Passing Events*), or steals into a room she had run to for safety (*Caroline Vernon*). Even when a woman is physically alone, she is often being watched; when Elizabeth Hastings, for example, paces back and forth in front of a picture window, she is being scrutinized both by her brother and by the male narrator, who is watching her from the bushes. Women's bodies are property, open to the man or men who enter them.

Not only do these women have no private space *within* these houses, but the entire house is open to all comers. Mina Laury, Zamorna's ever-pleasing mistress, is a caretaker for a house left completely unprotected with doors that are always open: "the door is constantly open & reveals a noble passage, almost a Hall, terminating in a staircase of low white steps, traced up the middle by a brilliant carpet . . . the mansion whose windows are up, its door as usual hospitably apart" (Gerin, *Novelettes* 42–3). A Freudian reading of this passage suggests that Mina's sexual availability—"the door is constantly open"—is destructive; Freud's dream analysis of his patients found that staircases and a hallway in dreams often meant a sexual act (228), and in Brontë's fantasy writing, stairs always appear when a character is being led to or into some form of danger. Stairs in the early juvenilia, for example, usually lead to a dungeon, a torture chamber, or some kind of tomb.

Mina's role in this house is to serve as a caretaker/hostess of all Zamorna's military friends who appear at sudden notice. And more importantly, her job, as she deems it, is to make this house satisfying to her lover's needs, submitting all her desires to make him comfortable: "it gave me a feeling of extasy [sic] to hear my young masters's voice, as he spoke to you or Arundel or to that stately Hartford, & to see him moving about secure & powerful in his own stronghold" (Gerin, *Novelettes* 45). Her house then, and symbolically, her body, are his "stronghold," and, in fact, Brontë says Mina is his property, as much as the estate on which she lives. Mina represents selflessness to the point of self-annihilation; a behavior Brontë both mocks (comparing Mina to a nun worshipping her god) and sympathizes with. For though she is, as Alexander says, a masochist who enjoys her masochism (*Early Writings* 167), she is only reacting in the most extreme form to the plight all the Angrian heroines share: they are all abandoned and exploited by the Byronic heroes whose "love" is neglectful at best. This is an extension of the earlier juvenilia, in which Brontë creates numerous children abandoned (Alexander, *Early Writings* 213) or forced to beg for attention from cold, apathetic fathers (all of whom imitate the emotional distance of Brontë's own father). Mina's desperate need to be loved by Zamorna just moves her more quickly towards self-annihilation; she will please Zamorna incessantly to gain his attention, until there is nothing left in her except the need to please. Mina stays with Zamorna because she has no other choice; she has no self apart from serving him: "I've nothing else to exist for," she says to one of Zamorna's aides. "I've no other interest in life" (Gerin, *Novelettes* 44).

When lecherous Lord Hartford invites himself into Mina's house (and body) in *Mina Laury*, we are not that surprised; Hartford has assumed that if Mina is "open" to Zamorna's needs, she will be compliant to his as well. Brontë emphasizes Mina's vulnerability at the beginning of this scene; it starts with Mina walking alone on her estate, a tiny figure passing through a huge, green lawn. The landscape image described here, a path bordered by trees, builds into a female sexual symbol:

> The forest of Hawkscliffe was as still as a tomb, & its black leafless wilds stretched away in the distance and cut of [sic], with a harsh serrated line, the sky from the country—That sky was all silver blue—pierced here & there with a star like a diamond, only the moon softened it, large, full, golden— the by-road I have spoken of received her ascending beam on a path of perfect solitude—Spectral pines & great old beech trees guarded the way like Sentinels from Hawkscliffe—farther on, the rude track wound deep into the shades of the forest, but here it was open & the worn causeway bleached with frost ran under an old wall—grown over with moss & wild ivy. (Gerin, *Novelettes* 140–1)

This path suggests the female vagina: lined with trees on either side it splits a huge lawn in two and is the entrance Hartford (on his rushing horse) uses to reach Mina. Walking in this pathway Mina is in a "female" landscape, which both reflects her body and nurtures it, the moon lighting her path as she walks along and bathing her in moonlight as she stands in front of her house. But this female landscape is as passive and helpless as Mina herself: the light that shines on her also leads Hartford to her more quickly, and the earth cannot protect Mina as Hartford attacks her inside the house, leaving her to beg and plead for his mercy.

These houses and lands symbolically portray how vulnerable these female characters are to the sexual advances of men. This vulnerability is further registered by the heroines' bodies. Most of them are locked inside the bodies of children, bodies too small and fragile to defend against what is defined as the "evil ways" (101) of their lovers, Zamorna and Northangerland.

The female heroines in the Angrian tales are tiny, beautifully-dressed dolls, a mixture of grown women and little girls. They represent Burke's ideal of the beautiful (as portrayed in the *Annuals*): a small, helpless and delicate creature, "delicate" to the point of "sickliness," "with a voice that is soft, sweet, clear, even, smooth—never shrill, harsh, deep or loud" (Mellor 109). Their bodies betray them; they are too small to defend themselves (the fiery Louisa Dance is laughable when she comes up only to Zamorna's elbow) and too weak to fight for their own needs (Mary Percy is left to freeze after her portly husband takes up all the space in front of the fire). Like the tiny adventurers against the giant geniis of Glasstown, these women cannot fight equally, and if cajoling and sweet talk are not successful, they must submit to their masters/lovers in order to survive. When Mary Percy wants to follow her husband, Zamorna (who wishes to visit his mistress), she begs and cries, but is finally talked into obedience: "Look at that weather & tell me if it is fit for a delicate little woman like you to be exposed to? . . . —you may well clasp those small, silly hands—so thin I can almost see through them—and you may well shake your curls over your face—to hide its paleness from me. . ." (130–131).

In their helplessness, these characters reflect Brontë's knowledge of the *Annuals*: the stories by women, especially Letitia Landon, stress female helplessness in the face of injustice and male aggression; women were consistently forced to submit and endure cruelty (Mellor 112–113). But Brontë goes a step further than Landon; for what makes her female characters helpless makes them infinitely desirable. The Angrian men are most attracted to women who resemble children, their tiny hands and slender feet (Gerin, *Novelettes* 303), their weakness compared to male strength. Zamorna, when tender, calls his wife and two mistresses "little girls" (Gerin, *Novelettes* 47), and it is when these tiny women are trembling and frightened that he most desires them.

Brontë takes the common Victorian assumption that women are by nature closer to children than adults (Kincaid 14), and sexualizes it, so that the more childlike the woman is, the more appealing she is to her lover. In this way Brontë's fantasy world is very similar to Victorian pornography, in which "the cult of the little girl" (Rush 56) was at its height, and the greatest sexual arousal derived from images of a man raping a young virgin, "the younger the better" (Marcus 156). A thriving prostitution market provided the product; as Stephen Marcus observed in *The Other Victorians*, "there was a considerable trade in the bodies of children that had been going on for years in London" (156). That "trade" included an international white slave market that serviced men in Europe and America (Rush 63) and a thriving prostitution ring in London, in which young girls were kidnapped, raped, and then sold to wealthy Englishmen for a price: "twenty pounds for a healthy working girl between the ages of fourteen and eighteen; a hundred pounds for a middle-class girl of the same age; and as much as four hundred pounds for a child from the upper class under age twelve" (Marcus 64).

In Angria, adult women are considered sexually attractive if they look and behave like little girls. If adult women are defined by men (and by themselves) as sexual objects, and if childlike women are especially desirable, little girls become sexual objects in themselves. The story *Caroline Vernon* in Brontë's juvenilia illustrates this point and goes beyond it; it is a clear adult-child romance, but it is also a fulfilled oedipal fantasy. The daughter (Caroline Vernon) desires her surrogate father, Zamorna. After an intensive sexual rivalry with her mother, she successfully banishes her mother and is, quite enjoyably, seduced by her father (Sadoff 126). Though the story in many ways parallels the conventional Romantic seduction tale, it is unusual because it is overlaid with Brontë's overt fascination with father-daughter love.

The story begins when the father, Northangerland, receives a proposal of marriage for fifteen-year-old Caroline from the black Ashantee Quashia (who represents, in Brontë juvenilia, male rage and lust). Quashia's description of himself as the perfect child-lover introduces the love theme of the story: ". . . she's young, you say, the more need she has of a father & won't I be both father & Husband to her in one?" (Gerin, *Novelettes* 284). Northangerland (Caroline's father) confirms Quashia's child-lust when he assumes that Quashia "wants to marry a little girl of ten or eleven years old" (Gerin, *Novelettes* 285).

This theme of father-lovers is not so shocking in the Angrian world, where mothers are neglectful or nonexistent (Alexander, *Early Writings* 215–16), and fathers frequently are dangerous or lustful towards their relations. Northangerland, for example, hates his sons and hires S'Death to kill them; the same pattern of a parent hurting his sons (by abandoning them) plays out later in *Ashworth* and *The Professor* (Alexander, *Early Writings* 221). Zamorna is constantly away from his own children, and in a very early poem (an unpublished poem addressed to "Justine"), Brontë has him betraying his responsibility to Mina Laury. He promises his foster-mother, Justine, that he will protect her daughter Mina as a surrogate-brother, and ends up seducing Mina instead (Alexander, *Early Writings* 214). Thus the pattern of the father/guardian as untrustworthy, dangerous, and uncaring is well established before this novelette.

Caroline Vernon's actual seduction begins when she is still a child. The first meeting between Zamorna and Caroline Vernon (in *Julia*) begins with a description of Zamorna's bedroom: a room that combines both the imagery of the red room in *Jane Eyre* with the phallic/palace room in earlier juvenilia: "... a large chamber, with a wide & lofty state-bed—windows shrouded in blinds, crimson carpets & curtains—& in four niches as many figures of marble, each holding out a bright candlestick that glittered strongly through the gloom" (Gerin, *Novelettes* 111). Zamorna is sleeping in a little office off from this main room, separate from the entrance hall.

In the classic incest story the child wakes up, either in early dawn or late at night, to find her father/molester by her bed (Blume 44). In Brontë's novelette *Julia*, Zamorna is awakened in his dark, moonlit room by the appearance of the child; the child is the intruder, the unknowing sexual temptress, and the adult must control his immediate, sexual desire. As ten-year-old Caroline creeps into Zamorna's room he calls out her name, and the child, eager to meet him, jumps into his lap: " '. . . come here, child'—The little girl needed no second invitation—in trembling excitement she sprang into the tall Officer's arms—Her nature was seen at once—her whole constitutional turn of feeling revealed itself—She cried & shook, & in answer to some soothing endearment clasped him in her childish embrace. . ." (Gerin, *Novelettes* 114). Zamorna, on feeling the child on his lap, is overcome with sexual excitement, partly because he has been fantasizing about his wife before Caroline arrived, and partly because Caroline reminds him of his wife (they are half-sisters, sharing the same father). In fact, Zamorna is amazed by the reflection of his wife in this child. He says, "You will make much such a woman as your half-sister Mary I fancy—child, I could almost imagine it was her little hand that clasped mine so" (Gerin, *Novelettes* 115).

As Caroline babbles away happily, expressing her innocent desire to be his wife, "That's your wife—am I like your wife? when I'm old enough I'll marry you—" (Gerin, *Novelettes* 115), Zamorna with difficulty restrains his desires. "The brightening moonlight, clearly revealed her features. That eye now bent on them, could distinctly trace even in their imperfect symmetry a foreign wildness, a resemblance which stirred sensations in his heart he would have died rather than yielded to—Sensations he had long thought routed out—but 'Heat and Frost and Thunder had only withered the stems, the roots still remained'" (Gerin, *Novelettes* 114). The openly sexual scene is on one hand culturally believable because the age of consent before 1861 was ten years old (Kincaid 70), but on the other hand it is also highly unusual for the literature of this time; this is a scene that Brontë is creating on her own, not borrowing from conventional Romantic literature. Similar scenes would be common in Victorian pornography, but Brontë, as a young Victorian woman and pastor's daughter, would have no access to that material.

This first meeting between Zamorna and Caroline is broken up by the appearance of Caroline's mother, Louisa Vernon, not by her angry reaction to the scene but by her deliberately ignoring it: "This singular little woman . . . paused at the threshold. 'It is dark,' she said 'I dare not come in.' 'Why madam?' asked her royal jailor as coolly as if he & she had been acquaintances of a century—She uttered a slight exclamation at his voice—'Oh God—I feel frightened!' " (Gerin, *Novelettes* 115). Louisa is finally cajoled into the room, and on entering it, throws Caroline out immediately. Caroline, angry at the dismissal, refuses, until she is ordered by Zamorna to comply.

In incest stories the child often wants the attention from the abuser on some level, and is angry at the mother for disturbing the affection (Malchiodi 145-6). Caroline's message to her mother, "I don't thank you, Mamma" (Gerin, *Novelettes* 115), begins an all-out war for Zamorna's affection between mother and daughter, which continues until Caroline's seduction by Zamorna at the age of fifteen. And as Brontë makes clear, Caroline's mother is silently recording the sexual play between the two for the next five years, blaming the flirtation not only on Zarmona, but on her child. It is Caroline upon whom she takes out her wrath, and Caroline whom she calls a whore, as in the scene where Louisa openly condemns her daughter in front of Zamorna and Caroline's father, Northangerland: " 'I'll tell you all—' almost screamed her ladyship—'I'll lay bare the whole vile scheme—your father shall know you, Miss—what you are & what *he* is—I never mentioned the subject before, but I've noticed, & I've laid it all up & nobody shall hinder me from proclaiming your baseness aloud' " (306–307).

Why would a mother attack her daughter like this, instead of protecting her? The reasons are common to mothers of incest survivors: the overwhelming power of the male/abuser and sexual jealousy (Malchiodi 145–6). In *Julia*, Brontë emphasizes Louisa's powerlessness—as Northangerland's mistress, Louisa is completely dependent, financially and emotionally, on her lover. When Northangerland rebels against Zamorna and begins civil war in Angria, Louisa becomes a political pawn. At the time of this first seduction, she's under house arrest in Zamorna's keeping. After Zamorna wins the civil war, Northangerland drops his mistress completely, and Louisa becomes a dependent of Zamorna: she lives in Zamorna's house, and Zamorna becomes the guardian of her daughter Caroline. Locked in this position, Louisa has no more power than the spouse of an abusive husband; she remains financially dependent on him, his virtual prisoner.

Not that Louisa is to be taken too seriously; she is, as Brontë makes clear, a selfish flirt, a bad mother, someone both Caroline and Zamorna would be better off without. In Freud's female oedipal complex, the daughter, subconsciously desiring the father, rejects the mother, and does not return to her until the father has rebuffed her sexual advances (Eagleton 155–6). In *Caroline*

Vernon, however, the stage is set for the daughter's forbidden desire to be fulfilled (Sadoff 126): Louisa will be in sexual competition with Caroline for Zamorna, and Caroline will win, "killing" the mother and having the father to herself.

As the novelette *Caroline Vernon* begins, Louisa is maintained in one of Zamorna's houses with her daughter, Caroline. Her old lover, Northangerland, has disappeared from the scene, and Zamorna has taken the place of father to the family; he pays the bills, he directs the little girl's studies and acts as her legal guardian. Louisa has determined that her power base with Zamorna would be stronger if she were involved with him sexually, and has attempted long and unsuccessfully to seduce him. Her main problem is that Zamorna is attracted to her teenage daughter, Caroline.

In Brontë's version of the mother-daughter sexual rivalry, the girl (Caroline) and the "father" (Zamorna) are not conscious of their sexual desires; it is only Louisa who is clearly aware of the triangle and is acting upon it. Louisa forces her daughter to wear clothing that hides her developing body: "this young lady's dress by no means accorded with her years & stature, the short-sleeved frock, worked trousers & streaming sash would better have suited the age of nine or ten than of fifteen" (Gerin, *Novelettes* 305). The mother refuses to buy her daughter an adult riding habit, and constantly belittles her appearance, calling her ugly (Gerin, *Novelettes* 312)—all things designed to stifle the young girl's sexuality and stall her development. And although Caroline is innocent of the real reason for Louisa's actions, she is aware that the main cause for all her mother's behavior is sexual jealousy:

> "She's like as if she was angry with me for growing tall—& when I want to be dressed more like a woman & to have scarfs & veils & such things, it does vex her so—then, when she's raving & calling me vain & conceited—a hussey—I can't help sometimes letting her hear a bit of the real truth . . . she's jealous of me—because people will think she is old if she has such a woman as I am for her daughter." (Gerin, *Novelettes* 308)

Brontë seems to endorse this view of Louisa as an older woman now aware that she has no sexual power over Northangerland or Zamorna (and is therefore of no worth in this male world), trapped as a prisoner in Zamorna's house, watching him prepare her young daughter for the sexual prominence she once enjoyed. There is very little concern shown by this mother for her daughter, only nostalgia for her old role as a sexual siren and resentment at her daughter's future success. Brontë makes clear that Louisa cannot win this sexual battle with her daughter because she no longer has any value: her worth in Angria was as a charming mistress, but now older and grayer, she is no match for her fresh fifteen-year-old daughter. Her hysterical fits of rage against Caroline and Zamorna are ignored; she is labelled a liar (Gerin, *Novelettes* 306) and is finally banished by Caroline, who locks her mother in her bedroom. This is the last time that Louisa appears in the novelettes.

Caroline's efforts to please the men and ignore her mother are rewarded; she is taken out of this unhealthy environment and sent to Paris to further her education, while her mother is left to rot at Hawkscliffe. Caroline agrees with Zamorna that her mother is "not fit to be let loose on society" (Gerin, *Novelettes* 314). But once Caroline returns from Paris, Northangerland's distrust of Zamorna keeps Caroline away from her guardian at all times, locked up in his house in Scotland during the great season in Angria. The reason for isolating Caroline is economic: Caroline can make a great social marriage only if she maintains her purity, and her father desires to maintain that at all cost.

This plot twist sets up the seduction attempt in which all the subtle sexual play comes to fruition. This guardian-ward seduction plot, which is, in reality, a displaced father-daughter romance (Mellor 91), was quite standard by the time Brontë was writing in 1839; the plot goes back to the early eighteenth century, and tended to have two basic structures: the guardian seducing and then abandoning the ward (Spencer 112–113), or the guardian persuading his coquette-like ward to accept a position as his wife (Spencer 142–147). Zamorna's change from father-protector to violator is also standard; after Radcliffe's novels, the father who is really a sadistic persecutor was a convention of the gothic romance (Mellor 91).

But Brontë is fascinated with this convention, and revises it so that the seduction is much more a forbidden fantasy (of the daughter winning the father's love) than a scene of violation. Though she attacks Zamorna's character, the tone of the passage is gently erotic; the daughter, though totally innocent and without guile, wins all her surrogate father's attention and love. Caroline now defines her once childish affection for Zamorna as "love" (Gerin, *Novelettes* 337) and sneaks out of her exile to surprise him at his friend's estate. Brontë makes it clear that Caroline's views of Zamorna are ill-formed and naïve: she never comes to a clear understanding of what she wants from Zamorna, and she has never clearly understood his character. She has divided him into two selves: the self of loving guardian, father-figure, and the self of passionate lover. Such a division is common in incest stories: the two selves of the parent, switching back and forth between kind parent and rough molester, the daddy at day versus the daddy at night. Fifteen-year-old Caroline is finally seduced by Zamorna in a room far to the back of the house where her protests could not be heard. Zamorna quickly turns from her kind guardian to an overpowering presence she cannot control:

> Here he was—the man that Montmorency had described to her—all at once
> she knew him—Her Guardian was gone—Something terrible sat in his place—

The fire in the grate was sunk down without a blaze—this silent lonely library, so far away from the inhabited part of the house—was gathering a deeper shade in all its Gothic recesses. She grew faint with dread—she dared not stir—from a vague fear of being arrested by the powerful arm—flung over the back of her chair—At last—through the long & profound silence, a low whisper stole from her lips. "May I go away?" No answer—she attempted to rise— this movement produced the effect she had feared, the arm closed round her—Miss Vernon could not resist its strength, a piteous upward look was her only appeal—He, Satan's eldest Son, smiled at the mute prayer— "She trembles with terror" said he, speaking to himself. "Her face has turned pale as marble within the last minute or two—how did I alarm her? Caroline, do you know me?" (353)

The woman/child, succumbing to her own passion and trust in Zamorna's tenderness toward her (his father personality), agrees to leave with him to his retreat, and thus seals her doom as his mistress. Her sexual worth goes down to nothing (except for Zamorna's needs), and she is kept, like her mother, as a woman/prisoner in Zamorna's house, rejected by the rest of society, and completely dependent on him for her economic survival. But she also, at least for a short while, wins the sexual love of her father. Jane Spencer, in *The Rise of the Woman Novelist: From Aphra Behn to Jane Austen*, says that the romance was attractive to women writers because it "offered escape from male-dominated reality through a fantasy of female power" (184). For Charlotte Brontë, however, the attraction was not female power but masochism, a revelling in erotic oedipal fantasies that promised only abandonment and pain.

With all the abuse overwhelming these female characters, is there any rebellion against the Angrian patriarchy; does Brontë ever attack the injustice of the world she creates? Gilbert and Gubar found Bertha Rochester of *Jane Eyre* to be radically rebellious (*The Madwoman in the Attic* 339), but how would rage appear (if it does) in this much earlier writing, where Charlotte, a still unsophisticated writer, is creating a fantasy world in which she herself is half in love with the Byronic romance?

The novelettes portray a world in which love for women equals self-annihilation: once an Angrian woman becomes sexually involved with a man, her need for his affection quickly becomes an addiction. Without the man, there is no "self" left; she is immediately in danger of death. This need for constant nurturance is made even more difficult by the man's response: both the Byronic heroes of Angria (Zamorna and Northangerland) are abusive with their love, neglectful and cold towards the women who are dependent on them. The Byronic heroes arrive and depart from their lovers at whim. When the women are compliant, the men stay until they get bored; when the women are irritable or angry, they leave quickly. The women's need to maintain whatever love they can get overcomes all other emotions, including anger.

The process of a woman's need for love burying her rage is most apparent in the story of the strongest woman character of the juvenilia, Zenobia Ellrington. Modelled in 1830 after the French feminist, Madame de Staël, Zenobia is wildly different from the other "angelic" women. Highly intelligent and educated (fluent in five languages, a classics scholar) (Alexander, *Early Writings* 22–24), Zenobia is furious at her limited choices. In a world where being large equals power, she is tall and physically threatening: big enough to take up space and be noticed, and strong enough to push one of the Duke's insulting sons down a flight of stairs with a "yell of ungovernable rage" (Alexander, *Edition Volume I* 303). The other women have pale ghostly skin like marble angels; Zenobia looks like the wild black Ashantees with a "dark, glowing complexion" and a "swarthy face" (Alexander, *Edition Volume I* 293, 313). The other women seem "silly" to her, their angelic behavior disgusting. She calls the Duchess merely a "handmaid for the imperious lord who domineers over her" (Alexander, *Edition Volume I* 302).

Zenobia's independence, however, is immediately shaken when she meets with the Duke's eldest son, Arthur Wellesley (who later becomes the Duke of Zamorna). Her unrequited passion for him drives her mad, and she follows the young Zamorna "five hundred miles" to confront him with her jealous love. When she meets him, she looks like a madwoman: her "dishevelled hair hung in wild elf-locks over her face, neck and shoulders, almost concealing her features, which were emaciated and pale as death" (Alexander, *Edition Volume I* 343). In her jealous rage she threatens Zamorna's true love, the angelic Marian Hume: " 'Viper! Viper! Oh that I could sheathe this weapon in her heart!' Here she stopped for want of breath and, drawing a long, sharp, glittering knife from under her cloak, brandished it wildly in the air. . ." (Alexander, *Edition Volume I* 343).

Alexander is right in describing this character as an over-the-top gothic villainess, a character the adolescent Brontë is having great fun creating ("Kingdom" 429). But it is telling that in this overblown, violent scene Zenobia's desire to be loved at all costs has turned her anger away from its real target, Zamorna. Instead, she expresses her rage at her rejection (with the phallic "sharp glittering knife") towards her female competition, the angelic and quite passive Marian Hume.

Zenobia's wild burst of rage seals her doom; the young Zamorna smiles at her "with contempt," and chooses Marian Hume as his wife, abandoning Zenobia for good. Five years later, Brontë brings Zenobia into the novelettes as the wife of the cruelest Byronic hero, the Earl of Northangerland. Brontë at twenty has banished the magic and archetypes of the old Angria, and Zenobia is left with just her defiance, a feeling she constantly represses to avoid her husband's verbal attacks. Northangerland, still disturbed by Zenobia's latent power, sexually rejects her for a string of frivolous, "silly" mistresses (Alexander,

Edition Volume I 302). To insure Zenobia's passivity, Northangerland also maintains a barrage of verbal attacks to destroy whatever independent self she may have left. He attacks her for her unfeminine appearance and conduct: she is not delicate or sweet, she is too hefty to be attractive; prostitutes are a more inviting sexual prospect than she is; she is, perhaps, not really a member of the nobility at all, but an illegitimate child by a mother who was secretly a whore (Alexander, *Edition Volume I* 41). In one of the many scenes where her sexuality is turned against her, Zenobia keeps her silence but lashes out in violence after her husband has left: "the Countess said nothing, she could not speak, but a destructive crack & the splendid fragments of a shivered mirror told what she felt" (Alexander, *Edition Volume I* 42).

Like a good little girl, Zenobia has learned to turn her hatred onto herself, shattering her own self-image. The Zenobia of Angria turns into a parody of her earlier fairy tale self, her huge size becomes extra girth; she is a "stout and portly" (Gerin, *Novelettes* 128) matron who, Brontë says, has no trouble filling up a chair with her behind (Gerin, *Novelettes* 128). And the wild woman who used to roam through the woods now locks herself in her husband's house, staring vacantly out the windows: ". . . a woman who in her thirtieth year has waxed so imperially stout & high that she will not even leave her own saloons for the benefit of fresh air" (Gerin, *Novelettes* 50). In the passage from teenager to young woman, Charlotte Brontë transforms the Glasstown's Arthur Wellesley into the raging, Byronic Zamorna, and the wild Zenobia into a depressed matron—a woman who stalks her sitting room the way that Bertha the madwoman will someday stalk her attic prison.

With the fate of Zenobia, Brontë refuses, even in her most secret writing, to create a woman who successfully rebels against patriarchy. The angry woman will appear in her mature novels, but always as a failed character: Bertha Rochester a self-destructive madwoman in *Jane Eyre*; Shirley Keeldar an outspoken feminist in *Shirley* who turns into a dejected wife once she marries Louis Moore. In Brontë's last novel, *Villette*, the rebellious woman has almost disappeared from the text; the only reflection of Zenobia is Vashti, the wild actress who appears very briefly and has no real impact on the heroine, Lucy Snowe.

In one of her last novelettes, *Captain Henry Hastings*, written in 1838, Brontë does create a way of avoiding female masochism, though the "cure" involves the woman isolating herself and repressing her sexuality. Elizabeth Hastings, the sister of the traitorous and destructive Henry Hastings, is Brontë's new response to male patriarchy; she avoids the real temptation towards self-annihilating, masochistic love by avoiding men altogether, a process made easier by her ugly, "little & thin" body (Gerin, *Novelettes* 180). Like Jane Eyre and Lucy Snowe, her lack of physical beauty makes her almost invisible to men; as a male observer says, she was a "little blighted mortal," a "pale under-sized young woman dressed as plainly as a Quakeress in grey" (Gerin, *Novelettes* 206). In defending her brother, Elizabeth has become a pariah in her father's house, and so is left to support herself as a lady's companion and teacher, becoming the first financially independent female character in the juvenilia.

Elizabeth Hastings is able to keep her clear rational mind and limited independence only by avoiding romance. This concept is not unique to Brontë; Wollstonecraft in her *Vindication of the Rights of Woman* had argued that a woman's rationality was only possible by the "repression, even elimination, of female sexual desire" (Mellor 34). For Brontë, however, this rationality is even more fragile, since there is no love in her world that is not defined by helpless masochism. When Elizabeth Hastings is approached by her first admirer, William Percy, she represses her own powerful sexual urges and rejects his proposition, a difficult decision since Percy is the first man to, like Rochester, see past her reserve to her "inmost heart" (Gerin, *Novelettes* 241).

Through the adolescent juvenilia, and especially the novelettes, we can see in crude form the disturbing fantasies (father-daughter seduction, masochism) and fatalism (the failure of rebellion) that reverberate through all of Brontë's mature novels, even as they are buried underground in complex characterizations and metaphor. The incestuous affair between Caroline and Zamorna becomes the disturbing flirtation between Polly and Mr. Home, or Jane Eyre in love with a man who "might almost be [her] father" (293). If the juvenilia is fulfilled erotic fantasy, and not just literary apprenticeship, then the uncomfortable themes that reoccur ten years later in *Jane Eyre* are entrenched in Brontë's psyche. If readers today are still disturbed by Brontë's novels, they have good reason.

Works Cited

Alexander, Christine. *The Early Writings of Charlotte Brontë.* Amherst, NY: Prometheus Books, 1983.

Alexander, Christine, ed. *An Edition of the Early Writings of Charlotte Brontë: Volume I: The Glass Town Saga 1826–1832.* Oxford: Basil Blackwell Ltd., 1987.

Alexander, Christine, ed. *An Edition of the Early Writings of Charlottte Brontë: Volume II: The Rise of Angria 1833–1835 Part 1: 1833–1834.* Oxford: Basil Blackwell Ltd., 1991.

Alexander, Christine, ed. *An Edition of the Early Writings of Charlotte Brontë: Volume II: The Rise of Angria 1833–1835 Part 2: 1834–1835.* Oxford: Basil Blackwell Ltd., 1991.

Alexander, Christine. " 'That Kingdom of Gloom': Charlotte Brontë, the Annuals, and the Gothic." *Nineteenth-Century Literature* 47 (March 1993): 409–436.

Blume, E. Sue. *Secret Survivors: Uncovering Incest and its Aftereffects in Women.* New York: Ballantine Books, 1990.

Brontë, Charlotte. *Jane Eyre.* New York: Penguin Classics, 1985.

———. *Shirley.* New York: Penguin Books, 1988.

———. *Villette.* New York: Bantam Books, 1986.

Chase, Karen. *Eros and Psyche: The Representation of Personality in Charlotte Brontë, Charles Dickens and George Eliot.* New York: Methuen, 1984.

Eagleton, Terry. *Literary Theory: An Introduction.* Minneapolis: University of Minnesota Press, 1983.

Freud, Sigmund. *The Interpretation of Dreams.* New York: Avon Books, 1965.

Gerin, Winifred. *Charlotte Brontë: The Evolution of Genius.* London: Oxford University Press, 1967.

Gerin, Winifred, ed. *Five Novelettes.* London: The Folio Press, 1971.

Gilbert, Sandra M., and Susan Gubar. *The Madwoman in the Attic: The Woman Writer and the Nineteenth-Century Literary Imagination.* New Haven: Yale University Press, 1979.

Hogg, James. *The Private Memoirs and Confessions of a Justified Sinner.* London: The Cresset Press, 1947.

Kincaid, James R. *Child Loving: The Erotic Child and Victorian Culture.* New York: Routledge, 1992.

Malchiodi, Cathy A. *Breaking the Silence: Art Therapy With Children from Violent Homes.* New York: Brunner/Mazel Publishers, 1990.

Marcus, Stephen. *The Other Victorians: A Study of Sexuality and Pornography in Mid-Nineteenth-Century England.* New York: Basic Books, 1966.

Mellor, Anne K. *Romanticism & Gender.* New York: Routledge, 1993.

Ratchford, Fannie. *The Brontës' Web of Childhood.* New York: Columbia University Press, 1941.

Ratchford, Fannie Elizabeth, and William C. DeVane. *Legends of Angria: Compiled from the Early Writings of Charlotte Brontë.* New Haven: Yale University Press, 1933.

Rush, Florence. *The Best Kept Secret: Sexual Abuse of Children.* New York: McGraw-Hill Book Company, 1980.

Sadoff, Dianne. *Monsters of Affection: Dickens, Eliot and Brontë on Fatherhood.* Baltimore: The Johns Hopkins University Press, 1982.

Spencer, Jane. *The Rise of the Woman Novelist: From Aphra Behn to Jane Austen.* Oxford: Basil Blackwell Ltd., 1986.

Safe Space or Danger Zone?:
Incest and the Paradox of Writing in Woolf's Life

Diana L. Swanson

I: Writing and Sexual Abuse

Recent work in critical theory and cultural studies concentrates on the functions of discourse in the construction of identities, histories, and social norms, suggesting an intimate, dialectical relationship between the stories people tell and the lives people live.[1] What is the relationship between writing and living as a "self" and an active agent in one's social world when one has been the victim of interpersonal violence that violates and denies one's personhood and agency? Can writing be a "safe space" in which women can tell—construct and convey—their stories of sexual abuse and assault and (re)construct competent, functional, integrated selves? Writing involves agency, active reconstruction of one's experiences and creation of one's ideas. And writing involves inter-relatedness, communicating with others in a common-enough language. Can these aspects of writing be an effective antidote to the experience of powerlessness, alienation, and obliteration of self that attends rape or incest, for example?

The words of Virginia Woolf (1882–1941), survivor of incest[2] and accomplished writer of fiction, biography, literary and social criticism, letters, and diaries, suggest that the answer is yes. In a diary entry for 1933, Woolf says, "I thought, driving through Richmond last night, something very profound about the synthesis of my being: how only writing composes it: how nothing makes a whole unless I am writing" (*Writer's Diary* 201). But if writing can be a "safe space" can it also be a "danger zone"? Given Woolf's well-known and at times extreme anxiety about publication, for example, she must have experienced danger in some aspects of the writing process.

In fact, for victims of sexual abuse to "speak out" about their experiences may at times have oppressive rather than liberatory consequences; the conditions of disclosure must be carefully analyzed before any judgments can be made about the effectiveness or consequences of "breaking silence" (Alcoff and Gray 263 and passim). Thus, answers to the questions outlined above must take into account the social and historical context, audience, and genre of the writing as well as what we know about the effects of sexual abuse and the process of recovery.[3]

Judith Herman, in her introduction to *Trauma and Recovery*, simply and eloquently outlines the dynamics of human response to trauma:

> The ordinary response to atrocities is to banish them from consciousness. . . . Atrocities, however, refuse to be buried. . . . The conflict between the will to deny horrible events and the will to proclaim them aloud is the central dialectic of psychological trauma. People who have survived atrocities often tell their stories in a highly emotional, contradictory, and fragmented manner which undermines their credibility and thereby serves the twin imperatives of truth-telling and secrecy. (1)

Sexual abuse inflicts severe emotional and often physical pain and, as an act, denies the personhood of the victim. It therefore instigates the dialectic Herman describes above, causing serious damage to the victim's memory, personality structure, and relationships to others. The recovery process must directly address and redress the victim's loss of control over her life, loss of memory, and loss of interpersonal connection.

Woolf's posthumously published memoirs and her fiction, particularly her first novel, *The Voyage Out* (1915), suggest that writing for Woolf created both a safe space for (re)constructing a self and developing a feminist critique of her family history, and a danger zone resonant with the threat of exposure, ridicule, and violation. Safety and danger, and the strategies Woolf employs to create the one and deflect the other, depend greatly on the genre—memoir or fiction—of a work and on its expected audience—self, friends and family, or the general public.

II: Writing as Self-Construction

In her last memoir, "A Sketch of the Past," written in 1939–40, Woolf speculates about the origins of her impulse to write and the function of writing in her life:

> The shock-receiving capacity is what makes me a writer. I hazard the explanation that a shock is at once in my case followed by the desire to explain it. I feel that I have had a blow; but it is not as I thought as a child, simply a blow from some enemy hidden behind the cottonwool of daily life; it is

> or will become a revelation of some order; it is a token of some real thing behind appearances; and I make it real by putting it into words. It is only by putting it into words that I make it whole; this wholeness means that it has lost the power to hurt me; it gives me, perhaps because by doing so I take away the pain, a great delight to put the severed parts together. (72)

These words describe, at least in part, how Virginia Woolf's writing is a response to and a triumph over emotional pain and psychic dismemberment, particularly over the trauma of her childhood in an incestuous family.

In this section of her memoir, Woolf distinguishes between "shocks," "blows," or "moments of being," that is, moments of emotional intensity and clarity, and what she calls "non-being" or "the cottonwool of daily life." Woolf explains that most of her days, as a child and as an adult, consist of non-being, a state in which life "is not lived consciously" (70), nothing "[makes] any dint upon me" (71), nothing is memorable. Then occasionally "there [is] a sudden violent shock; something [happens] so violently" that she remembers it all her life. This description of oscillation between cottonwool and shocks suggests the oscillation, described by psychologists and by sexual abuse survivors themselves, between the numbness acquired as a defence against the pain and/or memories of abuse and moments of intensity when memories and/or feelings intrude. The moments of being set off from the cottonwool also suggest the sealed off traumatic memories of abuse survivors (Herman 37–38). Many of the moments Woolf remembers so intensely, she says, "brought with them a peculiar horror and a physical collapse; they seemed dominant; myself passive" (72). Among these moments Woolf describes in the opening section of the memoir is a memory of her older stepbrother, Gerald Duckworth, exploring her "private parts" when she was perhaps six, perhaps younger.

Whether a shock brings incapacitation or revelation, Woolf says, depends on her ability to explain it by "putting it into words." Finding the words to explain a shocking "moment of being" brings that moment out of its frozen, non-verbal, sealed off state and makes it part of the ongoing narrative of her life—"puts the severed parts together." Woolf's passion for writing was, in large part, a passion for survival and self-healing from the fragmentation caused by abuse, a passion for creating and claiming power and efficacy, and a passion for explaining a threatening and unjust world.

Woolf's memoirs reveal how writing served to create a space for finding her own perspective on her experience, her family, and her society. In "Reminiscences" (1907–08), "22 Hyde Park Gate" (1920 or 1921), and especially "A Sketch of the Past" (1939–40), Woolf pieces together her memories to analyze and come to an understanding of the multiple pressures of a Victorian patriarchal family and society upon its daughters. As part of this project, she remembers, and analyzes the impact of, her experience of incest.

The Victorian middle-class family was organized around the needs and desires of the men. Woolf's mother, Julia Stephen, believed in conventional Victorian domestic values and trained her daughters to follow in her footsteps ("Reminiscences," "A Sketch"). Virginia states baldly that "my mother believed that all men required an infinity of care" ("22 Hyde Park Gate" 165). After Julia's death, Leslie Stephen expected his daughters to take on the roles his wife had performed. Especially after the deaths of their mother and their older half-sister, Virginia and her sister, Vanessa, then in their teens, were expected to minister to and sympathize with their father and their brothers, to run the household, to make their debut in society, and radiate charm around the tea table:

> While father preserved the framework of [upper-middle-class Victorian society], George filled in the framework with all kinds of minutely-teethed saws; and the machine into which our rebellious bodies were inserted in 1900 not only held us tight in its framework, but bit into us with innumerable sharp teeth. ("A Sketch" 151–152)

George Duckworth, their older half-brother, in particular, not only insisted that his sisters "sit passive and applaud the Victorian males" but also that they accompany him to social events, contribute to his social triumphs, and "share his views, approve of his beliefs" ("A Sketch" 154). Every party and dance was "a test" of their womanhood and social success (156); and George entreated and commanded their attendance with kisses, embraces, and tantrums. In "22 Hyde Park Gate," Woolf courageously revealed to her friends in the Bloomsbury Memoir Club that after these parties George brought these kisses, embraces, and more to her bed. George clearly felt that his claim to Virginia extended not only to her love, time, loyalty, and approval, but also to her body.

Thus, by their teens, Virginia and Vanessa Stephen had been well-trained in the duties of the Angel in the House. They had learned that it was their role selflessly to take "an infinity of care" for the needs and feelings of the men in the family, without expecting a commensurate attention on the part of others, or themselves, to discerning and responding to their own needs and feelings. In her dedication to exploring and interpreting her own feelings and memories in her memoirs, diaries, and novels, Woolf made a courageous break with this early training, implicitly affirming the importance and value of her own emotional life.

In her memoirs, she also remembers how writing helped her resist her own erasure. She describes how, while the outward organization of her life as a girl perforce revolved around the requirements of the men in the family and of social tradition,

> there was a spectator in me who, even while I squirmed and obeyed, re-
> mained observant, note taking for some future revision. The spectacle of
> George, laying down laws in his leather arm chair so instinctively, so
> unhesitatingly, fascinated me. Upstairs alone in my room I wrote a sketch of
> his probable career; which his actual career followed almost to the letter. ("A
> Sketch" 154)

Through writing, the young Virginia, up in her own room, could "revise" her
experience of the moment, setting it in "some order" different from that
assumed by George, reconnecting with her own feelings and perceptions. She
could criticize and distance herself from George's values and ambitions and
thus begin to assert her own different values and perspective on the world.
During a humiliating time at a dance: "I recall that the good friend who is
with me still, upheld me; that sense of the spectacle; the dispassionate separate
sense that I am seeing what will be useful later; I could even find the words
for the scene as I stood there" (155–156). Writing enabled her to distance
herself from her experiences of humiliation, exploitation, and silence in service
to her brother and through "finding the words" build a sense of her own
perspective and thus identity.

Victims of sexual and other forms of abuse generally use a survival strategy
of distancing, removing their minds from their bodies and numbing their feelings
and memories. Virginia's strategy of distancing herself through words and writing
bears an affinity to this survival strategy and shares some of its advantages and
disadvantages. The advantages are immediate: emotional and physical survival.
Louise DeSalvo, discussing Virginia's early journals and stories, makes the case
that writing literally "helped save Virginia Woolf's life" during some of her most
difficult and painful adolescent years by serving as the medium through which
she could express what was happening to her and start to forge an autonomous
and adult self (*Virginia Woolf* 261). In "Professions for Women," Woolf maintains
that her decision as a young writer to "kill" the Angel in the House was an act
of self-defense: "Had I not killed her she would have killed me. She would have
plucked the heart out of my writing" ("Professions" 238). In 1934, she explained
her continual experimentation with form and style throughout her adult career
as the result of having "to some extent forced myself to break every mould and
find a fresh form of being that is of expression, for everything I feel or think"
(*Writer's Diary* 213). For Woolf, being was expression, expression being. Linda
Brodkey maintains that Woolf "resists alienation by writing. It is not a unified
self she creates in words, but a self drafted and redrafted as possible verbal
repertoires—a self born in language use" (408).

This shifting and multiple self is not something to be uncritically celebrated,
however. It bears some disturbing similarities to the emotionally disconnected,

fragmented, and sometimes multiple personalities of many abuse victims who once they have learned to split off from their bodies and feelings do not know how to reconnect. DeSalvo points out, for example, that in her juvenile diaries Woolf employed an alter ego, a "Miss Jan," who was the one who had troubles, felt afraid or angry (*Virginia Woolf: The Impact*, 233–248). As an adult, Woolf does not simply say that writing helps her compose her being, but that "*only* writing composes it" (emphasis added). Again in 1937, as she began a memoir of her nephew Julian Bell in response to his death in the Spanish Civil War, she wrote: "I am so composed that *nothing* is real unless I write it" (Bell II 255, emphasis added). Woolf's words indicate an extreme dependence on writing to convince herself of her own reality, to coalesce her memories and present sensations. "My writing" and "me" are synonymous. Woolf's discussion of the interrelation of writing and being can be read as indicating her awareness of the complex ways language constructs reality and subjectivity, as well as her sophisticated understanding of "the two people," "I now" and "I then," and the way "this past is much affected by the present moment" and vice versa (75).

But the writing–dependent self is vulnerable in a number of ways. First, on a practical level, one cannot write all the time or about everything. Woolf often mentions in diaries and letters how disconnected and numb she gets when she cannot write for days or weeks at a time. Second, Toni A. H. McNaron has demonstrated that "Woolf's reliance on art to provide an order unavailable in life" and her technique of writing in scenes derived from moments of being, "moments of sharp recall," make her vulnerable to reliving those very moments of pain, chaos, and powerlessness that she depends on writing to control ("Uneasy Solace" 251 and passim). Third, when one shares one's writing with others or publishes it, it is one's *self* which one has spent such labor and pain creating that gets approved or rejected. Thus Woolf's extreme anxiety and vulnerability whenever one of her books was published. Finally, language is incapable of bearing the burden of realizing the self completely, of fully expressing the life of the body and its emotions. To be a self born *only* in language use is to be alienated from the body and distanced from experience, not rooted in an inner, felt knowledge of existence and desire. The "self born in language use" is Woolf's great achievement in the face of the abuse and appropriation which threatened to rob her of a vital, feeling self; it is also her tragedy. Writing for Woolf was both a symptom of her abuse and her triumph over it.

III: Writing as Reconnection

While writing was a lifeline, albeit tenuous, for Woolf through dangerous emotional waters, sharing that writing with others was often terrifying, for she was uttering forbidden and unspeakable truths about her family, patriarchal society, and her "own experiences as a body" ("Professions" 241). Yet, communicating with others and putting one's experience in a social, not only a personal, context is essential to overcoming the alienation caused by abuse. Hence, Woolf developed writing strategies of coding, self-censorship, and splitting of event and affect.

Alcoff and Gray's analysis of the subversive potential of "survivor speech" (the reports of [mostly] women who have suffered rape, incest, or sexual assault) and its silencing and recuperation by dominant discourses can help clarify the obstacles to public disclosure that Woolf faced and the efficacy as well as the limitations of her writing strategies. Survivor speech transgresses the dominant social order by authorizing discounted or disallowed speakers such as women and children and by presuming concepts such as "husband rapist" or "brother rapist" that are oxymoronic according to the assumptions of dominant discourses. Such moves allow and require the reconceptualization of social roles and power structures. The dominant order generally meets the threat posed by survivor speech by silencing or recuperation:

> Silencing works by physically denying certain individuals a speaking role—for example, through institutionalization, denial of access to listeners or readers, or the controlled administration of drugs. . . . Strategies of recuperation include categorizing survivor speech as mad, as evidence of women's or children's hysterical or mendacious tendencies, or even as testimony to women's essential nature as helpless victims in need of patriarchal protection. (268)

The confessional is the "discursive arrangement" most often deployed to recuperate survivor speech (270). Foucault traces the history of the confessional as a verifying and normalizing civil and religious ritual in Western society from the Lateran Council of 1215 through the development of psychoanalysis and criminal psychology in the twentieth century (*The History of Sexuality, Vol. 1*, cited in Alcoff and Gray 270–272). The confessional structure frames the survivor's testimony within the discourse of an "expert"—priest, doctor, judge, psychiatrist—purporting to evaluate and interpret her words and experience in order to arrive at the "truth." Alcoff and Gray elucidate several "dangers of the confessional" that are applicable to Woolf's situation. First, the confessional mode tends to focus "attention on the victim and her psychological state" and deflect it from the perpetrator and his actions, suggesting that the "problem" to be dealt with is the victim's psychology or morality not the perpetrator's violent behavior. Second, the confessional mode assumes a necessity for interpretation of the survivor's story by an "objective" "expert." Finally, the confessional sets up dichotomies between "experience and theory, feelings and knowledge, subjective and objective, and mind and body," dichotomies which, like the "need" for an expert, construct the survivor herself as the least authoritative source of testimony and interpretation of her own experience and the experiences of other survivors (279–280). In order to authorize survivor discourse, Alcoff and Gray argue that "we need to transform arrangements of speaking to create spaces where survivors are authorized to be both witnesses and experts, both reporters of experience and theorists of experience" (282). The challenge Woolf faced in her memoir and fiction was to transform the confessional mode of autobiography so as to authorize herself as witness and theorist.

In her life, Woolf experienced both silencing and recuperation of her story of incest. The circumstances of her life in a Victorian family in the late nineteenth century made it impossible for her to speak out about the incest while it was occurring. Quentin Bell alludes to the Stephen sisters' training in sexual "purity" and ignorance and explains that:

> it would have been hard for [George's] half-sisters to know at what point to draw a line, to voice objections, to risk evoking a painful and embarrassing scandal: harder still to find someone to whom they could speak at all. Stella, Leslie, the aunts—all would have been bewildered, horrified, indignant, and incredulous. (43)

To speak out would only have brought Woolf's own motives and purity of mind into question. The system of social credit, credibility, and authority was against her. As Lyndall Gordon points out, Woolf

> could not hope to combat the impeccable social front that George represented. . . . His mastery as effective head of the family, his age (he was thirty-six, his sister twenty), her dependence (he had a thousand pounds a year, she fifty) backed his overtures. (119)

Once George's behavior became known,[4] no serious connection was made by others between the abuse and Woolf's nervous breakdowns or sexual troubles, no action was taken against George, nor did Woolf find much support later in life for her interpretation of George's behavior as part of the patriarchal organization of the family and society.[5] George's behavior was not interrogated as indicative of mental dysfunction or criminal tendencies. Rather, Woolf was perceived by her doctors and her family as congenitally prone to insanity and/ or as hysterical and frigid.[6] For example, even Woolf's sister Vanessa, appealed to for advice after Virginia and Leonard's honeymoon in 1912, called her frigid (Gordon 152). The extent to which sexual abuse was not taken seriously by Woolf's family and doctors is indicated by the decision, in 1913, to send Woolf to George Duckworth's country house to recuperate from a breakdown and suicide attempt.

Woolf could not find much support in the social or political world beyond her family, either. The late nineteenth- and early twentieth-century women's movement in Britain did address sexual violence including stranger rape, marital rape, and child sexual abuse and incest, analyzing them as part of the system of male power over women and advocating legislative as well as social solutions. Women's rights advocates, however, were under concerted attack by the teens and twenties as anti-sex, puritanical, frigid, and neurotic (Jeffreys, *The Spinster and Her Enemies*). Freud and the sexologists were in the ascendancy in medicine and psychology. Their work variously tends to trivialize or deny rape and sexual abuse, to define normal, mature femininity as participation in conventional heterosexuality, and to label female celibacy as neurosis. Their ideas were being taken up by intellectuals, many social reformers, and even some workers in the women's movement. The Woolfs' own Hogarth Press published the English editions of Freud's work, translated by their friend, James Strachey.

Such a situation of gender inequality in all forms of power and authority and such a system of sexual meanings and definitions of normality could only cultivate indirect modes of writing about incest, what Woolf called her "side-long approach" ("A Sketch" 150). Yet she also says that "on the other hand, the surface manner allows one, as I have found, to slip in things that would be inaudible if one marched straight up and spoke out loud" (150).

Woolf's early mock-journalistic sketch, "Terrible Tragedy in A Duckpond, by One of the Drowned" (1899, 1904), may very well be her first attempt to communicate her incest experiences. This overtly humorous piece uses drowning as a metaphor for incest and "duckweed" as code for "Duckworth," according to Louise DeSalvo's analysis (255–261). Originally written in Woolf's private journal, and later sent to her cousin, Emma Vaughan, with instructions to "read my work carefully—not missing my peculiar words" (*Letters I* 28), "Terrible Tragedy" marks the beginning of Woolf's use of humor and coding to tell but simultaneously cover up her incest story.

Woolf's earliest memoir, "Reminiscences," and her first novel, *The Voyage Out*, continue these strategies of indirection. Woolf wrote "Reminiscences" in 1907–08, at the same time that she was in the early stages of her first novel, *The Voyage Out* (1915). As she completed them, she sent chapters of both to her brother-in-law, Clive Bell, who, while encouraging her writing, criticized her for her "prejudice against men" and was not receptive to her feminist insights (*Letters I* 383). Such an audience would not be conducive to the kind of full reconstruction of her incest story that therapists such as Herman or Bass and Davis call for. Woolf's letters at the time indicate that she was also concerned about the possible reception of her novel upon publication, admitting to Clive, for example, that it was difficult "to ignore the opinion of one's probable readers" (*Letters I* 383).

"Reminiscences," written for Vanessa's son, Julian, and unfinished, concentrates almost entirely on Woolf's mother and older half-sister and on Vanessa in its recounting of family history. However, near the end, it spends a long, two-page paragraph discussing George's behavior towards Virginia and Vanessa after their mother's death, when, Woolf says, "some restraint seemed to burst" (57). He seemed "immaculate" in character, and the Stephen children were taught so to think: "he showed himself so sad, so affectionate, so boundlessly unselfish in his plans, that the voices of all women cried aloud in his praise, and men were touched by his modest virtues" (57). But, says Woolf, such good-natured qualities were complicated in George by "a racing sea of emotions" and "violent gusts of passion." She attempts to explain George's character and actions: "nature, we may suppose, had supplied him with abundant animal vigour, but she had neglected to set an efficient brain in control of it" (58). The result was that "under the name of unselfishness he allowed himself to commit acts which a cleverer man would have called tyrannical; and, profoundly believing in the purity of his love, behaved little better than a brute" (58). This is all that Woolf allows herself to write at this time, but the connotations, particularly the Victorian connotations, of the words and phrases she uses—violent passion, animal vigour, the need of reason to control it, tyranny, purity of love vs. brutishness—hint at sexual indiscretion and coercion.

This early memoir of George concentrates on analyzing and explaining his character as a problem of human nature. Woolf also defends Virginia and Vanessa's early idealization of him and confusion over whether to trust him (common reactions of incest victims) as perfectly understandable given his standing in their social world (57). Thus, even in this short, early autobiographical fragment Woolf steers away from some of the pitfalls of the confessional mode, insisting on analyzing the perpetrator's behavior as the problem and placing the victims' silence in a context that explains it as a factor of social authority. By so doing she is also constructing her narrative voice as an authority on the family history, speculating about causes and effects, and avoiding presenting her adolescent self as a "case" to be analyzed or diagnosed by an expert other.

Woolf's first novel, *The Voyage Out*, is her first major, public articulation of her experience as a patriarchal daughter and an incest victim; her goal was to represent "a view of one's own" and "to give voice to some of the perplexities of her sex" (*Letters I* 383).[7] It is also her novel that concentrates most fully on a female protagonist who has suffered sexual abuse and on the effects this has on her development. *The Voyage Out* is about the struggle of Rachel Vinrace (a young middle-class British woman like Virginia Stephen) to become a knowledgeable, competent, adult person, and her defeat by the socio-sexual forces of British society. After becoming engaged, Rachel dies of a "fever;" that is, she dies of the heated (i.e. sexual) violence against women that marks her society.

Writing *The Voyage Out* inevitably raised Woolf's anxieties about her "probable readers." Symptomatic of her anxieties about publication is the extraordinary extent to which she revised and redrafted this novel. Louise DeSalvo's study of the manuscripts suggests that "no fewer than seven drafts of the novel once existed, but there may have been as many as eleven or twelve" (*Virginia Woolf's First Voyage* 9). DeSalvo also documents that, as Woolf revised earlier drafts with an eye towards publication, she consistently cut or made more obscure material concerning sexual abuse and feminist critique as well as autobiographical material. These concerns are left in the text as trace elements, in a sense, discernible if one pays attention to dreams, literary allusion, imagery, and Woolf's personal code words such as duckweed.

In *The Voyage Out*, incest is hinted at in the descriptions of the protagonist Rachel Vinrace's father and represented at a remove and by synecdoche by Mr. Dalloway's forced kiss. For example, Rachel's Aunt Helen suspects Willoughby Vinrace of "nameless atrocities with regard to his daughter" (24). And Willoughby's plans for Rachel's future reveal his desire to educate her to be his spouse-like companion; he tells Helen he wants Rachel to become his hostess and housekeeper. What is most insistently represented in the novel, however, is the alienated and split consciousness of Rachel and her consequent life-threatening inability to negotiate adult society and coming-of-age, particularly engagement and marriage. The novel makes clear that Rachel consistently moves through life in a distanced, dissociated state reminiscent of Woolf's cottonwool of non-being. For example, she had learned from her family not to feel or express intense emotions (36). The result is that Rachel feels disconnected from others, thinking "let these odd men and women—her aunts, the Hunts, Ridley, Helen, Mr. Pepper, and the rest—be symbols . . . symbols of age, of youth, of motherhood, of learning, and beautiful often as people upon the stage are beautiful. It appeared that nobody ever said a thing they meant, or ever talked of a feeling they felt" (37). The novel also represents some of the immediate effects of abuse. After Mr. Dalloway grabs and kisses Rachel,

> her head was cold, her knees shaking, and the physical pain of the emotion was so great that she could only keep herself moving above the great leaps of her heart. She leant upon the rail of the ship, and gradually ceased to feel, for a chill of body and mind crept over her. (76)

Rachel's reaction to the pain of violation is the typical reaction of victims of sexual abuse, who in order to survive numb themselves to what is happening. Thus Woolf implies a link between an experience of abuse and the detached fog in which Rachel tends to live.

The link between the cause (sexual abuse) and the consequences (Rachel's illness, nightmares and hallucination, inability to compose her life) is further suggested through imagery, coding and allusion. The night after Dalloway's "kiss," Rachel's fear and pain return to her in her dreams:

> She dreamt that she was walking down a long tunnel. . . . [which] opened and became a vault; she found herself trapped in it, bricks meeting her wherever she turned, along with a little deformed man. . . . His face was pitted and like the face of an animal. . . . Still and cold as death she lay, not daring to move. (77)

Instigated by Dalloway's violation, this dream expresses the horror and feeling of entrapment sexual abuse creates and the threat to survival it represents. Rachel freezes into terrified immobility, just as she numbs herself to her anguish after Dalloway kisses her. The "vault" suggests a burial vault, and indeed, Rachel lies "still and cold as death," while the bricks suggest the typical brick middle-class London home. Woolf implies that the family home can become a place of captivity for girls in which sexual violation is a terrifying threat to survival.

The image of men with animal-like faces surfaces again in *The Voyage Out* through allusion. Rachel's fatal "fever" comes upon her while the invocation to Sabrina, the virgin goddess of the river in Milton's *Comus: A Mask,* is read aloud, significantly, by her fiancé, Terence Hewet. Milton describes Comus as a male Circe who tempts travellers through his forest to drink from his "Crystal Glass," upon which their faces change "into some brutish form of Wolf, or Bear,/Or ounce, or Tiger, Hog, or bearded Goat" (ll. 71–72), and they become part of his rowdy and lascivious band of followers. The story of *Comus* centers on Comus's attempt to rape The Lady lost in his forest. Woolf's use of an allusion to *Comus* to introduce Rachel's fever might suggest to the general reader a link between sexual violence, Rachel's engagement, and Rachel's illness. The goddess Sabrina saves The Lady from Comus; Terence's reading of the invocation to Sabrina seems to invoke Rachel's fever, which "saves" her from her engagement and upcoming marriage. But this allusion also allows Woolf to use her private code about George Duckworth. The beast-faced men of Comus's band not only recall the animal-faced man of Rachel's nightmare but also Woolf's description of George in her memoirs: "though he had the curls of a God and the ears of a faun, he had unmistakenly the eyes of a pig." Again, "his face was sallow and scored with innumerable wrinkles, for his skin was as loose and flexible as a pug dog's" ("22 Hyde Park Gate" 166, 172). Woolf publicly, in code, links incest and Rachel's death, compares herself to Rachel, and suggests a connection between the sexual entrapment of girls in the family house and Rachel's impending marriage: they are both part of a patriarchal sexual system that threatens the survival and well-being of women.

That Woolf resurrects the metaphor of drowning and her code word "duckweed" in this novel as well underscores the validity of this reading. In Rachel's hallucinations during her fatal illness, she feels herself to be drowning in a pool of "sticky," semen-like water (340–341). Earlier in the novel, Mr. Dalloway had recounted a conversation in which the captain of the *Mauritania* had said that the danger he most feared for his ship was " *'sedgius aquatici,'* . . . which I take to be a kind of duck-weed" (42). The ship of Rachel's life has encountered in its maiden voyage out the danger most to be feared. Rachel, like Virginia Stephen, is "One of the Drowned," drowning in duckweed. Rachel's fate indicates the extremity of Woolf's pain and fear about sexual abuse and her knowledge that it produces serious obstacles to the achievement of a productive adult life. *The Voyage Out* is, in a way, a rewriting of "Terrible Tragedy in a Duckpond," and enlarges upon its strategy of coding.

While "Reminiscences" hints vaguely that George Duckworth has done something terrible and sexual to his sisters, in her first novel Woolf represents the emotional experience of incest and some of its psychological consequences through Rachel. Woolf thus splits autobiographical event and emotional content between the memoir and the fiction. Coding and splitting event and affect allow her to both tell and hide her story, to obey "the twin imperatives of truth-telling and secrecy." In this sense, these writing strategies can be seen as a replication of the psychological symptoms of trauma, as "hysterical" writing. But these strategies also allow her to avoid exposing her own emotions and psyche to the diagnosis of "the confessional" and instead to become the "expert interpreter" herself through her narrator who, by juxtaposition and comment, proposes an analysis of the sexual politics of Rachel's life.

Woolf's next memoir, "22 Hyde Park Gate," written years later in 1920 or early 1921, is the first in which she clearly states that George Duckworth sexually abused her, and in this way marks an important break with the earlier memoir. As in "Reminiscences," however, Woolf's own feelings about the abuse and interpretation of its significance for her own life do not come to the fore. The focus is on George's social ambitions, intense and muddled emotions, and plans for his sisters' social triumphs, again implying that he and his actions are the "problem case" to analyze, not Woolf herself. "22 Hyde Park Gate" concludes with a description of Virginia's first evening out to dinner and the theatre with George, ending with him tiptoeing into her room, flinging himself on her bed, and taking her "in his arms" (177). The final sentence ironically juxtaposes George's public image and private behavior: "Yes, the old ladies of Kensington and Belgravia never knew that George Duckworth was not only father and mother, brother and sister to those poor Stephen girls; he was their lover also" (177).

Woolf presented this piece to the Bloomsbury Memoir Club, a group of friends committed to openness and truth-telling, but also a group composed mostly of men, several of whom, such as Desmond MacCarthy, Woolf had already had conflicts with over women's issues. This would be an audience of "advanced" but not feminist views, open to talk about sex but not sympathetic to analyses of sexual politics nor necessarily a safe audience to whom to disclose the fear and pain of violation. Accordingly, "Reminiscences" resurrects "Terrible Tragedy's" strategy of deflecting attention through humor. The tone of the piece is sarcastic, ironic, witty. This approach allows her coolly to spear George Duckworth with her wit like an entomologist pinning a bug to a card, labelling him as a snob and a Victorian throwback as well as incredibly self-ignorant:

> His talk was all of ivory buttons that the coachmen of Cabinet Ministers wear in their coats; of having the entree at Court; of baronies descending in the female line. . . . His secret dreams as he sat in the red leather chair . . . were all of marrying a wife with diamonds, and having a coachman with a button, and having the entree at Court. But the danger was that his dreams were secret even to himself. (169)

The few times Woolf alludes to what it felt like to be George Duckworth's sister, she uses slightly melodramatic language, conveying a sense of how overwhelming it was but also making light of it. For example, "as [George's] passions increased and his desires became more vehement . . . one felt like an unfortunate minnow shut up in the same tank with an unwieldy and turbulent whale" (169).

A year later, for the same audience, she wrote "Old Bloomsbury," which mainly concerns the beginning of the Bloomsbury Group and a new life after her father's death. At the beginning of the piece, though, she brings her audience back to the end of her previous memoir, and indicates by a simple change in verb tense—would/did her audience catch it?—that George's abuse was not a single event but habitual:

> it was long past midnight that I got into bed and sat reading a page or two of *Marius the Epicurean* for which I had then a passion. There would be a tap at the door; the light would be turned out and George would fling himself on my bed, cuddling and kissing and otherwise embracing me. (182)

She also maintains that her breakdown after her father's death was "not unnaturally the result of all these emotions and complications" of the Stephen family life (183), suggesting an environmental cause of her "madness" and a link to George, among other sources, rather than simply a congenital, constitutional illness as her family liked to believe.

In the twenties and thirties, Woolf represented the emotional content of her experiences through her fiction, rather than her memoirs, continuing the early pattern of splitting affect from the overt autobiographical writing and placing it in the novels. The novels, her public texts, represent the emotions of the experience of abuse often without explicitly tying those emotions to the events or by displacing them to other kinds of people or to other, though often similar, events. In *Mrs. Dalloway* (1925), for example, Septimus Smith, a veteran of World War I, experiences dissociation, flashbacks, hallucinations, emotional numbing, alienation from other people, and a despairing lack of trust in social order or human nature. He encounters a medical profession that perceives him as a threat to the "normal" order, diagnoses him as morally cowardly and hysterical, and prescribes a rest cure at an asylum. To escape this normalizing regime, Septimus commits suicide by jumping from his window. Through this shell shock victim, Woolf represents many of the symptoms of sexual abuse victims, as well as their treatment by the medical establishment of her day. She thus anticipates Judith Herman's breakthrough: "the hysteria of women and the combat neurosis of men are one" (Herman 32). What men experience at war, women experience at home, in daily life.

In *To the Lighthouse* (1927), Woolf describes some aspects of the state of mind of an abuse survivor, but without tying them to any specific event. Cam Ramsay, sailing to the lighthouse with her father and her brother, finds herself painfully struggling with love, loyalty and anger for her father and her brother. Her mind gravitates towards images of underwater worlds or the faraway shore, seeking a state of no feeling: "They have no suffering there, she thought;" "They don't feel a thing there, Cam thought" (253, 272). Her mind, "numbed and shrouded" (272), flirts with images of death on land and underwater. She imagines sea changes to mind and body under the waves, and imagines that people on the faraway shore are peaceful, "free to come and go like ghosts" (253).

As a final example, Rose Pargiter, of *The Years* (1937), experiences a kind of sexual assault as a little girl; a man exposes himself to her on the street between her home and the corner store. In adulthood, Rose tells her sister and brother that she tried to commit suicide by slitting her wrists after this event when no one would listen to her tale about it. DeSalvo points out that "Rose recalls it [the assault] throughout her life as the moment that has shaped her very being. It has caused her to become a committed, political activist, a suffragist, who goes on hunger strike" (*Virginia Woolf* 185).

"A Sketch of the Past" is Woolf's final attempt to shape her life story. Begun as a diversion from her book projects at the time, the audience was unclear. Perhaps eventually it would be revised into something shaped, artistic, something for others, she suggests, but the draft that survives and is published in *Moments of Being* is a first draft that she wrote for herself. It is thus not

surprising that "A Sketch" is the most open, continuous, connected, and political of her memoirs. In this piece, Woolf speculates about the functions of
writing in her life, about the effect of Gerald's abuse of her at age six on her
personality and development, and places her family relations squarely in a
gendered political and historical context. Although this memoir does not go
into detail about Gerald's abuse and does not directly discuss George's sexual
behavior to her, Woolf concentrates much more fully on her feelings and the
effects of family members and events on her as a developing person than she
does in her earlier memoirs. She speculates, for example, that Gerald's abuse
may help to explain why she was "ashamed or afraid of my own body" (68)
and continues to feel fear and anxiety about her appearance and clothes. In this
memoir, as well, Woolf most clearly and completely combines autobiographical
detail and psychological and social analysis. She never stays in solely an autobiographical confessional mode; she interprets, sets in familial, historical, and
social context. By so doing, she obviates the split between theory and experience, mind and body, and the invalidation of the survivor as witness and
theorist that Alcoff and Gray analyze as one of the dangers of the confessional.
By taking on and combining the roles of witness, analyst, and historian, Woolf
models building theory upon experience and authorizes herself as an interpreter of the history and politics of the family.

In Woolf's memoirs, one can see a progression from vagueness and evasion to outspokenness and, in "A Sketch," to an explicit analysis of where the
incidents of abuse fit in her personal development, in the politics of her family,
and how these politics reflected Victorian social structures and gender roles.
Woolf moves towards greater clarity and detail in her telling of her story and
towards the kind of continuity of life story and reflection on the meanings of
the events that constitute the recovery process. But it is "A Sketch of the Past,"
the piece that most fully "puts the severed parts together," for which Woolf
could not imagine, or find, an audience. She was very much alone with her
experiences of incest and her political analysis of them, especially by 1940–41,
as the negative responses of her friends and family to her most overt political
critique of the patriarchal family, *Three Guineas* (1939), showed her. This reality
could only have contributed to Woolf's growing sense of isolation caused by
the death of friends and by World War II, a sense of being "adrift" that Toni
A. H. McNaron argues was central to Woolf's decision to commit suicide in
1941 ("Echoes").

IV: Conclusion

The example of Virginia Woolf suggests that writing can be a tool for
self-construction and for reconnection to past and future and to other people,

but that writing in itself is not enough. Audience and social context are crucial. The full potential of writing as a means of healing can only be fulfilled in the context of a supportive and responsive community and feminist renaming and rethinking of sexual abuse and its causes and consequences.

Through writing, Woolf remembers and represents events and feelings, moves away from a split sense of self, develops a more integrated, continuous sense of self in time and social context, places sexual abuse in childhood and adolescence in an ongoing narrative which explains their effects on psychological development, distances herself from and criticizes the perpetrators, and places what happened to her in the context of a feminist analysis of family and social gender politics. But her telling of her story remains split and incomplete. Events are not completely told nor told in a continuous narrative; different memoirs present parts of the story. Events and feelings are often hinted at or told in code or through allusion in the fiction and the memoirs. Direct or clear portrayal and analysis of sexual abuse in the fiction is often censored between draft and publication. Finally, affect is often split from the narration of her own story and put in the fiction, where it may be attached to characters or events analogous or similar to herself and her experiences but still disguised.

Thus, Woolf's strategy for creating a safe space to communicate publicly about sexual abuse is double-edged in its effects. On the one hand, Woolf's use of coding and indirection allows her to articulate experiences and imply political analyses of incest which she apparently did not feel safe in talking about more explicitly, especially early in her career and for a public audience. This indirection also allows the reader who is not open to such material to pass it by while the reader who is searching for such material will more easily perceive it. She thus creates a safe space both for herself and for the reader. Woolf's splitting of life event and emotional experience between memoir and fiction allows her to avoid the dangers of the confessional and to authorize herself as theorist of her own experience.

On the other hand, the space so created may be restricting for several reasons. Her strategy entails some self-censorship. She creates her "safe space" at the cost of clarity, of an outspoken naming of the crime and the perpetrator, and an explicit political analysis of their functions in maintaining the social status quo. Her strategy may make it easier for many readers to continue to deny that such material even exists in her life or writing. Finally, one of the symptoms of incest is an existential shame and guilt, especially about one's body. This shame and guilt must be among the sources of Woolf's evasion and self-silencing about bodily and especially sexual matters.

The indirection, coding, and splitting of Woolf's public writing is not only a strategy for creating safe space for self-expression and political analysis but also a symptom of the incestuous damage done to her. Woolf's accomplishments through writing should not be underestimated; she achieved an extraordinarily productive life, productive of many life-long friendships and of an enormous output of powerful writing in a wide variety of genres. However, writing functioned paradoxically in Woolf's life as both safe space and danger zone and Woolf's writing strategies constitute both a symptom of incestuous abuse and a means for (partially) healing. Knowledge of the pain and the costs behind Woolf's achievements can only increase our appreciation of them.

Notes

1. The title of Joanne S. Frye's *Living Stories, Telling Lives* encapsulates this relationship wonderfully.

2. In "A Sketch," Woolf reports an incident of abuse by her stepbrother Gerald Duckworth when she was about six (around 1888). We also know of ongoing abuse from George Duckworth in her adolescence, possibly beginning after her mother's death in 1895, certainly after her stepsister Stella's death in 1897, and continuing at least until sometime during her father's fatal illness in 1903–04.

3. In this article, I depend on knowledge about the effects of incest and other forms of sexual abuse and the process of recovery provided by a number of recent studies: Ellen Bass and Laura Davis, *The Courage to Heal*; Judith Herman with Lisa Hirschman, *Father-Daughter Incest*; Judith Herman, *Trauma and Recovery*; Patricia Love, *The Emotional Incest Syndrome*; Toni A. H. McNaron and Yarrow Morgan, *Voices in the Night*; Alice Miller, *The Drama of the Gifted Child* and *Thou Shalt Not Be Aware*; Florence Rush, *The Best-Kept Secret*; Diana E. H. Russell, *The Secret Trauma*.

4. Vanessa seems to have told Virginia's physician, Dr. Savage, about George's sexual abuse of Virginia during Virginia's mental illness of 1904–5, after her father's death. How soon anyone else was informed is hard to say. Woolf herself told Janet Case in 1911, and the Bloomsbury Memoir Club in 1920–21.

5. This minimizing of, or simple lack of analysis of, the seriousness and consequences of the sexual abuse Woolf suffered is repeated by many of her biographers, including Bell and Gordon, even though, as indicated above, they make clear its egregious nature and Woolf's powerlessness in her familial and social context. Louise DeSalvo's *Virginia Woolf* fills in this gap, and urges reconsideration of Woolf's "madness."

6. The medical treatment Woolf received indicates the extent to which medical theory and practice was entrenched in conventional gender ideology and that her doctors did not consider George's behavior as a possible cause of her illness. From Woolf's first breakdown in 1895 throughout her life, the prescriptions of her doctors included extreme restrictions on and/or complete cessation of reading and writing. Consider what this would mean given Woolf's dependence on writing to combat the symptoms of post-traumatic stress disorder. The rest cures she was made to endure in her breakdown of 1910 and at subsequent periods replicated the powerlessness, silencing, and isolation experienced during abuse, as well as the submission to a male

authority (in this case, the doctor). For history and analysis of the sexual politics of the rest cure as developed by the American physician S. Weir Mitchell, see Charlotte Perkins Gilman's *The Yellow Wallpaper* and Barbara Ehrenreich and Deirdre English, *For Her Own Good*. For more analysis of Woolf's illness and the politics of medicine, see Poole, Trombley, DeSalvo, Caramagno.

7. For a fuller discussion of my arguments about sexual abuse in *The Voyage Out,* see " 'My Boldness Terrifies Me': Sexual Abuse and Female Subjectivity in *The Voyage Out.*"

Works Cited

Alcoff, Linda, and Laura Gray. "Survivor Discourse: Transgression or Recuperation?" *Signs* 18.2 (Winter 1993): 260–290.

Apgar, Sonia. "Fighting Back on Paper and in Real Life." This volume.

Bass, Ellen, and Laura Davis. *The Courage to Heal: A Guide to Women Survivors of Child Sexual Abuse.* New York: Harper and Row, 1988.

Bell, Quentin. *Virginia Woolf: A Biography.* New York: Harcourt Brace Jovanovich, 1982.

Brodkey, Linda. "Modernism and the Scene(s) of Writing." *College English* 49.4 (1987): 396–418.

Caramagno, Thomas C. *The Flight of the Mind: Virginia Woolf's Art and Manic-Depressive Illness.* Berkeley: University of California Press, 1992.

DeSalvo, Louise. *Virginia Woolf: The Impact of Childhood Sexual Abuse on Her Life and Work.* Boston: Beacon, 1989.

———. *Virginia Woolf's First Voyage: A Novel in the Making.* Totowa, NJ: Rowman and Littlefield, 1980.

Gordon, Lyndall. *Virginia Woolf: A Writer's Life.* New York: W. W. Norton, 1984, 1993.

Ehrenreich, Barbara, and Deirdre English. *For Her Own Good: 150 Years of the Experts' Advice to Women.* Garden City, NY: Anchor/Doubleday, 1978.

Herman, Judith. *Trauma and Recovery: The Aftermath of Violence—From Domestic Abuse to Political Terror.* New York: Basic Books, 1992.

Herman, Judith, with Lisa Hirschman. *Father-Daughter Incest.* Cambridge: Harvard University Press, 1981.

Jeffreys, Sheila. *The Spinster and Her Enemies: Feminism and Sexuality 1880–1930.* London and Boston: Pandora, 1985.

Love, Patricia. *The Emotional Incest Syndrome: What to Do When a Parent's Love Rules Your Life.* New York: Bantam, 1990.

McNaron, Toni A. H. "Echoes of Virginia Woolf." *Women's Studies International Forum* 6.5 (1983): 501–507.

———. "The Uneasy Solace of Art: The Impact of Sexual Abuse on Woolf's Aesthetic." *Women's Studies International Forum* 15.2 (1992): 251–266.

McNaron, Toni A. H., and Yarrow Morgan, eds. *Voices in the Night: Women Speaking About Incest.* Pittsburgh and San Francisco: Cleis Press, 1982.

Miller, Alice. *The Drama of the Gifted Child: How Narcissistic Parents Form and Deform the Emotional Lives of Their Talented Children.* Trans. Ruth Ward. New York: Basic Books, 1981.

———. *Thou Shalt Not Be Aware: Society's Betrayal of the Child.* Trans. Hildegarde and Hunter Hannum. New York: New American, 1984.

Milton, John. *Comus: A Mask. Complete Poems and Prose.* Ed. Merritt Y. Hughes. Indianapolis: Bobbs-Merrill, 1957. 86–114.

Poole, Roger. *The Unknown Virginia Woolf.* 1978. Atlantic Highlands, NJ: Humanities, 1982.

Rush, Florence. *The Best-Kept Secret: Sexual Abuse of Children.* Englewood Cliffs: Prentice-Hall, 1980.

Russell, Diana E. H. *The Secret Trauma: Incest in the Lives of Girls and Women.* New York: Basic Books, 1986.

Schulkind, Jeanne, ed. *Moments of Being.* 2nd edition. New York: Harcourt Brace Jovanovich, 1985.

Swanson, Diana L. " 'My Boldness Terrifies Me': Sexual Abuse and Female Subjectivity in *The Voyage Out.*" *Twentieth Century Literature* (forthcoming).

Trombley, Stephen. *All That Summer She Was Mad: Virginia Woolf: Female Victim of Male Medicine.* New York: Continuum, 1981.

Woolf, Virginia. "22 Hyde Park Gate." *Moments of Being.* Ed. Jeanne Schulkind. 2nd edition. 162–177.

———. *The Diary of Virginia Woolf.* 5 vols. Ed. Anne Olivier Bell. Intro. by Quentin Bell. New York: Harcourt Brace Jovanovich, 1977.

———. *The Letters of Virginia Woolf.* 6 vols. Eds. Nigel Nicolson and Joanne Trautmann. New York: Harcourt Brace Jovanovich, 1975–1980.

———. *A Passionate Apprentice: The Early Journals, 1897–1909.* Ed. Mitchell A. Leaska. New York: Harcourt Brace Jovanovich, 1990.

———. "Professions for Women." *The Death of the Moth and Other Essays.* 1942. New York: Harcourt Brace Jovanovich, 1970. 235–242.

———. "Reminiscences." *Moments of Being.* Ed. Jeanne Schulkind. 2nd edition.

———. "A Sketch of the Past." *Moments of Being.* Ed. Jeanne Schulkind. 2nd edition 61–159.

———. *The Voyage Out.* 1915. New York: Harcourt Brace Jovanovich, 1948.

———. *A Writer's Diary.* 1953. Ed. Leonard Woolf. New York: Harcourt Brace Jovanovich, 1982.

"One need not be a Chamber—to be Haunted":
Emily Dickinson's Haunted Space

Mary Jo Dondlinger

Emily Dickinson produced an imposing quantity of poems in the early 1860s, a period of her life which biographers, such as Mabel Loomis Todd, Martha Dickinson Bianchi, and Richard Sewall, agree was ridden with emotional agony and grief. Sewall describes the period as "crucial, a time of extraordinary stress and inner turmoil" (465). Millicent Todd Bingham writes, "All that is known points to a crisis in the early 1860s. The inner turmoil which beset her throughout her life was intensified at that time" (417). The enormous amount of artistic expression, over three hundred and sixty poems in one year, was a means of dealing with and overcoming this anguished period of her life. Emily Dickinson, herself, suggested that her writing assuaged her pain when she wrote of her poetry to T. W. Higginson, "I felt a palsy, here—the Verses just relieve" *(Selected Letters* 174*)*. She felt that writing possessed healing power; it was therapeutic. Despite Dickinson's assertions and universal agreement that this was a "crisis" period, various biographical accounts of the period are not satisfying primarily because they fail to account for the sexual explicitness of such poems as "A Bee his burnished Carriage" (1339) and the violence in such poems as "Rearrange a 'Wife's' affection! (1737). The sexual references in these poems are misinterpreted as affectionate and loving; the violence is simply ignored.[1] Another explanation, which accounts for such allusions, is that Emily Dickinson was sexually abused and wrote as a means of creating safe space.

I contend that Emily Dickinson was a survivor of a sexual abuse, specifically incest, and like many sexually victimized women, used writing as a means of reconstructing a sense of safety. I support this argument first by illustrating how Dickinson, given her family background, was at high risk for sexual victimization. I will then offer an interpretative reading of six poems, labelled the "Wife" poems, which suggest that Dickinson was a victim of father-daughter incest. Finally, I will show how Dickinson's perception of home, normally the quintessential "safe space," as represented in her poetry, is threatening. Yet through this poetry, Dickinson constructs alternative safe spaces, such as the heart, soul, mind, and even the grave.

I would like to stress that my intent is only to speculate upon a provocative explanation of the cause of Emily Dickinson's suffering. Cultural restrictions have prevented this type of supposition in the past and it has only recently been feasible, because of contemporary feminist criticism, to entertain the possibility that Dickinson's suffering resulted from sexual victimization. Entertaining a possibility is not synonymous with providing a definitive interpretation of Dickinson's entire canon, nor is such my intent. My design is simply to suggest a biographical interpretation of Dickinson's "crisis" which accounts for the inadequacies of previous interpretations.

Many circumstances in Dickinson's family background indicate that she was at a high risk for sexual victimization. Studies on sexual victimization outline factors which are conducive to sexual abuse. While these factors describe both the social conditions and family backgrounds of victims, the findings concerning the social factors are ambiguous and inconclusive. The family structures that encourage sexual abuse, however, are consistent in many studies.[2] The main factors, according to David Finkelhor, are marital conflict or disruption, absence or inability of the mother, and the ordinal position of siblings (118–130). Each one of these factors applies to Emily Dickinson's family background.[3]

Marital conflict refers not only to parents fighting excessively; marital disruption is the absence of either parent for extended periods of time or permanently. Conflict and disruption seem to be factors because children are less supervised and more vulnerable to sexual advances. They may also receive contradictory messages about sex and what is appropriate, making them less able to discern, refuse, and report inappropriate behavior (Finkelhor 119).

While there are reports of husband and wife quarrels in various Dickinson biographies, there is no reason to believe it was excessive. It is normal for couples to disagree occasionally. There is evidence, however, that Edward and Emily Dickinson's marriage was disrupted. Edward was frequently out of town for extended periods of time, sometimes for years. He spent four years in Washington as a representative to the U.S. Congress. His legal practice took him away from home as well. Emily Norcross spent much time away from the home seeking treatment for illness. When she was at home, she was bedridden and prone to despondency. These periods of withdrawal and depression, which began shortly after her marriage to Edward Dickinson, continued until her death. Because the marriage was disrupted in this way, a disintegration of affection and communication between parents and a decrease in supervision of the children is likely.

The absence or inability of a mother is another risk factor. According to Finkelhor, one theory suggests that she abdicates her maternal responsibilities. Another proposes that she tries to exchange roles with her daughter. Still another sees the weak or absent mother as unable to protect her daughter from abuse or fails to report the abuse if she discovers it (120). Whatever the reason, the statistical evidence that absent or ineffectual mothers are a factor is conclusive. Three times as many girls with absent or passive mothers were reportedly victimized than those whose mothers were present on a regular basis (125).

Emily Norcross Dickinson's repeated absence from the home for treatment of illness and her debilitation when in residence is well documented. When she was not bedridden, she was often depressed and withdrawn. From a very young age, both Emily and Lavinia had to manage the household and care for their mother. Emily's comment in a letter that she "never had a mother" is often quoted and speculated upon. Although an exaggeration on Dickinson's part, the statement indicates a perception of her mother's effectuality. She seems to have recognized and resented her mother's disability.

The ordinal position of siblings is another factor in father-daughter incest, with the oldest daughter receiving the highest probability of abuse. While the ordinal position of a daughter is significant for victimization in general, it is a decisive factor in father-daughter incest. Finkelhor writes, "It has been found that victims of father-daughter incest are almost always the oldest daughters" (129). Emily Dickinson was the oldest daughter in the Dickinson family. If Edward Dickinson had any inclination toward incest, his daughter Emily would have been the victim.

The most powerful support for the contention that Dickinson was a victim of sexual abuse, particularly incest, lies in an interpretation of the "Wife" poems. The "Wife" poems are a group of six poems, in which Dickinson seems to imagine that she is married by calling herself a wife. These poems are 199 "I'm 'wife'—I've finished that—," 461 "A Wife—at Daybreak I shall be—," 463 "I live with Him—I see His face—," 732 "She rose to His Requirement," 1072 "Title divine—is mine!", and 1737 "Rearrange a 'Wife's' affection!" The significance of these poems is that in trying to interpret what Emily Dickinson may have meant by the word "wife," the reader is forced to reevaluate Emily Dickinson's relationship with her father. In her biography, Barbara Antonina Clarke Mossberg writes:

> It is readily apparent to the reader of both the poetry and the letters [of Dickinson] that the father is the central—if not the only—figure in Dickinson's thought. Consequently, Edward Dickinson is one of the most notorious fathers in literary history, his importance an issue which every biographer has had to resolve. (68)

Dickinson's relationship with her father figures prominently in these six poems. This analysis will begin by outlining the various characteristics of a "wife"
and the possible ways in which Dickinson might have been using the term.
The characteristics and usage can then be compared with the "wife" that
Dickinson depicts in the poems.

The word "wife," which currently refers to "a married woman," archai-
cally referred to any woman, married or unmarried. The word "woman" is
derived etymologically from the word "wife." While "wife" did not always
possess the specificity of the modern meaning, it is most probable that Emily
Dickinson was referring to this definition of wife; namely, a married woman.
Because she was unmarried herself, she likely used the word to connote some
aspect of "womanhood" closely associated with the qualities and experience of
a wife.

The term "wife" has implications metonymically associated with its literal
definition, a married woman. For example, a married woman can be characterized as sharing a home with a man. A woman gains a measure of social
status upon marrying, as marriage is perceived as a rite of passage. This status
carries a measure of social obligation and responsibility. Historically, marriage
placed a woman and her assets under the patriarchal control of her husband.
A married woman also was understood to have sexual experience, which led
to the conception and raising of children. Sharing a home, patriarchal control,
social status and responsibility, sexual experience, and child-rearing are experiential aspects of a "wife," and a woman possessing any one of these characteristics might justifiably be termed a "wife."

Dickinson might have adopted the perspective of a "wife" for a number
of reasons. She may have been pretending to be married or imagining what
marriage would be like. It is also possible that the "wife" poems may relay
attitudes about marriage or wifehood that she observed in other married
women such as her mother or her sister-in-law, Susan. Another conceivable
explanation is that her referent may not be a literal "wife" but is a metaphor
for another relationship to which the husband/wife relationship bears much
similarity. In this sense, the "wife" in the poems might be one not literally
"married," but who possesses several of the characteristics previously defined.

Dickinson may have been merely fantasizing herself a wife in these
ambiguous poems. Marriage was an important social distinction, although
unmarried women were not social outcasts. However, even today, when the
importance and distinction placed upon marriage is decreasing, young girls
fantasize about weddings and getting married. It would not be unusual, then,
in a society where marriage did have greater prestige, for young girls to engage
in the same fantasies and for Emily Dickinson to fantasize about marriage or
even call herself a wife in a few poems and letters. Nevertheless, her girlhood
letters do not express such fantasies. Rather, she seems to express such profuse

affection for her girlfriends that she leaves no room in them for the anticipation of a future husband.[4] Nor does she seem to aspire to wifehood in the poems; she seems to ridicule and scorn it. She calls it a "soft Eclipse" (199, line 6); it is something that blots you out, makes you fade, grow dark and become dim. To get married is to be "Born—Bridalled—Shrouded—/In a Day—" (1072, line 10). That is to say that you are "Born" into a new identity, "Bridalled" like a horse under the will and control of its rider, and "Shrouded" like a corpse, all in a single day. Her view of marriage is not a positive one. If these are truly her perceptions toward marriage, it is ludicrous to believe that she is fantasizing about being a wife. If such were the case, the poems would celebrate the virtues and benefits of marriage, not take such an ironic tone.

Another possibility is that the attitudes and experiences of the "wife" in the poems refers to those she gleaned from other marriages. She observed the marriage of her parents and could comment on marriage based on these observations. Since she was such a close friend and confidante to her sister-in-law, Susan, it is probable that she would have held intimate discourse with her upon the subject of marriage. The wife in poem 732 could plausibly have been either her mother or sister-in-law. However, it seems inconceivable that the "wife" in the other five poems could possibly be anyone but Dickinson. Every one of these poems are in the first person singular. In many instances, the first person "I" is metrically placed as the stressed syllable of the iamb, emphasizing this first person perspective. In poem 199, "*I'm* "wife"—*I've* finished that—" (line 1), "*I'm* Czar—*I'm* 'woman' now—" (line 3), "*I* think" (line 7) all refer to first person I's, which are emphatically stressed by the meter. The same is true in poem 463 in the first two lines "*I* live with Him—*I* see His face/*I* go no more away." This is repeated in lines 9 and 10, "*I* live with Him— *I* hear His Voice—/*I* stand alive—Today." The emphasis placed on this perspective seems to decree that the "wife" can refer to none other than the writer, herself.[5] Only in poem 732, which is written from the third person singular feminine point of view, does it seem credible that the "wife" be interpreted as someone else.

The final possibility regarding Dickinson's application of the term wife is as a metaphor for a similar relationship in Dickinson's life. Dickinson had close relationships with a handful of men, Edward and Austin Dickinson, Samuel Bowles, Thomas Wentworth Higginson, and Charles Wadsworth, to name a few. Many of them, however, do not bear enough similarity to a marriage relationship to be the metaphorical referent to these poems. Her relationships with Bowles, Higginson, and Wadsworth, for example, did not involve cohabitation, social distinction, or patriarchal control.

Her relationships with both her father and brother, on the other hand, do have some parallels to a marriage-like relation. They both meet the criterion of cohabitation, since she lived with them most of her life. As such, her relationship with either of them bears that specific similarity to a married relationship. The characteristic of patriarchal control indicates a stronger connection with her father than with her brother. Austin did become her patriarch after Edward's death, but Emily was already forty-four. Up to this point and after, their relationship was close and fraternal. Although Sewall likes to downplay assertions made by Lavinia Dickinson and Mabel Todd that Edward Dickinson was tyrannical, he does maintain that Edward was the patriarch. Emily, herself, remarks in a letter to Austin, "What father says, he means" (*Letters*, Johnson Letter 82). He was the person in control and was not to be defied or refuted. Thus, since her relationship with her father bears this similarity to the married relationship as well, if she is referring metaphorically to some real relationship with a man, her relationship with her father seems to be the most likely referent.

This father-daughter relationship can be assessed based upon the other characteristics of "wife" as well. Social status depends upon social recognition consequent to taking marriage vows. If a woman does not literally take the vows, she does not obtain the status. It is not requisite to performing wifelike domestic responsibilities, however. When Dickinson's mother became ill, she was forced to take on many of the domestic and social responsibilities of a married woman. She writes in a letter of 7 May 1850, "I have always neglected the culinary arts, but attend to them now from necessity, and from a desire to make everything pleasant for father, and Austin" (*Selected Letters* 38). The roles of hostess and housekeeper did sanction a share of status along with the responsibility. Emily would have merited some "wifely" status in playing hostess to her father's guests. She comments on her status and duty in a satirical passage in the same letter:

> I am yet the Queen of the court, if regalia be dust, and dirt . . . Father and Austin still clamor for food, and I like a martyr am feeding them. Wouldn't you love to see me in these bonds of great despair, looking around my kitchen, and praying for kind deliverance. . . . *My* kitchen I think I called it, God forbid that it was, or shall be my own—God keep me from what they call *households,* except that bright one of 'faith'! (*Selected Letters* 40)

She recognizes the rank of a wife; she calls herself a "Queen of the court." Yet the "court" is one of "dirt" and "dust." She compares the subservient station of a wife to that of a "martyr." The comparison is not an incredible one since the will and desires of a wife are sacrificed to her duties to husband and family. Emily Dickinson, though unmarried, made this same sacrifice. She maintained the station of a wife and mother in her mother's stead. Consequently, her relationship with her father bears that similarity as well, making it the most likely metaphorical referent.

Since "wife" as metaphor seems the most plausible hypothesis for Dickinson's use of the term—as opposed to an unwed girl's fantasy or the experiences of some "wife" other than herself—it is necessary to examine how this metaphor works in the poems. Poem 463 ("I live with Him—I see His face—") discusses cohabitation. She literally states in the opening line and repeats in line 9, "I live with Him—." The reference to cohabitation in poem 461 ("A Wife—at Daybreak I shall be—") is less obvious. This poem examines the thoughts and feelings of a "Maid" on her wedding night, about to become a "Bride." While she waits in her bedroom, fumbling at her "Childhood's prayer" (9), her husband or "Future climbs the Stair" (8). Although more obscure than 463, it is plausible that the couple live together in this house with the bedroom and the "Stair," even if they have only recently taken up residence together.

The quality of "wife" as obedient to patriarchal command is also manifest in the poems. Beginning with the most literal example, poem 732 opens with "She rose to His Requirement," depicting a wife rising to meet the "Requirement" or command of a patriarch or master. The subservience of a wife to patriarchal control is also evident in the repeated capitalization of the masculine pronouns. While Dickinson's use of punctuation and capitalization is often disregarded as erratic and therefore not worthy of decisive interpretation, the capitalization of the masculine pronouns is decidedly consistent throughout these poems and deserves consideration. Although masculine pronouns, when capitalized, often refer to God, in the context of these poems, that is not the best interpretation. The poems deal directly with the subject of wifehood, not religion. The reference might be to the religious notion of being "married" to God, but this concept refers to an elevated, spiritual commitment to God. It isn't a relationship that entails housework. Given the mundane tone in the poems, it seems more credible that the pronouns allude to a father, patriarch, or husband. That they are capitalized gives a strong emphasis to the prominence of the patriarch. In fact, they invoke the power and eminence of the ultimate father/patriarch/husband; namely, God.

The social status and responsibility of a wife are especially pronounced in this series of poems. She grants the "wife" in the poems various elevated titles because of her marital status. She refers to the wife as "Czar" (119, line 3), as "Empress" (1072, 4), and "Royal" (1072, 5). These terms describe the rank and position associated with marriage. In 1072, she hails "wife" as a "Title divine," a reference to the social distinction given to married women. These seemingly laudatory titles, however, are quite ironic. Her "Empress" is the "Empress of Calvary!", an empress of pain and anguish, not land, people, wealth, or even happiness. Such irony suggests that Dickinson's attitude toward this distinction was dubious and it was not a title that she seemed to desire.

The poems also associate wifehood with responsibility and duty; the first stanza of poem 732 is a good example.

> She rose to His Requirement—dropt
> The Playthings of Her Life
> To take the honorable Work
> Of Woman, and of Wife—

This stanza describes the young girl leaving her childhood pastimes to take on the responsibilities of womanhood. It is quite interesting to consider that she is not doing this of her own accord, as she naturally matures or grows up. She does this because of "His Requirement." This can be an autobiographical comment on the situation previously discussed—that she and her sister were forced to take care of her father and brother during the course of their mother's illness. She didn't have to be married to feel like a wife. She did the "honorable Work" of one already.

Another attribute of wifehood that must be analyzed is that of sexual experience. Poem 461 "A Wife—at Daybreak I shall be" deals exclusively with this subject. Also the sexual explicitness of 1072 ("Title divine—is mine!") and 1737 ("Rearrange a 'Wife's' affection!") is too prominent to be avoided. If Dickinson's "wife" in the wife poems is a metaphor for her relationship with her father and the poems introduce the subject of the sexual experiences, then it is conceivable that there was a sexual event in Dickinson's relationship with her father. In treating this sensitive subject, it is perhaps best to proceed line by line through each of the poems and attempt to ascertain where the meaning of "wife" in a sexual sense applies.

The first stanza of 199 states, "I'm 'wife'—I've finished that—/That other state—/I'm Czar—I'm 'Woman' now—/It's safer so—." In this stanza the term "wife" is contrasted to "That other state." Clearly that other state refers to being unmarried, more specifically to girlhood. The interpretation of "That other state" as girlhood is supported by the statement in line 3, "I'm 'Woman' now." Line 4, however, introduces a contradiction. Dickinson has stated in her letters and in other poems an amount of disdain for wife and womanhood. How can she thus say, "It's safer so"? It is either an inconsistency or she is referring to a different aspect of womanhood. In the other allusions, she was referring to the duties and subservience associated with a wife. She must now be referring to something different. The line makes sense if that attribute is sexual experience. Sex is "safer" after it has been experienced. It is less physically and psychologically painful. As such both "wife" and "Woman" might refer to a female who has experienced sex, as opposed to "That other state," virginity. This interpretation also makes sense in light of the last stanza. "This being comfort—then/That other kind—was pain—." Womanhood in terms of duty and responsibility would not be a "comfort." In fact, Dickinson saw it as martyrdom. Childhood, not womanhood, was ease and comfort in comparison. Womanhood in terms of sexual practice, however, would be more comfortable;

intercourse as a child would be painful. Just when she begins to divulge the source of this pain, she cuts herself short saying, "But why compare?/I'm 'Wife'! Stop there!"

The sexual implications in poem 461 are more distinct. This poem is unmistakably about a young girl becoming a woman through sexual experience. She literally goes to bed at night a "Maid" and is a woman or "wife" in the morning, "at Daybreak." Lines 3 and 4 read, "At Midnight, I am but a Maid,/How short it takes to make it Bride." What possibly can occur overnight to transform a child into a woman, if not sexual intercourse? The second stanza suggests this interpretation. "Softly my Future climbs the Stair,/I fumble at my Childhood's prayer/Soon to be a Child no more." The interpretation of these lines as a bride awaiting her groom on their wedding night was discussed earlier. The last line, however, is quite puzzling. The poet writes, "Savior—I've seen the face—before!" In earlier versions of the poem, Dickinson did not use the word "Savior"; it was instead "master." While the word "master" certainly makes a connection to patriarch or husband, as does "Savior," this bride seems startled by her recognition. Surely, a bride must have met her master before this moment. Why should she be surprised at recognizing him now? Perhaps, he is a figure that is too familiar, one whom she recognizes, but who should not be sharing her bed.

Poem 463 supports the suggestion of a familiar face, like that in poem 461, that is somehow *too* familiar. In this poem, she admits, "I live with Him— I see His face—/I go no more away" (1–2). This is a strong indication that the indeterminate "Him" is her father. The reference to a sexual connection between the two comes in the second stanza.

> The Only One—forestalling Mine—
> And that—by Right that He
> Present a Claim invisible
> No Wedlock—granted Me—

The word "Mine" in line 5 refers to "privacy," which occurs in line 4. The only person forestalling her privacy then is the "Him" with whom she lives. This "Him" forestalls her privacy by right of some "Claim invisible." The invisible claim is contrasted with the visible claim of "Wedlock" mentioned in line 8. Wedlock presents to a husband the claim of a sexual intercourse. Once wedded, the husband is free to claim the sexual favors that his wife dutifully renders. The man in this poem, however, appears to be making such a claim upon the persona of the poem, most likely Dickinson, without the overt legality of "Wedlock." Further, after reiterating in the third stanza that the "Him" is someone with whom she lives and "hear[s] His Voice," she reveals in the fourth stanza that the He has taught her that she has no power to stop him.

"Taught Me—by Time—the lower Way—/Conviction—Every day—/That Life like This—is stopless—." The word "stopless" is replaced later by "endless." Both words suggest her utter powerlessness against this man. She can only submit to the "Claim invisible" that he makes of her.

Poem 1072 further develops the idea of "wife" without the external or overt manifestation of marriage. The first two lines read, "Title divine—is mine!/ The Wife—without the Sign!" Here, again, she possesses a "title" or "claim" to be a "wife" without the outward "Sign" of marriage, such as a ring, a certificate, or even a husband. If she claims the title of wife despite no outward sign, the claim is conceivably on account of sexual activity. The "Empress of Calvary" image in line 4 could support such an interpretation. Calvary, of course, refers to the place where Christ was crucified. By titling herself "Empress of Calvary," Dickinson sees her own suffering as comparable to that of Christ's. The piercing and penetrating nature of the wounds that Christ received are often interpreted as analogous to sexual penetration.[6] As previously noted, she saw herself as a "martyr," yet another comparison to Christ.

The last in this series of poems, 1737, is the most baffling. Because of its complexities, it will be cited here in full with a brief analysis following.

> Rearrange a "Wife's" affection!
> When they dislocate my Brain!
> Amputate my freckled Bosom!
> Make me bearded like a man!
>
> Blush, my spirit, in thy Fastness—
> Blush, my unacknowledged clay—
> Seven years of troth have taught thee
> More than Wifehood ever may!
>
> Love that never leaped its socket—
> Trust entrenched in narrow pain—
> Constancy thro' fire—awarded—
> Anguish—bare of anodyne!
>
> Burden—borne so far triumphant—
> None suspect me of the crown,
> For I wear the "Thorns" til Sunset—
> Then—my Diadem put on.
>
> Big my Secret but it's *bandaged*—
> It will never get away
> Till the Day its Weary Keeper
> Leads it through the Grave to thee.

The first stanza is loaded with violent and disjointed anatomical imagery. The word "affection" in line one could refer either to a fond or tender feeling or to a pathological mental or physical condition. The fact that it is a " 'Wife's' affection" and that it is being "rearranged" is very jolting. The words "dislocate" and "amputate" in the next lines add to the sense of violent action upon the "Wife's affection," "Brain," and "Bosom." The second stanza suggests humiliation and embarrassment at "Fastness" and "troth." The word "Blush" is repeated twice. Stanza three is full of acute pain and a feeling of betrayal. The anguish is "bare of anodyne!"; there is no relief from the pain. The fifth stanza begins with the idea of a "Burden." This "burden" is likely a painful secret, an interpretation confirmed in the last stanza. That it is "borne so far triumphant" indicates that no one has discovered the secret. In comparing the burden to the crown of "Thorns," she indicates its painful nature and alludes again to an identity with Christ. The reference to Diadem is also significant. Diadem comes from the Greek "dia," meaning across, plus "dein," meaning to bind. She seems to be bound to a painful burden. In the last stanza, the line "Big my Secret but it's *bandaged"* confirms this meaning. The word "bandaged" modifying "Secret" indicates not only the hidden nature of the secret, but suggests that the secret concerns some sort of injury. No one will ever know for sure, however, since she will carry it to her grave. The context of the whole poem suggests that the secret involves the violence, humiliation, betrayal, and anguish set forth in the preceding stanzas.

While the "wife" poems can be interpreted in a number of ways, one interpretation seems most satisfactorily to explain the diversity of expression in all of the poems. This is the interpretation that the "wife" in these poems is a metaphor for a real relationship in Emily Dickinson's life. The relationship which best fits this metaphor is that with her father. The sexual explicitness, symbols, and images in these poems suggest that this relationship involved a sexual event.

The ways in which Dickinson uses space in her poetry also offer evidence of her possible victimization. Her description of space suggests that writing for her was a means of constructing a sense of safety or coping with threat. There are many poems in which she describes the house or home, often the model safe space, as a threatening place. In contrast, she describes the grave as a safe, cheery place, often comparing it to a home. In yet other poems, she gives non-physical human characteristics, such as the mind, heart or soul, architectural features, in an attempt to construct safe spaces internally. In all these instances, she seems to be trying to cope with a sense of threat, quite probably from within her own home, by recreating a sense of home or safety elsewhere.

British psychiatrist Anthony Fry describes safe space as "the conditions that sustain us" (1), including family, good health, and interpersonal relations, as well as environmental conditions such as home and community. Since the home is where people eat, sleep, and spend time with the family, it is the primary place of nourishment, rest, and loving companionship; it is the primary place of safety. When the home is threatened, by financial difficulty, burglary, even sickness, people often suffer psychologically, sometimes severely. Threats to the home endanger a person's sense of safety and consequently their psychological stability.

Interestingly, in many of her poems, Dickinson describes the home as a threatening yet inescapable place. In poem 1334, "How soft this Prison," she compares home to a prison. The prison is described as "soft" and the restricting bars as "sweet" because it refers to a home, not an actual prison. Despite such positive adjectives, it is also seen as "sullen," giving the house a brooding, depressing air. The varied references to "Prison," "Dungeon," and "Incarceration" add to the gloominess and indicate the inescapability she associates with home. In poem 127 " 'Houses—so the Wise Men tell me," she expresses her skepticism that any house, including the "Many Mansions" which Christ attributes to "his Father," is "snugly built" enough to keep out "the tears" and "the storm." The distrust that she describes in "The way I read a letter's this" also indicates that she felt unsafe in her own home. She goes to great pains to make sure the door is secure and the room empty before she "pick[s] the lock" of the envelope. This mistrust, gloom, inescapability, and skepticism toward "home" suggest that Dickinson perceived home with apprehension, that it was not entirely "safe."

In contrast, Dickinson describes the grave as a place of safety, often comparing it with a house or home. She seems to anticipate gaining a measure of security in death that she cannot find in life. In poem 457 she describes tombs as "Sweet—safe—Houses" and as "Glad—gay—Houses," demonstrating the gaiety, security, and happiness which she envisions a home should provide. In poem 1743, she describes the grave as "my little cottage," in which she "make[s] the parlor orderly" and "lay[s] the marble tea." Once again the grave is described as a cheery and inviting place. Ironically both places are the residences of the dead. Poem 1701 "To their apartment deep" also employs the grave as dwelling metaphor, although it lacks some of the cheerfulness of the above poems. Nevertheless, the poem does see the grave as a place of safety and invulnerability as it is a place where "No ribaldry may creep." Feeling threatened and apprehensive about her own home, she yearns for a home that is safe. Envisioning the grave as a safe, cheery space, she anticipates a sense of security in death that she did not receive in her own home.

Dickinson also turned inward, seeking comfort and security internally. Evidence of this is signified in the many poems in which she describes nonphysical interior "spaces," such as the heart, mind, and soul, in physical, architectural terms. The heart, however, is not seen as a safe space, nor is the mind. Both are vulnerable to violation. The soul, however, seems to be impervious to such encroachment.

In poem 1567, the heart is described in spatial and architectural terms; it has "many doors." Poem 928 "The Heart has narrow Banks" describes the sea in spatial terms as a metaphor for the passions of the heart. Bounded by "narrow banks" and "measur[ing] like the Sea," the heart has "insufficient Area" when it encounters a hurricane or emotional trauma. The heart in this state "learns/that Calm is but a Wall/of unattempted Gauze"; tranquility is unprotected within such a wall. "An instant's Push demolishes/A Questioning—dissolves." While architecturally defined with area, measurements, even walls, the heart does not have sound, impenetrable enclosures. Rather, it is fragile and vulnerable as a space. It is unsafe.

In 632, "The Brain is wider than the Sky," Dickinson describes the vastness of the mind, giving it dimensionality in breadth, depth, and weight. In 280 "I felt a Funeral in my Brain" the mind has the physical space to accommodate a social gathering. The lines, "And creak across my Soul" and "then a Plank in Reason, broke," suggest the mind has a floor, a boundary defining physical space, and tangible material construction. While this construction is sounder than the gauze walls of the heart, it is still penetrable. A "plank in reason" can, despite its rigidity, be broken.

In poem 1142 "The props assist the House," Dickinson asserts that the "perfected Life," like a house, is built into a "Soul." Just as props are used in the building of a house, they also asssist in the building of the soul. The poem sets up a comparison between the physical architectural space of a house, including the way it is constructed, and the interior space of the soul. The comparison works well because a house also frames the development of the soul, a development which occurs for the most part in the home. Dickinson also describes the soul architecturally in 1055 "The Soul should always stand ajar," giving it tangible space and a bolt and door. The metaphor is similar to that of 303 "The Soul selects her own Society," except in the latter poem, the soul is personified as inhabiting a physical space instead of being that space. As a space, the soul seems to be the most sound, an idea consistent with Dickinson's equating the grave with a safe home.

Ultimately, it is poem 670 "One need not be a Chamber—to be Haunted" that best illustrates how Dickinson compares the inner regions of the psyche to unprotected physical space. In this poem, she does not distinguish between mind, heart, or soul. She refers to "Brain" and "Body" alike, comparing the whole being to the space of a house with chambers and corridors. The entire poem follows:

> One need not be a Chamber—to be Haunted—
> One need not be a House—
> The Brain has Corridors—surpassing
> Material Place—

Far safer, of a Midnight Meeting
External Ghost
Than its interior Confronting—
That Cooler Host.

Far safer, through an Abbey gallop,
The Stones a'chase—
Than Unarmed, one's a 'self encounter—
In lonesome Place—

Ourself behind ourself, concealed—
Should startle most—
Assassin hid in our Apartment
Be Horror's least

The Body—borrows a Revolver—
He bolts the Door—
O'erlooking superior spectre—
Or More—

In representing a human being as a tangible space, she suggests that the mind can be violated and it can be haunted. Dickinson then asserts that it is horrifying to examine one's own haunting or to recognize one's own violation. The power with which she expresses this idea also attests to the possibility that Dickinson was personally violated. She seems to wrestle with this internal "Ghost" and with her own psychological stability regularly. Some threatening event not only penetrated her own home but her own person, as well.

Some event occurred in the early 1860s that caused Dickinson an enormous amount of pain. An interpretation of Dickinson's relationship with her father in terms of the "wife" poems suggests that Dickinson saw herself as fulfilling the role of wife to him. Given the sexual references in the poems, some sexual event in the father-daughter relationship is likely to have been a cause for Dickinson to adopt the voice of a "wife." That Dickinson seems to view her home as unsafe, even threatening, seems to support such an argument. In contrast, she visualizes the grave as a homey place of safety and happiness and the soul as an internal space, which is impervious to violation. While she materializes the mind and heart into physical spaces, ultimately both are vulnerable to emotional and psychological "haunting." Through spatial imagery, defining non-physical spaces in architectural terms and imbuing them with the characteristics of home, Dickinson uses her writing to create safe space, a sense of comfort and security that she never fully attained in her lifetime.

Notes

1. I was unable to locate a study that dealt with the violence in Dickinson's poetry. While the biographical explanations of her "crisis" period that I consulted generally ignore the violent images, my research was not exhaustive. The authoritative biographers such as Sewall, Bianchi, Todd, Johnson, and Whicher do not treat this subject.

2. While I only cite directly from Finkelhor, I consulted Jean Goodwin, *Sexual Abuse: Incest Victims and Their Families* (Boston: John Wright, 1982) and Judith Lewis Herman and Lisa Hirschman, *Father-Daughter Incest* (Cambridge: Harvard University Press, 1981).

3. Emily Dickinson was the middle child of the three children of Edward and Emily Norcross Dickinson. Emily had an older brother, Austin, who married Susan Gilbert, one of Emily's close friends. She also had a younger sister, Lavinia, who, like Emily, never married.

4. The first volume of Johnson's collection of Dickinson's letters contains these early letters to Abiah Root, Susan Gilbert, Jane Humphrey, and others.

5. The personal nature of her poems, written only for herself and for close friends and family members and not for publication, also suggests that she was writing about herself. The first person pronoun, I, is the most frequently occurring word in all 1775 poems. With the exception of only a handful, these poems were not even discovered until after her death. She wrote them, sorted them, tied them in little bundles with thread and hid them. It seems undeniable, given the introspective and secretive nature of her writing, that all of those first person I's could refer to no one but herself.

6. The ecstacy of St. Theresa being pierced by the angel's arrow is a similar analogy. Visually represented in the famed Bernini sculpture, this ecstacy is interpreted as both spiritual and physical.

Works Cited

Bianchi, Martha Dick. *Emily Dickinson Face to Face: Unpublished Reminisciences and Letters.* Boston: Houghton, 1932.

———. *The Life and Letters of Emily Dickinson.* Boston: Houghton, 1924.

Bingham, Millicent Todd. *Emily Dickinson's Home: Letters of Edward Dickinson and His Family.* New York: Harper, 1955.

Dickinson, Emily. *Emily Dickinson Selected Letters.* Edited by Thomas H. Johnson. Cambridge, MA: Harvard University Press, 1958.

———. *Letters of Emily Dickinson.* Edited by Mabel Loomis Todd. New York: World, 1951.

————. *The Letters of Emily Dickinson*. Edited by Thomas H. Johnson. Cambridge, MA: Harvard University Press, 1958.

————. *The Poems of Emily Dickinson*. Edited by Thomas H. Johnson. Cambridge, MA: Harvard University Press, 1995.

Finkelhor, David. *Sexually Victimized Children*. New York: The Free Press, 1979.

Fry, Anthony. *Safe Space: How to Survive in a Threatening World*. London: J. M. Dent & Sons, 1987.

Mossberg, Barbara A.C. *Emily Dickinson: When a Writer Is a Daughter*. Bloomington: Indiana University Press, 1982.

Sewall, Richard S. *The Life of Emily Dickinson*. New York: Ferrar, Straus and Giroux, 1974.

Wolff, Cynthia Griffin. *Emily Dickinson*. Reading, MA: Addison-Wesley, 1988.

"There is no home there": Re(his)tor(iciz)ing
Captivity and the Other in Spofford's "Circumstance"

Lisa Logan

I.

Spaces can be real and imagined. Spaces can tell stories and unfold histories. Spaces can be interrupted, appropriated, and transformed through artistic and literary practice.

—bell hooks, *Yearning: Race, Gender, and Cultural Politics*

In *Hard Facts*, Phillip Fisher argues that the nineteenth-century American novel "executes the past" through popular forms. This "retroactive" use of the past—in popular settings and stories that recognize, repeat, and "work through" it—"transform[s] the present" by rationalizing and making acceptable "hard facts," including the killing of Indians, the system of slavery, and industrial capitalism (3–8). The historical novel thus rehistoricizes and naturalizes an American history that is already complete. Fisher's point is that historical fiction imposes on its subject a narrative that suits the ideological present—that the *spaces* of American history, including the wilderness, home, and city, are, to paraphrase bell hooks, subject to appropriation and tranformation through literary practice. Fisher's argument illustrates how the uncomfortable facts of American history can be contained and *made safe* through narrative.

This safety is often achieved through the use of racialized discourses. As Toni Morrison's *Playing in the Dark* has shown, a reexamination of the Africanist presence in American literature uncovers the assumptions and ideologies of Anglo American writers. Morrison demonstrates that figures of race are central to narratives of Anglo American selfhood; through these figures, Anglo writers confront their own national and cultural identities. The Africanist presence, Morrison argues, has permitted American writers to contemplate risky subjects in safety (28).

Narratives of cultural identity are closely tied to the ideologically charged spaces of American national and individual histories. As Biddy Martin and Chandra Talpade Mohanty point out, identities are linked to ideologically grounded "homespaces." They argue that the perceived safety of home is founded on unquestioned assumptions about self and Other:

> [Home] refers to the place where one lives within safe, protected boundaries; 'not being home' is a matter of realizing that home was an illusion based on the exclusion of specific histories of oppression and resistance, the repression of differences even within oneself. (196)

For Martin and Mohanty, "home" becomes a metaphor for identity. "Home" represents a set of positions that we occupy unself-consciously; the ideological underpinnings of these positions are covered over and unacknowledged.

I wish to locate the captivity narrative and Harriet Prescott Spofford's short story "Circumstance," a nineteenth-century revision of this genre, at the interstices of Fisher's, Morrison's, and Martin and Mohanty's theories. To convey and stabilize the cultural meaning of American selfhood, the captivity narrative depends on configurations of the American landscape, such as home and wilderness, in which gendered and racialized ideologies are imbedded. According to Fisher, the captivity narrative "miniaturizes" early national history, casting Anglo Saxon "invaders as prisoners" (43) and legitimizing their campaign of genocide against Native Americans. It typically traces the white victim's capture, imprisonment, rescue, and restoration against the dramatic and binarily opposed settings of home and wilderness. For women writers, this movement between home and wilderness, safety and danger, is further complicated by their disempowered positions in a dominant culture that maps its racialized and gendered ideologies onto their bodies and which struggles to make women's acts and words "safe." In a culture that determines when and how women can be subjects in discourse and that imposes material sanctions on women who do not comply, women who write about captivity tread a tricky path between safety and danger.

Mary Rowlandson's captivity narrative *The Sovereignty and Goodness of God* (1682), for example, explicitly underscores her position of safety within a culture that aggressively contains women's difference and disorder within hegemonic structures. Throughout her narrative, Rowlandson negotiates safe spaces from which to speak, spaces which have been disrupted by her Indian captivity and by Puritan attitudes toward "public" women and their speech. Rowlandson fashions acceptable narrative positions for herself, including that of chaste and pious Christian, Puritan goodwife and deputy husband. She constructs her captors as her polar opposite, the savage and heathen racial

Other.[1] Against this fixed and stereotyped notion of the Other, the woman writer negotiates a safe discursive position.

At the same time, however, the very presence of the Other disrupts and brings into question that safety. The captivity experience unsettles the spatial categories of home and wilderness, exposing the ideologies on which they rest as tenuous. The certainty of these spaces is predicated on unexamined assumptions about and uncontested distinctions between self and Other, right and wrong, truth and lies. The captivity experience destabilizes these assumptions and distinctions and challenges the ideological foundations underlying the safety of home. In the captivity narrative, as in Martin and Mohanty's essay on identity politics, home becomes not only a physical space but a metaphor for women's unsettled and unsettling position.

In revisiting the captivity narrative, Harriet Prescott Spofford's short story "Circumstance" is similarly concerned with woman's cultural and discursive "place." The story transpires in the wilderness and domestic spaces of America's early national history. In representing the captivity narrative from a nineteenth-century perspective, Spofford's story engages in the politics of historicization; she "interrupts, appropriates, and transforms" history's spaces. In Spofford's narrative, as in the early American captivity narrative, domestic and wilderness spaces serve as metaphors for hegemonic definitions of safety and danger which are mapped onto "woman" and which threaten to erase female subjectivity. As in nineteenth-century romantic fiction, Spofford invokes cultural configurations of race as she engages questions of American space and woman's "place." Like Rowlandson's narrative, "Circumstance" is concerned with woman's negotiation of safe spaces in culture and in discourse. In negotiating woman's position, Spofford's story brings into tension women's literary traditions, American romanticism, and figures and discourses of race. Ultimately, she seems to challenge the stability of these categories and, in doing so, to question the safety of woman's "place" in the national spaces of home and wilderness.

II.

> There is no home there. The log-house, the barns, the neighboring farms, the fences, are all blotted out and mingled in one smoking ruin. Desolation and death were indeed there, and beneficence and life in the forest.
>
> —"Circumstance"

Spofford sets her story in the margins, at the edge of the northern forest of Maine and, as Anne Dalke has pointed out, explores the tenuousness of experience. That tenuousness, I argue, stems from the text's collapsing of typical categories of home and wilderness. The heroine has spent the day at the "home" of a sick friend, a home associated with illness, pain, and death. Unlike Rowlandson, who often "can not find her way," she is not afraid to enter the forest alone and perceives "the sweet *home*feeling of a young and tender wintry wood" (84, my emphasis). As this "sincere and earnest woman" "sallie[s] forth" into the evening wilderness, her husband remains at home with the baby. She must traverse three miles of woods to get home, described as "one of a dozen log-houses . . . with their half-cleared demesnes separating them . . . from a wilderness untrodden save by stealthy native or deadly panther tribes" (84). The ominous proximity of the "stealthy native" and "deadly panther tribes" undercuts the security and safety of home. Home is situated at the edge of a "great forest," in "half-cleared demesnes"; while Spofford's language is apparently oppositional, it also suggests the mutually dependent natures of home and wilderness—one is made possible only by the "clearing away" of the other. This language undercuts and problematizes the opposition of home to wilderness and recalls Martin and Mohanty's observation that home is "an illusion of coherence and safety based on . . . exclusion . . . [and] repression" (196). While nineteenth-century culture represses what lies outside home as "Other," Spofford's story seems to forward home's uncertain and illusory qualities. Home is never quite "cleared" of the wilderness; the forest compromises its "domain"—questions the rights and privileges which it assumes.

The heroine's "captivity" aloft in a tree in the "arms" of an "Indian Devil" panther reenacts the captivity narrative's concern with home and wilderness, and the relationships between these categories and women's subjectivity. Like Rowlandson, who negotiates safe speaking positions before an audience wary of women's public speech, Spofford's heroine's voice—her singing—meets the demands of her captor, satisfies her instinct, and represents conscious choices and strategies. Her song at once complies with and questions essentialist definitions of women's words: "Again her lips opened by instinct but the sound that issued thence came by reason. She had heard that music charmed wild beasts. . ."(86). Her singing is a choice, a substitution of song for scream. What she sings is inadvertent and unconscious: "[A] little thread of melody stole out, a rill of tremulous motion; it was the cradle-song with which she rocked her baby. . ."(86). Although she sings an expected song, one seemly for a woman and a mother, the circumstances of her singing disrupt the "safety" of cultural images of "woman." The picture of a mother singing her child to sleep before the hearth, which a lullaby invokes, alters to a woman rocking and singing in the arms of a dark and savage panther. By shifting the circumstances of the heroine's singing from home to wilderness, Spofford suggests that a woman's voice might be heard in other spaces than the home.

"Circumstance" questions safe categories of home and wilderness in other ways as well. One of the first images to cross the heroine's mind following her capture is of her child "sleeping rosily" and "the father cleaning his gun, with one foot on the green wooden rundle" (86). The home, traditionally the domain of the wife, is here secured by the father; the wife, typically safe at home, confronts the wilderness alone. The images of her husband's well-oiled gun and his foot that rocks the cradle bring into view exactly who "keeps" the home and at what cost. Distinctions between home and wilderness are blurred and uncertain. As the heroine endures her torture, she dreams of home:

> She fancied the light pouring through the chink and then shut in again, with all the safety and comfort and joy, her husband taking down the fiddle and playing lightly with his head inclined, playing while she sang, while she sang for her life to an Indian Devil. Then she knew he was fumbling for and finding some shining fragment and scoring it down the yellowing hair. . . . (88)

Here Spofford juxtaposes the heroine's night peril with the idyllic "safety and comfort and joy" of the lit cabin. The heroine's singing to her husband's fiddle seems to merge with her wilderness singing. She imagines her husband "playing while she sang, while she sang for her life to an Indian Devil." Her husband's safety and comfort is almost at the expense of her danger. His "fumbling for and finding some shining fragment" parallels the fumbling of her captor's claws in her clothing, his "scoring it down the yellowing hair" recalls the beast's "scoring" of her white flesh. In this passage, distinctions between the safety of home and the danger of the wilderness are made murky as the figure of the husband blurs into that of the beast.[2]

Perhaps most ambivalent and uncertain is the story's attitude toward rescue. In Rowlandson's narrative, restoration constitutes reassimilation into her former home and position. Yet her text questions this restoration through its depiction of her sleepless nights and constant worry over the uncertainty of her physical and spiritual safety. "Circumstance," too, insistently challenges notions of rescue and the promise of safety held out by husband and home. With her husband's appearance, the heroine forgets her "fervent vision of God's peace" and imagines only her log home:

> Cheerful home sound then, how full of safety and all comfort and rest it seemed! what sweet morning incidents of sparkling fire and sunshine, of gay household bustle, shining dresser, and cooing baby, of steaming cattle in the yard, and brimming milk-pails at the door! what pleasant voices! what laughter! what security! (95)

The heroine may recover this idyll only through the loss of her spiritual vision, her voice, and, of course, through more danger. Since the panther's body covers her own, her husband's bullet must "pierce her body" before "reaching any vital part of the beast" (94). Domestic bliss is possible only at the expense— indeed the annihilation—of her voice and self. Her vision of her happy home is followed by her discovery that "her voice was hoarse and sharp,—every tone cut like a knife,—the notes became heavy to lift,—withheld by some hostile pressure,—impossible. One gasp, a convulsive effort, and there was silence. . ."(95). Home and safety, the passage seems to imply, are exclusive of woman's voice. Her silence is effected by some "hostile pressure," which is at once the physical strain of singing all night and, perhaps, the presence of cultural forces militated against women's expression.

Ironically, it is the beast—the Indian Devil, the violent Other—who saves her. The panther, spying her husband, springs up and seizes her, and her husband fires. The Indian Devil's body breaks his captive's fall and rescues her from her husband's gunfire. "Circumstance" seems to ask who the Other really is, who has the power to rescue, and what that rescue implies.

But Spofford has still more questions about home and safety. Returning to their log-house, the family discovers "no home there" (96). Their settlement has burned to the ground in an apparent Indian attack. As the two look on, the husband's gun falls away from him, reinforcing his inability to "rescue." They are faced with a curious truth: "Desolation and death were indeed there, and beneficence and life in the forest" (96). "Circumstance" questions the boundaries between safety and danger and inverts the assumptions beneath early America's opposing definitions of home and wilderness.

III.

> Fire is not half ourselves; as it devours, arouses neither hatred nor disgust; is not to be known by the strength of our lower natures let loose; does not drip our blood into our faces from foaming chops, nor mouth nor slaver above us with vitality. Let us be ended by fire, and we are ashes, for the winds to bear, the leaves to cover; let us be ended by wild beasts, and the base, cursed thing howls with us forever through the forest.
>
> —"Circumstance"

In *Playing in the Dark,* Toni Morrison links the Africanist presence in American literature to nineteenth-century American romanticism. The roman- tic tradition, she observes, offered Anglo American writers a strategy for deal- ing with their "New World" fears and for exploring Americans' boundless capacity for uncertainty; the African American served as a metaphor for the limitless terror Anglo Americans faced and which they termed the "power of blackness." These romantic fears are, of course, cast in a different light for women, whose marginalized positions in nineteenth-century culture necessarily complicate Morrison's characterization of the romantic "terror of human freedom." Throughout "Circumstance,"[3] Spofford's use of race exists in tension with her more explicit critique of dominant cultural narratives about woman's "place." I suggest that we read this tension as a cultural politics. We might ask, how do figures of race and racialized discourses allow Spofford to contemplate dangerous subject matter safely?

The captivity narrative relies on figures of race to negotiate American history and cultural identity. The threat of national and cultural disorder is expressed in the unsettled wilderness and mapped onto an inexplicably "savage" racial Other. Spofford's nineteenth-century captivity narrative negotiates the spaces of American history from a woman's perspective, exploring home and wilderness as positions from which women might speak. Spofford's story challenges categories of home and wilderness, a challenge which depends on the story's use of the racial Other, onto whom ideas about violence, power, and sexuality are displaced. I wish to consider how this displacement at once questions and conserves racialized categories of self and Other. Specifically, the figure of the Indian Devil affords Spofford a site for exploring in safety culturally disruptive notions about woman's "place."

Judith Fetterley has argued that Spofford's Indian Devil is a metaphor for "unrestrained male sexuality . . . often let loose on the bodies of women" (226). The Indian Devil "lick[s] her bare arm with his rasping tongue and pour[s] over her the wide stream of his hot foetid breath" (86). She "saw instinctively the fierce plunge" of his claws, and feels them tear her with "agony" and "quivery disgust" (86). Caught in his "great lithe embrace," she sees with horror white and red—his white tusks, red glaring eyes, and long red tongue, her own white flesh and crimson blood. As Fetterley notes, the passage can be read as "an experience of 'rape,' a nightmare as likely to occur in the home as in the woods" (266). This violence, I argue, at once historicizes and sexualizes nineteenth-century relationships between Native American men and Anglo American women. In this way, the "Indian Devil's" death is made "safe."

The image of the husband with his gun seems consistently and closely linked to sexual violation. When her captor first seizes her, she calls not upon God but on her husband. Her singing is punctuated by images of her husband safe at home, rocking the baby, cleaning his gun, rosining his bow. At one point, his fingerwork at the fiddle blurs into the Indian Devil's clawing at her body. Her husband's approach is heralded by "[a] remote crash of brushwood [that] told of some other beast on his depredations" (93). His intrusion marks yet another violation—her loss of voice and vision. It may be, as Fetterley contends, that Spofford's Indian Devil encodes the violence men promise for women at home, an encoding that Spofford anticipates her women readers will understand. The racialized "beast," then, offers a safe space for Spofford to articulate such a revolutionary notion.

But I suggest that this reading needs to be complicated for a number of reasons. First, I suggest that we consider the violence the heroine endures from her sexualized and racialized captor within other paradigms. Fetterley asks us to view the story in terms of the "violation and vulnerability" women faced when they entered into art. Invoking Hawthorne's remarks that literature should "exhibit women's bodies, naked, without restraint of decency," Fetterley argues that the violence in "Circumstance" represents women's sense of "shame and loathing at such enforced and public exposure" (265). I contend, however, that dominant cultural constructions of "true womanhood" are equally violent in that they threaten to erase women's subjectivity. Essentialist definitions of "woman" and her "place" violate women by demanding that they enact their lives and works according to hegemonic definitions. The panther promises punishment if the singing fails to please. Similarly, nineteenth-century American culture's expectations for women's acts and words promise the withdrawal of those privileges extended to feminine "virtue" if women fail to live up to those expectations. The promise of privilege to the virtuous implies that certain women may *deserve* a whole range of violent and punitive remunerations, which could include bad reviews, failure to find work, abandonment, and rape. Violence, therefore, is linked not only to women's vulnerability or wish to remain private. Rather, one's biological circumstance, being born a woman, invites exposure, scrutiny, and, possibly, violation. The heroine's vocal response to her capture and violation places in tension woman's voice and her violation. The juxtaposition of these terms recalls that captivity has historically been a pretext for women's writing as well as a place where the meaning of women's subjectivity has been struggled over. The captivity narrative, produced in an era that punished women's public speech with excommunication and banishment, concerns women's negotiation of discursive space. Spofford substitutes the Indian Devil of her maternal grandmother's legend for Rowlandson's "heathens," and the heroine's singing replaces Rowlandson's "true story."[4]

As Anne K. Mellor argues, romanticism "requires the construction of an Other, which is seen as a threat to the originating subject . . ."(3). The romantic artist constructs *his* beloved as Other, who must be possessed, consumed, effaced, and destroyed if he is to achieve his goal. According to Mellor, consummation "can only be achieved through the literal annihilation of the consciousness of the division between the lover and his beloved" (26). Mellor's comments recall the famous American romantic heroines, Ligeia, Madeline Usher, Beatrice Rappaccini, all victims of violent male artist figures. Spofford, whose style and subject matter place her within traditions of American romanticism,[5] writes from a discursive moment that mythologized the male artist and predicated his aesthetic transcendence on the possession and destruction of the female Other. In returning to the captivity narrative to imagine her female artist (the singing heroine), Spofford returns to a genre in which the *racialized* Other enables the subject's spiritual vision and conversion. The racialized Indian Devil provides both a safe *and* dangerous site for exploring the woman artist's position and voice.

But the panther does not merely represent the Other. As in Rowlandson's captivity narrative, in which the wilderness experience destabilizes categories of self and Other, and as in romantic fiction, in which, as Morrison writes, the "subject of the dream is the dreamer" (17), Spofford's text conflates categories of self and Other. The narrator observes that, unlike fire, beasts such as the Indian Devil are "half ourselves" when "the strength of our lower natures [are] let loose" (89). I find it significant that the beast's consonance is with "our" natures, implying that boundaries such as human/beast, white/Indian, Christian/heathen, and male/female are indistinct. This indistinctness is perhaps most visible when the husband shoots the panther out of the tree, and there follows "a terrible yell of desperation . . . that filled her ears with savage echoes" (95). Here Spofford removes the agency from this "terrible yell." Whether these "savage echoes" issue from the panther, the husband, or the woman herself is left—deliberately, I think—ambiguous. The question of agency here foregrounds the collapsing of categories that Spofford effects and hints quietly that woman's voice *might* articulate the unseemly. The panther—the racialized figure, the easy stereotype—affords Spofford a strategy through which to explore this possibility obliquely and in safety.

IV.

Oh, was there no remedy? Was there nothing to counteract it, nothing to dissipate that black drop, to make it colorless, powerless, harmless, a thing of air? Were there no sweet, good people among all those dead and gone women? . . . What gifts were these grandmothers going to give the child then? she asked.

—Spofford, "The Godmothers"

"Circumstance," a revision of the early American captivity narrative, "interrupts, appropriates, and transforms" the spaces of American history as they map dominant ideologies onto women's bodies. The story is concerned with "place," which I have tried to define as at once the physical settings of home and wilderness and the ideological categories of self/Other, man/woman imbedded in them. "Circumstance" struggles with the meanings and uses of the past from the nineteenth-century present Spofford occupied. In considering what those

meanings and uses might be, I turn to Spofford's short story "The Godmothers" (1896).

Like "Circumstance," "The Godmothers" focuses on the collision of two
worlds. The heroine, Rosomond, has left her American home for marriage to
a L'Aiglenoir and has just given birth to an heir in her husband's "ancestral
stronghold." As the heroine lies "faint and weak" in a "dim vast chamber," the
L'Aiglenoir grandmothers "step from [the] frames" of their sea-gallery portraits
(207), reminding the heroine of their history of scandal, forgery, counterfeit,
adultery, opium, poison, cruelty, the guillotine, and the madhouse—a history
of "black blood" (214). Rosomond responds to these visitors with terror,
crying "What gifts were these grandmothers going to give the child then?"
(215).

Like "Circumstance," this story is concerned with a history of "blood,"
only the politics of possession and empire are displaced onto the French
aristocracy. Its concern with national "color" is displaced onto the "purples and
scarlets" of the European grandmothers versus Rosomond's own wan and
pallid American ancestors. Rosomond's question—what shall be passed on to
her child?—is, according to Phillip Fisher, the question of all American writers:
What is the relationship of history to the national identity of the present? I
suggest that "The Godmothers" speaks intertextually to the American romantic fiction and women's captivity traditions which Spofford worked within by
engaging this question. Spofford attempts to work out a safe and "usable past"
from which to speak and which to pass on.

The story seems expressly concerned with woman-centered traditions.
Rosomond's husband is "away on the water, or in the hunt, or at the races"
(208). The L'Aiglenoir stronghold has historically been kept by its women,
who, to bring the family its lands and titles, traded themselves and their
integrity. Rosomond at first discounts them as "all only tradition," saying that
their lives "would have been dreadful if [the stories] were true" (209). Her
husband reminds her, however, that "happiness has no history," "virtue has few
adventures," and that "the big wills, the big passions" are "memorable . . . and
drown out the others" (209–10). His words seem to address directly Spofford's
own position within women's and canonical literary traditions. What is her
"place" to be? What is her relationship to her literary descendants and ancestors? What will be remembered and how?

"The Godmothers" centers its treatment of American history and literary
traditions, as in "Circumstance," on color. Rosomond contrasts the "pallor of
her colonial and nineteenth-century New England grandmothers with the
"purples and scarlets of [European] women of great passions, of scope, of
daring and deed and electric force" (214). Rosomond views Anglo American
women's histories and traditions as wan and disempowered. She imagines her
New England ancestors:

> Far off, by the curtain of the doorway, huddled together like a flock of frightened doves—gentle ladies, quiet, timid, humble before heaven, ladies of placid lives, no opportunities, small emotions, narrow routine, praying by form, acting by precedent, without individuality, whose goodness was negative, whose doings were paltry, their drab beings swamped, and drowned, and extinguished. . . . (214)

Rosomond's grandmothers are colorless as drab doves, adhering to the outward forms of religion and culture in dull lives that fail to question the "narrow routine" of woman's "place." In leaving America for Europe, Rosomond rejects her American grandmothers' "passive virtues" of self-effacement, self-sacrifice, and quiet acceptance for "great drama" and a "larger nature." Her choice seems to suggest a failure to locate within American culture a place from which to counter its "pallid" narratives of femininity.

"The Godmothers" represents Spofford's engagement with divergent narratives of American history and literary tradition. The L'Aiglenoirs recall the uncomfortable truths about America's past that "Circumstance" invokes: colonial expansion and the genocide of Native Americans. The L'Aiglenoir family was borne of rape, after a "sea-rover had scaled the heights" of a lady's castle and "taken her, loathing and hating him, to wife" (212). This family history speaks to both the disturbing history of American expansionism *and* the impact of patriarchal culture on racialized and gendered Others. Out of these tensions emerged a tradition of Anglo women's writing based on the domestic and wilderness captivity of women's lives, a tradition which, like dominant cultural narratives and canonical literary traditions, often relied on figures of race and color.

"The Godmothers" seems to respond to troublesome American histories and traditions by reimagining a whitewashed and safe space from which the young child, the L'Aiglenoir of the twentieth century, like the woman writer, might emerge. Such a space is figured forth in the beautiful and "original savage," "swift and supple . . . with free and fearless foot, large-limbed and lofty as Thusnelda, clad in her white wolfskin, with the cloud of her yellow hair fallen about her, carrying her green bough, strong, calm, sure" (216). In Spofford's "original savage" a romanticized Native American woman blurs into a curiously Nordic goddess. Her values are ". . . scorn for the ignoble, trust in thy fellow, dependence on thine own lust sinew and unconquerable will,—familiar friend of hardship and content, spare, and pure, and strong,—joy in the earth, the sun, the wind, faith in the unseen" (216). This noble savage, her blonde whiteness a product of nineteenth-century aesthetics of feminine beauty, represents "the unpolluted, strong, wild strain in [her son's] blood, the vital savage" (216).

"The Godmothers" attempts to rewrite American history onto an Anglo woman's body, to construct a history and tradition that is safe to pass on. The story evinces an incredible amount of anxiety about nation, Anglo American women, and American history and literary traditions. Spofford maintains the integrity of "blood" by positing the pre-colonial, pre-slavery, and insistently white body of a European ancestral godmother. In this way, she makes the spaces of history and tradition "safe." Rosomond's husband tells her that "pictures are no more certified than the traditions" (210). "Circumstance" and "The Godmothers" attempt to reimagine and transform American history and traditions. Her fiction presents its own gallery of pictures that revises the spaces in which history and tradition have mapped discursive and cultural meanings onto women's bodies. In trying to make these spaces "safe," her fiction is no more or less "certified" than those histories it appropriates and transforms. Spofford's is a whitewashed "picture" in the gallery, illustrating what is at stake in making American spaces safe.

Notes

1. For a more detailed discussion of Rowlandson's negotiation of discursive space, see my "Mary Rowlandson and the 'Place' of the Woman Subject."

2. Judith Fetterley writes about the sexual overtones of the panther's attack, arguing that it represents the displaced and menacing sexual power of men "who cannot be the woman's husband," that is, Native Americans. Fetterley argues that, although the text hints that "home is where the beasts are," it "stops short" of identifying the husband with the panther (267). Fetterley concludes that Spofford's story exemplifies the pervasive racist imagination of nineteenth-century white writers. My reading, however, suggests that Spofford's boundaries are less explicit than Fetterley implies. I wish to explore the relationship of Spofford's use of race to American literary and historical spaces.

3. Spofford's other works, such as "The Amber Gods," "The Black Bess," "The Moonstone Mass," and "The Godmothers," operate this way as well.

4. Halbeisen describes the story's inception in Prescott family legend. Spofford's links to Rowlandson are even more coincidental than her use of captivity conveys: the Prescott family settled in Lancaster, Massachusetts and was probably living there at the time that Rowlandson was taken captive.

5. Bendixen makes this point in more detail, xxii.

Works Cited

Bendixen, Alfred. "Introduction" to *'The Amber Gods' and Other Stories* by Harriet Prescott Spofford. Ed. Alfred Bendixen. New Brunswick: Rutgers University Press, 1989.

Dalke, Anne. " 'Circumstance' and the Creative Woman: Harriet Prescott Spofford." *Arizona Quarterly* 41.1 (Spring 1985): 71–85.

Fetterley, Judith, ed. *Provisions: A Reader from Nineteenth-Century American Women.* Bloomington: Indiana University Press, 1985.

Fisher, Phillip. *Hard Facts: Setting and Form in the American Novel.* New York: Oxford University Press, 1985.

Halbeisen, Elizabeth K. *Harriet Prescott Spofford: A Romantic Survival.* Philadelphia: University of Pennsylvania Press, 1985.

hooks, bell. *Yearning: Race, Gender, and Cultural Politics.* Boston: South End Press, 1990.

Logan, Lisa. "Mary Rowlandson and the 'Place' of the Woman Subject." *Early American Literature* 28:3 (Winter 1993): 255–77.

Martin, Biddy and Chandra Talpade Mohanty. "Feminist Politics: What's Home Got to Do With It?" *Feminist Studies/Critical Studies.* Ed. Teresa de Lauretis. Bloomington: Indiana University Press, 1986.

Mellor, Anne K. *Romanticism and Gender.* New York: Routledge, 1993.

Morrison, Toni. *Playing in the Dark: Whiteness and the Literary Imagination.* New York: Vintage, 1992.

Spofford, Harriet Prescott. *'The Amber Gods' and Other Stories.* Ed. Alfred Bendixen. New Brunswick: Rutgers University Press, 1989.

"Entirely Unprotected": Rebecca Ketcham's Trail Diary

Mary Sylwester

Safe space for women on the overland trails was complicated by the coordinates of the adventure. In the early nineteenth century, overwhelming physical danger was perceived to arise from the geographical region between the Missouri and Columbia Rivers, a space inhabited by alien peoples and fraught with unknown hazards. To step across the western border of Iowa or Missouri in those days meant to expose oneself and one's family to the insecurity posed by a lack of regulation. No towns, and few forts, intervened in the vast expanse from Council Bluffs to the Columbia River. In leaving friends and family, emigrants risked losing support networks and social frames of reference and thus entered a cultural danger zone. Within the emigrant space, protection lay in the temporary dissolution of the wall between public and private. A group economy satisfied the needs for organized physical protection and for ongoing social interaction. Strangers shared campfires, and the family space merged with public areas. With the creation of that practical *ad hoc* community, however, persisted expectations that such a space, with its particular rules and responsibilities, would be a transient phenomenon, limited to the emigrant project. Eastern social values and boundaries would reappear once the trip was over. In emigrant narratives of the experience, however, the geographical danger zone occasionally disrupted social patterns to the extent that the end of the story could not be played out in the fashion forecasted at the beginning of the narrative. For nineteenth-century women, who drew their identities in large part from their role within the private sphere, that disruption became a danger in itself. For trail diarist Rebecca Ketcham, the writing of the experience grew to be impossible as the predicated ending of her story lost its connection in the emigrant space to the subject position she came to inhabit.

Within the borders of the United States at mid-century, the rhetoric of domesticity made the private home an island of safety and serenity presided over by the mother. Nineteenth-century female writers such as Catharine Beecher, Lydia Sigourney, Lydia Maria Child, Susan Warner, and the popular

Fanny Fern preached that the individual family home was meant to be a special and secure feminine domain, in which the moral character as well as the physical health of future generations was formed. Catharine Beecher declared in *The American Woman's Home* that "the family state . . . is the aptest earthly illustration of the heavenly kingdom, and in it woman is its chief minister"(19). The walls of the home sheltered women from the worldly pursuits of trade and legislature and guarded the moral well-being of the family as the key to national virtue.

Leaving the eastern enclosure of the home for the wide-open West, then, exposed women to worldly influences and even endangered the sanctity of the family. That so many women were willing to go seems extraordinary. Historians and critics have speculated that they must have been coerced by insistent husbands, or held captive to masculine impulses to conquest.[1] From the perspective drawn in this scenario, the outdoor world of men, mud, and money-making reached in and swept women out of their comfortable homes. Pioneer women are thus to be pitied. Another view, however, is possible. Women, according to the contemporary popular press, were a source of formidable cultural power. The trek westward might be seen, therefore, not just as a dangerous ordeal, but also as an opportunity to recreate what was culturally perceived as the safe spaces of home within an unbuilt landscape. From this alternative perspective, women were not exactly captives to the all-powerful male world of commerce and conquest, but rather comprised a cultural Trojan Horse that depended on the outside world of men and machinations for movement.

At the beginning of her 1853 journey, Rebecca Ketcham saw herself in just such a position of power. She aligned herself squarely within a Beecheresque view of women's role as cultural missionary. In the 1840s, Catharine Beecher organized a legion of female teachers to serve on the frontier, binding Christian duty, womanly character, and national good: her National Popular Education Board sent dozens of single women westward, starting in 1847. The scheme of exporting women teachers to the West found support in some of the most popular literature of the day: in *Godey's Lady's Book* of 1849 editor Sarah Josepha Hale wrote that the "plan of sending female teachers from the Eastern States to the West" was of "far more importance to the improvement, and, we may add, prosperity of our land, than will be all the gold of California."[2] Hale appealed for continued public dedication to such service:

> While the young men are thus going forth to gather gold, will not the benevolent and pious of our land contribute to send forth our young women to disseminate that wisdom which must be taught, or the gold will prove a curse and not a blessing? (295)

Hale's metonymic identification of men with gold and women with wisdom seemed to elevate the position of the feminine, and yet reinforced a cultural separation between the world of men and the realm of women. Wealth, apparently, was a "blessing," if its accumulation in the rough world of commerce could be supported by the pleasant and gentle influences of teachers, wives, and mothers. The profession of teaching for women, although it may have seemed finally a way for spinster ladies to support themselves in the workaday world, was hardly separable in contemporary discourse from the protected sanctuary of the home. Hale proclaimed the role as "teacher of the young" to be woman's "office, her mission"(355). Out of such rhetoric emerged women like Rebecca Ketcham, for whom teaching in the wilds of Oregon was a once-in-a-lifetime opportunity.

At first, Ketcham's expectations for that opportunity guided the development of her narrative; as the unaccustomed life of the trail stretched on, however, her vision of life "at home" in Oregon blurred into an increasing awareness of the interim space. Because a diary kept is as much a record of the efforts to work out a preconceived narrative structure as it is a shaping of a new one, it is possible in the emigrant's journal to follow two stories at once: the development or disintegration of the forecast plot of settlement together with the emergence of an independent story of the road. The well-bordered space of the home, so important to the success of women's mission in the West, broke down in the fluid environment of the trail. Maintaining a separation between home and public areas was a near-impossibility as cooking, washing, sleeping, and even more personal matters had to be accomplished outdoors within view of other people. In that exposed situation, the social distance between men and women was diminished and borders between public and private became permeable. A symptom of that permeability was that women's household chores were open to bargain: for example, women often cooked and baked for people outside their own families in exchange for supplies or draft animals. Or, as in the case of Rebecca Ketcham, women might be required to provide such domestic services as part of the fee for their passage. The role of women, so well-confined within walls at home, on the wide-open trail leaked into the world of public commerce.

In this disconcerting moment, when indoors became outdoors and the protecting borders of home were replaced by tentative lines on a map, the story of the road impinged upon the narrative of progress. Michel Butor compares the movement of travelers through space to a writer's movement across a page: he draws an analogy between the white space dividing units of meaning in a text and the waiting times between stops on a train route (Butor 1–16). For pioneers driving wagons across the continent, unlike passengers on a faster trip, that white space could not be ignored. Between the beginning and the end lay a vast space punctuated only by the occasional fort or trading post: a space in which significant living was to be done, but for which there was little except sketchy guidebooks and travelers' tales as patterns. In this unwritten space, journalizing for many was a way of negotiating the experience: even the barest of diaries, including only mileage and weather, might provide a kind of map, or at least an understandable pattern. The result of such attention to the interim space itself, however, was to make it signify all out of proportion to the destination. The space of the trail competed with the overarching fantasy of home.

Rebecca Ketcham is one of the most satisfying diarists of the trail, because she wrote copiously not only about the landscape and the schedule of the trail, but also, and most interestingly, about the personality conflicts that drove people apart. Ketcham was not one of the teachers sent West by the National Board, but her aim seems to have coincided with the missionary zeal of that organized effort. She had collected donations from friends and relatives to support her trip, an action which suggests that her trip was considered worthwhile by other people in her community. Her diary offers no clue as to her reasons for undertaking the journey or her plans for settlement after her arrival. Lillian Schlissel speculates Ketcham may have gone West to escape a soured romance; but this guess, like any other, is unsubstantiated by the journal (Schlissel 101). Her pious sentiments and firm resolution to continue reflected in her diary, and the record of her eventual teaching occupation in Oregon, cast her within the general mold of the feminine teacher/activist of the era. After teaching in Clatsop Plains, Oregon for somewhat less than two years, however, she married an upstanding citizen named Finis E. Mills, a member of the Board of Trustees of the First Presbyterian Society. Within five years after her marriage, she, Mills, and their two young sons left Oregon for Kentucky, apparently her husband's family home (*Ketcham* 248).

Ketcham traveled with a small group of people under the authoritarian leadership of William H. Gray, one of the original 1836 missionaries to the Oregon Indians and a veteran of overland travel. In 1853, Gray was on his third east-west journey across the continent. His prickly and overbearing personality is well-documented in the diaries of Mary Walker and others who traveled west with him in 1838.[3] Ketcham recorded the general complaints of the 1853 party about his restrictions on food consumption, baggage weight, and sleeping time. At one point she wrote with horror of Gray's whipping a fifteen-year-old boy for the crime of falling asleep on guard duty, and the next day with satisfaction noted that Gray himself could scarcely stay awake while driving the team. As a leader, he was opinionated and absolutist, but his policies were calculated to ensure survival. Indeed, he was an amazing survivor not only of the general hazards of the road such as lack of food and bad water, but also of Indian attack (he was the sole survivor of a Sioux ambush near Ash Hollow on a return trip East in 1837), and of financial ruin, changing occupations several times during his long life. His project that corresponded to Ketcham's trip was the transport of a large flock of sheep to Oregon.[4] Despite his personality flaws, he was a veteran of the trail and knew how to respond to its rigors. One of Ketcham's major complaints early on was that he disregarded what she understood to be implicit rules of social behavior, such as protecting women from dangers and inclement weather.

Perhaps because she perceived herself as part of a powerful social force for good, Ketcham assumed she would receive deferential treatment and that her opinion would be valuable. Early in her 1853 journal, she frequently reminded herself to follow the example of her Savior, and to remember what it meant to be a Christian, despite the unending discord around her. The first sign that such a position was not to be hers in Gray's company was his autocratic decision to travel on Sunday (*Ketcham* 249). Gray repeatedly disrupted Ketcham's preferred subject position by insisting on a military-style organization for their company (in which she is decidedly subordinate) instead of recognizing cultural or family patterns that would allow her a more protected role. To her great irritation, Ketcham was required to cook and clean for the company much more often than she found convenient. Gray refused to make distinctions between people in terms of the amount of work required, other than assigning men to the animals and women to the care of the camp. She decreased the work she did, however, after finding out that her passage cost nearly twice as much as that of fellow traveler James Van Renssalaer. She wrote "Charge me one hundred and fifty and then expect me to work my way! I think I shall find more time to write hereafter"(263). "Working [her] way," apparently, was something Ketcham had not anticipated. The financial transaction of her passage, in her mind roughly similar to the act of buying a steamboat ticket, should have been over when she paid her fare. The kind of workaday employment Gray demands was distasteful, for it placed her in the role of servant rather than of paid and protected passenger.

Ketcham's outrage at Gray's dealings with her appeared to be aimed not strictly at gender-based inequality, but rather the idea that she should be dragged out of her rightful social position and thus denied the protection she felt she deserved. That her ideas about social position were firmly based in her feminine identity became clear a few days later, when she was left out in the rain during a storm instead of being invited to ride with the other women in the covered carriage. Riding alone when the rain began, she assumed Gray would stop and let her get into the carriage. Instead, he found her a rubber overcoat, and another woman gave her an old bonnet to wear so hers would not be ruined. According to Ketcham, she rode in the thunderstorm for two or three hours and through a deep stream that further soaked her dress until they arrived at a camping place and the rain stopped. In the carriage at last, she waited with the others for the ground to dry enough for a fire to be laid and tents to be set up:

> So there I sat in the carraige [sic] for more than an hour, my feet and limbs cold as ice, and my face and head like fire. Every time anyone spoke to me I had the greatest difficulty to keep from crying. If it had really seemed necessary for one to ride, and there had been anyone with me, I could have laughed it off, but to have all the rest riding along in their carraige, and me taking all that terrible storm alone when there seemed to be not the least necessity for it, I can assure it was a good deal more than I could bear without being very indignant, and I would not have felt so badly then if Mr. Gray had shown the least disposition to have a fire made and a place for me to change my clothes and be made comfortable. I was not much afraid of taking cold, but the idea of being treated in so heartless a manner was the main thing. (265)

Alone, ignored, and soaked, Ketcham feels abandoned by the man who, she feels, has contracted to take care of her, and therefore unnecessarily exposed to dangers. It is important to point out, for the sake of context, that the men in the company regularly got wet in taking care of the sheep and oxen. The rubber coat given Ketcham during the storm was a man's. For her it was inadequate, and not just because it didn't cover her skirts.

What seemed truly "heartless" to Ketcham is that she felt her woman-hood merited more careful treatment. Gray, however, was in service to the exigencies of the weather, not to social convention. She chose to ignore the practical fact that the ground was too wet to lay a fire or set up a tent, and instead focused on her outrage at the discomfort to which she is subjected. At home, no doubt, she would have been invited indoors and offered warm clothes while her wet things hung by the fire to dry. Here on the plains, however, the only "indoors" places available were the transient sleeping tents they bring along; and the availability of those was completely dependent on the cooperation of the environment. The fire that was the very symbol of hospitality and concern at the heart of the home, could not practically be kindled. The trail controlled this particular turn in her narrative, yet she attrib-uted the twist to Gray. At this point in Ketcham's journal, Gray came to personify the dangers placed in her path. Her insistence that he could alter her miserable circumstances if he chose, de-emphasized the role of the weather and the landscape and assigned control to him. Safe space on the trail, then, de-pended upon his good graces.

Ketcham thus set up Gray as her protector. His actions in that role, however, were decidedly unsatisfactory. After the ordeal of the rainstorm, Ketcham felt the insult to her womanhood was compounded by Gray's failure to recognize her sacrifice. Her assumptions about the appropriate treatment of women had been challenged, and she began to perceive that she was mistaken about the social codes that would be operative on the trail. The social differences between men and women at home in New York were simply not recognized in Gray's company, because he saw no practical purpose in them. The financial inequality revealed by Ketcham's inquiries to James revealed that Gray's attitude with regard to women was far from worshipful: apparently, he felt ladies were trouble. Far from the reassuring walls of home, Gray was inclined to expose her as much as possible to the hardships of the outdoors.

Gray's disregard for culturally-defined feminine prerogatives showed itself in his control of such traditionally feminine matters as cooking and nursing. As far as Gray was concerned, domestic routines and rationales were best left behind for the duration of the journey. He prepared meals himself and restricted portions; and, when diarrhea or other maladies struck the group, he prescribed and administered remedies. His standard remedy for diarrhea was a diet of stewed fruit and rice; or, in severe cases, abstention from solid food altogether and a regimen of liquids only. His dictatorial administration of even these helpful cures, however, chafed the members of his party. In June Ketcham, troubled with constipation, wrote in exasperation:

> rice and peaches have been provided for those who had diarhea, and I have eaten of them. I have never before been where I had no choice as to what I could eat, nor the privilege of saying what I would like. A pretty dear passage across the Rocky Mountains I call it. (280)

For Ketcham, Gray's control over the traditionally feminine arts of food and medicine was much harder to accept than his dictatorship over the more masculine issues of navigation and care of stock. Her emphasis on her own powerlessness is particularly acute at this point: to have no "choice" or "privilege" in these matters was particularly galling. Gray's actions actively impinged upon her subject position.

Despite his disregard for the routines of home, William Gray was in fact acting as the head of a family group during this trip: most of the members of the company were his wife's relatives. The family model, however, clashed disastrously with his management of the group. One of the principal sources of conflict during the trip, and one that Rebecca Ketcham invoked when she wrote of her disappointment in failing to become part of an harmonious family, was that in spite of Gray's militaristic discipline, people in the group tended to follow pre-existing family habits rather than accept new rules. Camilla Dix, for example, the spinster sister, was forever doing younger sister Martha Godley's work; the Godley boys were pampered by their mother, and the matriarch Sarah Dix was accustomed to unquestioned authority on matters of health and cooking. Gray, however, was in the business of moving people and stock across the continent as quickly and as safely as possible, and he had no patience with those who shirked what he defined as obligation or who objected to policies he understood as necessary. He readily whipped his fifteen-year-old nephew, Henry Godley, for falling asleep on duty. Family feelings were irrelevant beside the demands of the road. Ketcham writes that she was disappointed in the rapport of the company: "I had expected we would all cling together and to be one family, but we are anything else. I presume I shall have some heartache after I get there, before I get settled" (266). "Family" and "settled" at mid-journey were words that still inhabited the preconceived narrative of her trip; but at this juncture she perceived that the story was becoming more complicated than she expected. Significantly, however, settlement, coterminous with happiness, was yet the implied end.

In order to make that end possible, Ketcham suspended her own judgment about Gray's behavior. She excused his abuses of power by citing the different space of the trail, no longer blaming him for the vicissitudes of the weather, but rather assigning him a mediating role between the dangerous transitional space of the road and the safety represented by home and hearth. The "heartache" brought on by his autocratic authority and the subsequent disintegration of the "family" on the road would, in her mind, be restored after the ordeal of the passage was behind her. Even William Gray, she considered, might be different within his own home. She resolved to suspend judgment on Gray's behavior until the space of the journey was done, and recognizable frameworks of home reestablished:

> I believe it will not do to judge of character on this journey as one would anywhere else. The incidents or circumstances here develop character as nothing else can, and if allowances are not made, we cannot come to correct decisions. At all events, I don't think I can understand Mr. Gray till I see him at home. (271)

In trying to understand Gray's seemingly inappropriate behavior, Ketcham reasoned that the rules of conduct were not the same as "at home." This suspension of judgment is an important conjunction between the narrative of expectation and the narrative of the road in her journal, for it marked the place from which she loosened her own control on the imaginative shaping of events, and began to rely almost entirely on Gray's mediation of her experience.

As Ketcham's diary progressed, it revealed a growing alliance with Gray and his authority. Indeed, the narrative began to depend on his actions rather than hers: Ketcham became a commentator on Gray's actions rather than the recorder of her own emotions. Near the end of the trip, she even admitted that she favored Gray over the seemingly more congenial men and women in the party: "I do not know why it is I always feel inclined to side with men like him against everyone else. Still I believe my judgement tells me he is far from being the only one in the fault in the difficulty they have had"(352). She began to see other members of the company as disrupters of the codes laid down by Gray, instead of the other way round. Gray, as the arbiter of the narrative imposed by the journey, took precedence over the increasingly in-appropriate actors still preoccupied with maintaining the standards of Ithaca. Despite the hardships he imposed in terms of food and rest, Ketcham reassured herself in her journal that he must have had reasons for his behavior. After one river crossing where the sheep were nearly beyond control, she wrote: "I am sorry for the man anyway. He has a terrible temper to control, and with so much care on his mind, so much to irritate and vex him, I don't wonder he acts like a crazy man"(375). Without admitting it, Ketcham transformed Gray in her diary from a "crazy man," one whose actions are inappropriate, to a man whose behavior is at least understandable.

In her journal, this suspension of judgment and dependence upon Gray as arbiter of the road extended from personality even to features of the land-scape. Everything she previously knew and understood almost instinctively became suspect. She wrote with surprise about the deceptive nature of the landscape for Ithaca-trained eyes. Height, distance, even expectations of weather patterns were not to be trusted. Camped on the Platte River, she wrote: "It is surprising to see how easily one is deceived in the distance here on these plains, and in size of objects. I have a great many times mistaken a crow some distance before us for a man"(279). This illusion of perspective, commonly reported by overland emigrants, was paralleled in Ketcham's writing by a certain disjunction of expectations. Her account of Fort Kearney, for example, exposed the vast difference between her idea of what a fort looked like and the way this one presented itself: "We saw no mounted guns, nor in reality anything that looked like a fort except the dress of those we saw about"(274). Gray was also of the opinion that Fort Kearney fell far short of its name. Ketcham recorded that he commented that it looked like "the commanding officer liked strong drink better than anything else"(274). In other situations, Ketcham's tentative views of the environment gave way to those of the trail-hardened Gray. About Independence Rock, a landmark near the Platte on which emigrants traditionally carved their names and dates, she wrote:

> It is said to cover an area of 5 acres. I [think] that is correct, but that it is four hundred feet high I doubt very much. Of course we cannot judge of distances nor heights as we could at home, but thinking steadily of what we

> have passed, and comparing this with the other given heights, I doubt it very
> much. (348)

The qualifiers she added to the statement undermined her empirical defense
of her opinion. The superfluous repetition of "I doubt . . . very much" especially neutralized her initial tone of confidence. Similar hesitations dogged her
descriptions of other parts of the landscape. Describing the landscape around
Independence Rock earlier in the paragraph, she repeated the word "seem"
three times in rapid succession, as if her view of things were at best a hazy and
ill-remembered recollection of a dream:

> We seemed to be in a large prairie, . . . with great mountains of rocks seem-
> ingly thrown up from the earth. . . . As we passed around the ends of them,
> we could see all around. They appeared strangely enough to me. These chains
> of mountains seemed to be on every side of us, and we could see no way
> of getting out of the valley. . . . (348)

William Gray, of course, was her guide out of the valley, and he did not seem
to be lost or confused for a moment. Over the course of the journey, she
became a keen listener to him as he drove the carriage, noting that she was
learning much from him about driving the team, identifying flora and fauna,
understanding Indian behavior, and even about writing in a journal. With her
acceptance of a distinction between home and trail, she seemed also to have
accepted Gray as an authority.

Near the end of the journey, she had learned so well to disregard her own
instincts that she occasionally defied common sense. For example, despite
noting that "If we had been at home [we] would have expected rain"(383),
she made no preparations for the wetting that followed within a few minutes.
This time, she and the other women, who had been preparing to dry clothes (!),
climbed into the carriage and waited out the rain, which shortly "began to
come down in large drops" (383). In the context of her changed frame of
reference, the rain was a surprise, proof not that her Eastern sensibilities were
right, but rather evidence of the unpredictability of Western weather. This
episode, although recorded without commentary in her diary, served to underline her complete subjection to Gray. She assumed that her own opinion, even
about domestic routines learned at home in New York, was valueless. Lack of
confidence in her own powers of discernment seemed to undermine Ketcham's
ability to take care of herself. In order to take advantage of Gray's protective
powers, she had to give up the self-sufficient attitude that led her to make the
trip as a single woman in the first place.

Perhaps because of the fact that she placed herself at the mercy of forces
outside her control, Ketcham's diary revealed no sense of personal insecurity.

She felt so confident in Gray's skill and judgment, in fact, that the occasional skittishness of the other women irritated her. For example, when the elderly Mrs. Dix requested permission to avoid a dangerous river crossing with the wagons and ride instead as a passenger on the ferry, Gray became angry and this time Ketcham, surprisingly, was on his side: "Mr. Gray did not like it at all that the request was made. He likes to have us have confidence in him and let him manage his own affairs without a word of interference, and I think it would be very much for the happiness of this company if Mrs. Dix and Mrs. Godley would cease to interfere as they do"(357). In contrast to her earlier outrage about the stony treatment she received in the rainstorm, Ketcham was surprisingly complicit in Gray's refusal to make allowances for age and gender. Mrs. Dix's request showed a preference for protection from the elements and for organized public transport (a shadow of the social structures they had left behind) over the exposure to wild water Gray's plan offered. Such a preference seemed entirely reasonable for an elderly lady, accustomed to social conveniences. Her request, however, revealed Mrs. Dix had not relinquished the life of the home for the life of the trail, and that revelation enabled Ketcham to feel superior. She had realigned herself completely, from representative of Eastern manners to virtual deputy of frontier behavior. The "heartache" she expected to suffer through seemed to have dulled as her expectations were deferred.

Just as her own sense of loss had lost its sting, the griefs of others in Ketcham's journal were subject to a William Gray-styled reduction. Like many other emigrants, she counted graves when they appeared by the roadside,[5] but she did not record very many (a surprising lack only one year after the cholera epidemics on the trail in 1851 and 1852); and those she did write about she suspected of merely appearing to be graves:

> Before this morning we had seen five graves; today we have seen four, making nine. Mr. Gray said some person who was considered reliable had made a statement which was published for a fact in regard to the graves seen on this route, which we account for in this way. (The number was very great—I forget what it was, and beside, he said what was singular, no grass grew on these graves.) We have noticed all along long, narrow holes in the ground which look like a grave sunken in. But as we leave such an one wherever we camp, we take it for granted those we see are made in the same way. Indeed, we are sure of it from the signs around. They take a spade and dig such a hole to make a fire in. . . . when it rains upon the ashes we leave, an alkali is formed which prevents the grass from growing upon them. (269)

Ketcham's phrasing here tells a great deal about her increasing separation from Easterners and growing allegiance to Gray's frame of reference. Her qualifications of the report ("*considered* reliable" and "*published* for a fact") served to underline the naivete of the Eastern readers who took such reports at face value. The sentimental horror of thousands of graves lining the route became for her a picture drawn by overinspired writers for a gullible public. Her own sketch of the experience was drawn by William Gray. That Ketcham repeated his explanation of the apparent "graves" in her journal not only eliminated the possibility for her own emotional response, but also implied an emerging gulf between the Gray-Ketcham unit and the imaginary mass of uninitiated Easterners. At this point in the journal, the twin focus on the home behind and destination beyond blurred: far from wishing herself at the end of her wanderings, Ketcham lamented the haste at which the group traveled and stated her desire to return someday to better enjoy the scenery. The geographical expanse that for her was originally merely a space of transition had become a place with its own logic and its own particular meanings.

That logic and meaning, however, depended entirely on Gray's interpretation. From the beginning of her journal to the end, Ketcham's outlook changed from that of an independent woman out to fulfill a cultural mandate to that of a follower whose own subjectivity depended upon the authority of her captain. His abrupt departure near the Columbia River when the party was still weeks from their destination, then, left her bewildered and afraid. Although the most significant dangers of the passage were behind them, Gray's abandonment seemed to Ketcham to be inexcusable. In her journal she complained:

> Mr. Gray was very much tried, but I cannot think he did quite right in leaving us as he has. I felt badly enough when he went away. . . . I have not felt so much anxiety and dread on the whole trip as I do now; feel so entirely unprotected. (400)

At this point on the trail, the only significant geographical hazard left was the passage down the Columbia, a venture handled by ferryman entrepreneurs on the river itself. Local Indians were interested in trade, not attack. Yet, the departure of William Gray stripped her of the sense of security her dependence on his judgment allowed. Her feeling of exposure at this point seemed to arise from the disjunction between her trail-adjusted point of view and her renewed need, near her long-planned destination, to recover meaningful social structures. Having ceased to regard the trip as white space to be endured between the meaningful loci of Eastern home and Destination West, she had begun to recognize significance in the landscape itself. Without Gray as her interpreter of that landscape, she was suddenly without referent in an unfamiliar syntax. The geographical isolation she enjoyed and wished to linger within just a few pages earlier became not only a threat, but a barrier to the reassumption of her accustomed position within a social grammar.

Without a secure social or geographical place, Ketcham seemed also to have lost her ability to find a safe subject position from which to write. Shortly after Gray's departure, but before the end of her journey, the entries in her diary ceased. Her angry and self-assured "I shall find more time to write hereafter" at the beginning of the trip (263), a statement which made the act of writing a defense against the unwelcome space created by Gray, belonged to a completely different writer. The Rebecca Ketcham writing, or not writing, at the end was not powerful enough to erect those kinds of defenses. The pages she was so determined to fill at the beginning of her journey despite Gray's demand on her time were left blank at the end of her book, before the end of the trail. The frameworks of home still unbuilt, she dropped her narrative altogether. The ending of her journal, forecast from the very beginning as the reestablishment of familiar structures and values, was unwritten. Her foreshadowed observations of William Gray at home came to nothing, and her dreamt-of success as a teacher and bringer of civilization in the frontier regions of Oregon went unrecorded. The alien space of the trail bound her so effectively to authority other than her own that, when she found herself unprotected in that space, her own ability to muster authorial power ended. She left her written self as Gray left her: on the road.

Rebecca Ketcham's slide from self-sufficient, confident young teacher to fearful emigrant follows a delicate border between protection and exposure. The conflict between the need for group security against dangers in the landscape and the desire for individual protection against ambiguities in the social sphere engendered difficulties for emigrants, especially for women, who by mid-century presided over the cultural sanctuary of the home. Although Ketcham suspended judgment about human behavior on the trail and thus was able to fit into the military-style order Gray demanded, she planned to teach in Oregon when she arrived, to help reconstruct the stable social framework that gave special power to her feminine position. The process of her movement through the alien space of the trail, however, changed her options. What she had assumed to be the trivial space of the journey imprinted itself on her writing in a way that made the completion of her story impossible. Like the furniture jettisoned from wagons and left to bleach in the sun, the fantasy of domesticity was at once fragile and difficult to move. Forced to condense both physical and intangible components of home into the most basic elements, emigrants sometimes found their dreams of home replaced by an unending sense of uprootedness.

Notes

1. For the most extensive literary analysis of pioneer women's narratives, see Annette Kolodny, *The Land Before Her* (Chapel Hill: The University of North Carolina

Press, 1984). Lillian Schlissel's historical collection, *Women's Diaries of the Westward Journey* (New York: Schocken Books, 1982), is now a classic. Other studies include Julie Roy Jeffrey, *Frontier Women* (New York: Hill and Wang, 1979); Sandra L. Myres, *Westering Women and the Frontier Experience 1800–1915* (Albuquerque: University of New Mexico Press, 1982); and Susan Armitage and Elizabeth Jameson, eds. *The Women's West* (Norman, Oklahoma: University of Oklahoma Press, 1987).

2. 38 (April 1849): 294. For information about women teachers in the West, see Polly Kaufman, *Women Teachers on the Frontier* (New Haven: Yale University Press, 1984). *Godey's Lady's Book* addresses the subject of women teachers in two issues: April, 1849: 294–295 and May, 1850: 354–355.

3. See Clifford Drury, *First White Women over the Rockies* 3 vols. (Glendale, CA: Arthur H. Clark, 1963). Mary Walker's diary is reproduced in vol. 2.

4. The movement of the sheep was a frustrating project that nevertheless succeeded until the very end of the journey, when Gray was tying up the boat containing the animals at the mouth of the Columbia River. A sudden storm pulled the boat back out into the waves and capsized it, drowning the entire flock. He had mortgaged his farm to buy them. See Ketcham 240–245.

5. Lillian Schlissel calls women emigrants in particular "actuaries of the road" for the prevalence of running totals in their journals. For more on this diaristic phenomenon, see Schlissel, *Women's Diaries of the Westward Journey*, 15.

References

Anderson, Benedict. *Imagined Communities: Reflections on the Origin and Spread of Nationalism*. London: Verso, 1983.

Beecher, Catharine and Harriet Beecher Stowe. *The American Woman's Home, or, Principles of Domestic Science*. 1869; rpt. Hartford, Connecticut: The Stowe-Day Foundation, 1991.

Bercovitch, Sacvan. *The American Jeremiad*. Madison: University of Wisonsin Press, 1978.

Bushman, Richard L. *The Refinement of America*. New York: Alfred A. Knopf, 1992.

Butor, Michel. "Travel and Writing." *Mosaic* 8:1 (Fall 1976): 1–16.

Child, Lydia Maria. *The Mother's Book*. 1831; rpt. Old Saybrook, Connecticut: The Globe Pequot Press, 1992.

Drury, Clifford M. *First White Women over the Rockies*. 3 vols. Glendale, CA: Arthur H. Clark, 1963.

Faragher, John Mack. *Women and Men on the Overland Trail*. New Haven: Yale University Press, 1979.

Hale, Sarah Josepha. "Editor's Page." *Godey's Lady's Book*. April 1849: 294–295 and May, 1850: 354–355.

Kaufman, Polly Welts. *Women Teachers on the Frontier*. New Haven: Yale University Press, 1984.

Ketcham, Rebecca. "From Ithaca to Clatsop Plains: Miss Ketcham's Journal of Travel." Eds. Leo M. Kaiser and Priscilla Knuth. *Oregon Historical Quarterly* 42 (1961): 237–87, 337–402.

Kolodny, Annette. *The Land Before Her: Fantasy and Experience of the American Frontiers, 1630–1860*. Chapel Hill: University of North Carolina Press, 1984.

Schlissel, Lillian. *Women's Diaries of the Westward Journey*. New York: Schocken Books, 1982.

Stowe, Harriet Beecher. *House and Home Papers*. Boston: Ticknor & Fields, 1865.

Unruh, John D., Jr. *The Plains Across: The Overland Emigrants and the Trans-Mississippi West, 1840–1860*. Chicago: University of Illinois Press, 1979.

Urry, John. *The Tourist Gaze: Leisure and Travel in Contemporary Societies*. London and Newbury Park, CA: Sage Publications, 1990.

Safe Space and Storytelling:
Willa Cather's *Shadows on the Rock*

Linda K. Karell

The tension between the desire for home, for synchrony, for sameness, and the realization of the repressions and violence that make home, harmony, sameness imaginable, and that enforce it, is made clear in the movement of the narrative by very careful and effective reversals which do not erase the positive desire for unity, for Oneness, but destabilize and undercut it.

—Biddy Martin and Chandra Talpade Mohanty

The above epigraph is drawn from Biddy Martin and Chandra Talpade Mohanty's essay, "Feminist Politics: What's Home Got to Do With It?"[1] In that now well-known essay, Martin and Mohanty examine Minnie Bruce Pratt's autobiographical narrative, "Identity: Skin Blood Heart," in order to theorize "the power and appeal of 'home' " (191). Martin and Mohanty's essay investigates how the desire for "home" and its subsequent constructions within the various communities inhabited by Pratt always exist in tense relationship, buttressed by the illusion of safely demarcated spaces, and contested by the realization that others' stories must be violently suppressed in order to maintain that illusion. Throughout their essay, Martin and Mohanty question the desirability of "home" in relation to feminist and lesbian feminist theory and as a component of Pratt's narrative itself. Defining what they mean by "home," Martin and Mohanty argue that

> "Being home" refers to the place where one lives within familiar, safe, protected boundaries; "not being home" is a matter of realizing that home was an illusion of coherence and safety based on the exclusion of specific histories of oppression and resistance, the repression of differences even within oneself. (196)

The relationships between concepts of "home," "safe space," and "storytelling" are multiple, but for the purposes of this essay, I want to suggest that safe spaces, whatever their form, designate "home." In other words, to be "home" or to be "at home" always connotes a form of safe space. That space may be material, such as the house in which one grew up and felt secure, or it may be psychological, such as a particularly familiar or comfortable pattern of emotional responses. For women, however, the physical and psychological safe spaces that resonate as "homes" have often been linked to women's bodily, sexual, or artistic containment and violation within those structures. In my reading, the critical challenge of Martin and Mohanty's analysis is its insistence that "home" relies upon the relentless exclusion of difference for its maintenance. As Martin and Mohanty implicitly argue by their use of Pratt's autobiographical narrative as an example of their insights, the stories women tell about their lives can disrupt a belief that the safe spaces of home can be had without a concomitant cost to the women who inhabit them or, for that matter, to those others excluded from those homes. Without denying the psychological necessity, the "positive desire," for safe space, unheard or unacknowledged stories hold the potential to undermine and sometimes even shatter "home's" claims to security and protection from difference. For women, then, it is important to consider the wide-ranging implications of what we call safe space. Is safe space desirable? Is it even possible and, if so, under what circumstances? In this chapter I argue that constructions of "home"—and thus of safe space—are invariably tenuous; they are often desired for their promise of safety, but they are simultaneously always vulnerable to disruption. Desire for a safe space to call home that is coupled with a realization that home is vulnerable and tenuous is the central tension in Willa Cather's 1931 novel, *Shadows on the Rock*, and it is through Cather's use of storytelling that we witness the disruption of safe space. As critics have already noted, there are a range of stories within the pages of *Shadows on the Rock*: legends of historical saints and pioneers, tales of warring Indians and devout religious explorers, and recounted memories of historical figures all interweave with the narrative of the daily comings and goings of the Canadian settlers. Susan Rosowski stresses storytelling's unifying and universalizing potential when she argues that each character in *Shadows on the Rock* "participates in rituals of storytelling, by which individual lives are joined to timeless legends" (179). But in *Shadows on the Rock*, seldom do any two characters tell the same story. The discrepancies between stories steadfastly resist a single coherent reading; stories contradict each other and simultaneously work to question the very assurance of home they are called upon to create. The stories in *Shadows on the Rock*, their content and the manner in which they are told, enact the novel's internal debate between the liberating potential of safe spaces that signify "home," and the threats of women's socialization, erasure, and silence that structure those homes.

Moreover, in *Shadows on the Rock*, race as well as gender impact which stories can be told and by whom, and whose stories will be believed. In fact, Cather's insistence on the importance of the position from which one speaks in this novel foregrounds differences from the universal and insists upon the impossibility of stability. Cather mounts her largest investigation of universality with her examination of religious space as a potentially safe space for women. Here too, however, while the text's representations of religious spaces reveal an obsession with coherence and stability, the contradictions between those representations simultaneously force the reader, through the characters' storytelling and through the content of the stories they tell, to acknowledge that coherence and stability may come at a cost to women and are highly tenuous. What is up for grabs in *Shadows on the Rock*, in other words, is the possibility and the desire(ability) of an uncontested, universally human story.

In addition to the resonance that the metaphor of home has for my reading of the many layers of *Shadows on the Rock*—the surface text, the subtext, the multiple and often contradicting stories—the safety promised by a stable home is apparent in Cather's writing process and in the novel's reception. In other words, the desire for safe space figures in specific ways in Cather's attempts to control interpretations of her life as well as in the reputation for being a marginally canonical writer that has stuck to Cather relentlessly through the years. Written when Cather was fifty-eight years old and nearer to the end of her career than to its beginning, *Shadows on the Rock*, like the rest of her late fiction, has been consistently considered inferior to her early novels. In fact, to the degree that Cather is valued as a canonical writer, she is valued for a reductive selection of work, one that emphasizes her earlier pioneer novels. Interpretations of her work based on these novels frequently judge Cather's art to be most significant when most readily digestible as a universal story. In *Cather, Canon, and the Politics of Reading* (1992), Deborah Carlin argues that "What designates [her] early novels as canonical then is their appeal to reading publics as stories already inscribed within the national imagination. . . . What is identifiably canonical within Cather's nearly fifty years of fiction writing then is, paradoxically, a small number of texts that embody the expansive West of the American imagination" (7–8). Certainly the reason for this truncated critical assessment is not a lack of range on Cather's part. Throughout her writing career, which spanned the length of her adult life, Cather wrote prolifically and diversely. Her writing covers a wide range of subjects, and she experimented with dramatically different composing processes and literary styles. But the novels that have secured Cather's literary reputation, *O Pioneers!*, *My Antonia*, and *Death Comes for the Archbishop*, for example, have often been read as transcendently "human" stories that resonate across time. *Shadows on the Rock* shatters this promise of a familiar—and consoling—story of nation-building.

Working on behalf of the universal, critics have praised Cather as an intuitive artist, one who possesses a "naturalness so great that one is tempted to think of her almost as not a writer at all," since this naturalness "lies far below the surface of conscious endeavor" (Tennant ix). As feminist scholarship has shown, however, crediting a female author with intuitive greatness at the expense of rationality satisfies cultural expectations about what and how a woman should write and effectively bars her from creative agency: not masters themselves, women are mastered by their intuition, which proves more capable than their intellects. At the risk of belaboring what I hope is the obvious, even a quick skim through Cather's early non-fiction writing will severely tax any reading of her as solely an intuitive writer, rather than as one who is consciously directing (if not fully in conscious control of) her writing energies and abilities. Scores of her articles, entertainment and literature reviews, and cultural commentaries reveal a young woman very much engaged with the cultural questions of her time and carefully and deliberately defining for herself the potential of art and the role of the female artist.[2]

Gendered expectations for women's writing in America have allowed critics to construct a Cather whose literary works uphold interpretations of America's colonizing history as justified, even divinely ordained. Cather's focus on Westward expansionism through her positive representation of the pioneer, especially of the pioneer woman, her frequent emphasis on landscape and on what has been interpreted as "the archetypal and eternally human," as well as "that effortless symbolic quality that is Cather's distinctive note" (Rose 132, 128), mesh well with historical renderings of America's past as the discovery and morally sanctioned occupation of a "new" land. In contrast to her contemporary Gertrude Stein's radical linguistic experimentation, for instance, the placid surface of Cather's novels, her focus on exteriority rather than interiority, her insistence on precise word choice, on traditional grammar and syntactical structure in order to render meaning exactly, have all been invoked to uphold critical readings of Cather as conservative and apolitical. Although Cather has sometimes been dismissed as simplistic, naive, or escapist in the literary celebration of Modernism's self-conscious complexity, many critics who argue for Cather's "greatness" agree that she is able to achieve anonymity, thus transcending gender, race, and class.[3] Cather's writing has been judged most aesthetically pleasing when least politically disruptive, helping to create what Carlin describes as "the early critical formula that Cather's novels climax in the twenties, then spiral downward in a trajectory of despair, decline, and artistic degeneration" (16). The critical silence that envelops *Shadows on the Rock* consistently avoids confronting a Cather who is more politically engaged than most readings of her earlier novels suggest. We can see this engagement in her essay, "On *Shadows on the Rock*," where Cather was openly skeptical of the desire for ceaseless stability that so structures her novel: "There another age persists. There . . . I caught something new to me; a kind of feeling about life and human fate that I could not accept, wholly, but which I could not but admire" (15). Her description is evenhanded, suggesting that the premise of stability that permeates her novel was not only "new" to her, but also somewhat unconvincing. While we need not read Cather's retrospective statement of her intentions as fixing the meaning of her text, her statement intervenes in the conflation of author and text that upholds readings of Cather as either transcendent or naive, and it shows her to be quite able to tolerate, even to admire, ambiguity.

Shadows on the Rock is plotted to create the "illusion of coherence" (Martin and Mohanty 180). The novel's structure of repetition emphasizes stability: set during 1697–1698 in French Quebec, Canada, *Shadows on the Rock* spans one year of twelve-year-old Cécile Auclair's life. The seasonal arrival of ships carrying the supplies from France necessary for survival is a comforting repetition, as are the characters' daily rituals of labor, religious observation, food preparation, and storytelling. However, the atmosphere of certainty that predictable events and cyclical time generate within the text is almost immediately suspect, when challenges to the possibility of stability erupt. The rock upon which Quebec is built is equally a symbol of stability and a reminder of vulnerability. Buffeted by "the ever-changing northern light and weather," Quebec is bounded by a forest which keeps difference—and the terrors it is believed to contain—perpetually within view:

> [O]n the West, behind the town [of Quebec], the forest stretched no living man knew how far. That was the dead, sealed world of the vegetable kingdom, an uncharted continent choked with interlocking trees, living, dead, half-dead, their roots in bogs and swamps, strangling each other in a slow agony that had lasted for centuries. The forest was suffocation, annihilation; there European man was quickly swallowed up in silence, distance, mould, black mud, and the stinging swarms of insect life that bred in it. . . . The river was the one thing that lived, moved, glittered, changed,—a highway along which man could travel, taste the sun and open air, feel freedom, join their fellows, reach the open sea . . . the world, even! (6–7)

Representing the forest as living terror may be consonant with historical perceptions of the vast unknown North American continent at this period of colonization, but something in addition to the quest for psychological or historical realism is also registered here. In a text that so relentlessly insists on the need for a stability possible only through the absence of change, this description of the forested landscape of Quebec posits exactly the opposite: changelessness is terrifying stagnation, while the movement of the river offers life *because* it changes. Even at this early point in the novel, with her description of Quebec's forest,

Cather contradicts her characters' desires for a secure place to call home and begins crafting a rich subtext that will continue throughout the novel.

An equally disruptive element of that subtext is the racial difference that poses a threat to the colonists' new home in Quebec. Cather's description of the forest is a New World nightmare filled with repulsion and dread. It is also a screen onto which fears of racial difference are projected as a chaos that threatens to annihilate the French settlers. Besides breeding insects—or perhaps, the paragraph suggests, as an example of them—the forest is home for Native peoples. Unlike her representations of Native Americans in *Death Comes for the Archbishop*, in *Shadows on the Rock* Cather deploys predictable stereotypes and records a historical prejudice. For example, Cécile "liked to think of things of their own in Canada," and some of the stories that fascinate her are about the "wonderful" and "terrible" "tortures the Jesuit missionaries endured at the hands of the Iroquois, in those savage, interminable forests" (101, 102). Although Cather's emphasis is on Cécile's adolescent romanticization of suffering (Cécile's father, for instance, wonders "whether there has not been a good deal of misplaced heroism in the Canadian missions,—a waste of rare qualities which did nobody any good" [155]), Cécile's romanticization of the missionaries' tribulations requires the opposition of a savage tribe of Indians. During his visit with Cécile and her father, one of the novel's contemporary male religious figures, Father Hector, also portrays the Indians as entirely alien and malicious in his story of another male religious leader's encounters with the Hurons: "Everything about the savages and their mode of life was utterly repulsive and horrible to him; their filth, their indecency, their cruelty" (151). Throughout *Shadows on the Rock*, Native people are generally savages, occasionally cannibals and, like children, are blissfully unaware of their uncivilized ways, requiring the salvation of the Jesuit priests. In the above passage, Cather projects this paralyzing fear of racial difference onto the forest, and she records the European desire to contain otherness *elsewhere* in order to maintain safe—white—homes.

For a transplanted white European community, the racial difference represented by the Indians in *Shadows on the Rock* is a constant threat to the colonizing project and the European definitions of home that the novel privileges. For Cécile's mother, Madame Auclair, the Indians are the chaos her homemaking is aimed at excluding: "Without order our lives would be disgusting, like those of the poor savages. At home, in France, we have learned to do all these things in the best way, and we are conscientious, and that is why we are called the most civilized people in Europe. . ." (24). The home Madame attempts to leave Cécile as her legacy is comprised of innumerable acts of ritualistic ordering designed to "make the new life [in Quebec] as much as possible like the old [life in France]" (23). From the start, however, the unity of their home is undone as we see these characters' homes built upon the denied or devalued homes of others: despite the unceasing ordering that is

Cécile's maternal inheritance, the presence of the Native peoples and the forest that is *their* home remain as mute stereotypes in a text that can neither fully suppress nor completely acknowledge their presence. That presence of a hostile and alien culture is constructed as an attempt to justify Madame and Cécile's domestic ordering even as it condemns their efforts to failure.

If the domestic sphere fails to provide women with safe space, then what about the spiritual sphere? Cather gives her fullest treatment of the contradictions created by conflicting stories and their implications for safe space for women, in her representation of Jeanne Le Ber, the intensely ambiguous female religious figure at the center of the text. Le Ber is the character through whom Cather explores the potential of religious spaces to offer safe homes to women. Le Ber is a nexus of competing stories, a series of contradicting interpretations; her "meaning" depends upon who is telling the story, to whom, and where. Le Ber first enters the text as a legend when Cécile, who is repeatedly transfixed by romanticized stories of female religious figures, reviews the "whole story" in her mind (130). The public story currently circulating throughout Quebec tells of a recent visit to Le Ber by angels who fix her broken spinning wheel. This story renders Le Ber miraculous and mysterious—a spiritual authority as suspect as it is liberating for women. It is significant that, despite appearances, Le Ber does not speak for herself. Initially, the words ascribed to Le Ber are part of Cécile's memory of the legend of Le Ber, prompted by the recent news of the angels' visit. Later, Pierre Charron reports Le Ber's words, along with his interpretation of their meaning, in the stories he tells about her to Cécile's father.

At seventeen, as the legend Cécile reviews goes, Le Ber imitates the domestic retreat of the medieval mystic, Catherine of Siena, isolating herself in her father's house, speaking only to a personal attendant. At the end of ten years of religious seclusion, Le Ber uses her dowry to have a three-tiered cell built behind the church's high altar where she continues to live in isolation, embroidering altar cloths, knitting for the poor, and steadfastly observing her religious convictions. In *Felicitous Space*, Judith Fryer claims Le Ber's three-tiered cell is a literary example of "the female discovery of felicitous space" (50), and the public legend Cécile lovingly reviews includes Le Ber's ecstatic description of that space: "[M]y room is my terrestrial paradise; it is my center; it is my element. There is not any place more delightful, or more nourishing for me, not any castle, not any palace, which is more agreeable to me. I prefer my cell over the rest of the universe" [my translation] (136). The earthly paradise Le Ber creates specifically excludes heterosexual marriage and motherhood. If we recall Martin and Mohanty's theory of "home," we see that with Le Ber, Cather excludes precisely those institutions which traditionally structure domestic homes for women, and which will entirely define Cécile's eventual home with Pierre Charron, Le Ber's girlhood suitor. In this instance, the exclusion of "specific histories of oppression" (Martin and Mohanty 196) is a force of resistance, a method of struggle that can redefine home as a site of potential liberation for women. Yet, whether or not we agree that Le Ber's space is felicitous, she gains it by intensifying precisely the domestic space she rejects in order to establish her new home. In other words, Le Ber embraces metaphorically those institutions she rejects physically: she is still quite literally "within her own chamber within her father's house" (132).

Although the religious space Le Ber occupies replicates in many aspects the domestic space she rejects, her isolation becomes a focus for the novel's investigation of the consequences for women of female resistance through religious devotion. Le Ber's retreat is founded on female isolation, which the novel represents simultaneously as Le Ber's "entombment" and as the cause for public "conversation and wonder" (134). As the story describing how Le Ber's spinning wheel was repaired "was told and retold with loving exaggeration," it becomes an "incomparable gift":

> The people have loved miracles for so many hundred years, not as proof or evidence, but because they are the actual flowering of desire. In them vague worship and devotion of the simple-hearted assumes a form. From being a shapeless longing, it becomes a beautiful image; a dumb rapture becomes a melody that can be remembered and repeated; and the experience of a moment, which might have been a lost ecstasy, is made into an actual possession and can be bequeathed to another. (137)

Judith Fryer discusses this paragraph as "a description of the process of writing" and describes Jeanne Le Ber as a legend (330–331). This rhetorically elusive paragraph, much as Le Ber herself is elusive, can certainly be a description of writing, but it also describes storytelling and its rewards. And like stories, the paragraph's meaning exceeds even these interpretations, transforming and taking up other meanings. "Flowering of desire" is at once desire's culmination, and the blossoming forth of more intense desire. Desire for a stable form infuses the stories of Le Ber, prompting their retellings, creating the miracle that is the story. Cather may want a stable form for her narrative authority, but her desire for a spiritual home that will produce permanence in the stories she tells is undone by precisely the desire motivating the stories. The "actual possession" is inherently unstable because while bequeathable in retellings, it will also change with the inevitable revisions and exaggerations of retellings. The image and the melody signify longing and rapture transformed by desire, but simultaneously represent their loss, the desire for their return, and the impossibility of their fulfillment as "an actual possession."

With the public legend of Le Ber, Cather reiterates the familiar apotheosis of woman into worshipped icon. The legend of Le Ber seems to posit religious space as a site of authentic power for women, one outside the prescribed heterosexual marketplace. Yet a closer examination of the legend, coupled with Charron's stories, counters that possibility with increasing ambivalence. Filtered through Cécile's perspective, the public legend of Le Ber emphasizes her mystery as well as her resistance to an expected trajectory of development that would end in marriage to Pierre Charron. Her mystery depends upon her elusiveness, and her resistance has required it. Succeeding stories about Le Ber, told from rejected suitor Charron's perspective, present the female recluse as a failed woman in a religious exile of despair. His stories about her de-emphasize her mysteriousness and undercut the possibility of conscious agency, pointing instead to female socialization as the source of her devotion: "If the venerable Bourgeoys [sic] had not got hold of that girl in her childhood and overstrained her with fasts and penances, she would be a happy mother today, not sleeping in a stone cell like a prisoner" (177). Ultimately Cather resists final authority over Le Ber's meaning; the reader must sift through contradictory stories to determine Le Ber's status in the text. In this way, Cather cautions against claims of religious authority or transcendence as methods of defining autonomous subject positions for women.

In fact, whoever the teller is, the stories told about Le Ber show her performing, with alternating success and failure, depending upon the gendered expectations of the storyteller, an expected femininity, one assumed by the characters to be knowable and stable. Her performances, when filtered through her storytellers' expectations, shape the dramatically contradictory interpretations of her. That gender does indeed play a substantial role in interpretation is evident when Cather shows that Le Ber's public performances of femininity were successful during her rare public appearances in church. The spectacle of Le Ber generates public fascination and approval, and "On such occasions people used to come in from the neighboring parishes for a glimpse of that slender figure, the richest heiress in Canada, clad in grey serge, kneeling on the floor near the altar, while her family, in furs and velvet, sat in chairs in another part of the church" (133). However, if Le Ber is able to resist cultural pressure to accommodate conventional female subject positions, she is nonetheless constrained by those subject positions. The novel stresses that the public legend of Le Ber not only privileges but eroticizes her self-denial, her isolation, and her intense physical discomfort: "On bitter nights many a kind soul . . . lay awake for a little, listening to the roar of the storm, and wondered how it was with the recluse, under her single coverlid" (135).

That such piety is interpreted as authentic only when enacted by a woman is suggested by Cather's opposing representation of a male religious, Bishop Saint-Vallier. Saint-Vallier is described as "a man of contradictions," and Euclid Auclair's patron, the Count, describes him as "an actor" (121). Like Le Ber, Saint-Vallier similarly garbs himself in the severest dress, but his actions are interpreted as "lacking in good taste," with a "piety too conspicuous. . . . He had a hundred ways of making himself stand out from the throng, and his exceptional piety was like a reproach to those of the clergy who were more conventional and perhaps more worldly" (123). In her article, "Female Grotesques: Carnival and Theory," Mary Russo sees a liberating potential in the performance of femininity. Russo argues that "deliberately assumed and foregrounded, femininity as a mask, for a man, is a take-it-or-leave-it proposition; for a woman, a similar flaunting of the feminine is a take-it-*and*-leave-it *possibility*. To put on femininity with a vengeance suggests the power of taking it off" (224). For Russo, femininity is an act of agency performed by a subject, rather than a constitutive aspect of a biologically-female individual. Indeed, many critics have investigated Cather's masculine masquerades: in particular, Cather's high school cross-dressing and her focus on male subjectivity in such novels as *The Professor's House* and *Death Comes for the Archbishop* have led critics to speculate on whether she assumes masculine masks, positioning herself within male literary traditions in order to legitimate an exploration of lesbian themes, or even to continue writing within a culture with few successful female authors as models.

The stability of the female identity Le Ber creates depends upon the stability of the home she creates. As Martin and Mohanty's theorizing suggests, Le Ber's home is maintained by exclusion and suppression. Both the public legend Cécile reviews and Charron's subsequent stories about Le Ber are precipitated by intrusions that undercut the possibility of maintaining a stable home. In Cécile's story, angels miraculously appear and fix her spinning wheel. In Charron's story, he describes his two forced meetings with Le Ber. Both of these meetings undermine the possibility of constructing an inviolable space for women to call home; he keeps intruding, bringing with him male expectations about what a woman's home should be and then telling stories that position him as a victim of Le Ber's refusal to meet those expectations: "There are plenty of girls, ugly, poor, stupid, awkward, who are made for such a life. It was bad enough when she was shut up in her father's house; but now she is no better than dead. Worse" (177–178). Although Charron identifies a religious coercion invisible to Cécile because it is withheld from her, his complaints are also influenced by his disappointment that other institutions which would more directly benefit him—marriage and motherhood—did not claim Le Ber first. Despite Charron's sense of masculine entitlement, his description of Le Ber refuses the text's earlier stories that imply that Le Ber's religious commitment is the natural fulfillment of an essential feminine nature. Charron's stories suggest that "safe" religious homes are already constructed by a culture that desires women be located there.

Charron's stories reveal an increasing concern with female performance, with Le Ber's failure to perform a femininity that allows Charron to retain her as a sexualized "Other." Charron portrays a Le Ber who moves progressively away from an accepted standard of femininity. His description of her before her self-imposed seclusion focuses on her hostessing ability and her beauty. He recalls Le Ber "when she first came home from Quebec and used to be at her mother's side, at the head of a long table full of good company, always looking out for everyone, saying the right thing to everyone" (178). Then, describing their first meeting four years after her first retreat, Charron says, "She was gracious and gentle, as always, and at her ease. . . . There was still colour in her cheeks,—not as rosy as she used to be, but her face was fresh and soft, like the apple blossoms on that tree where we stood" (179). Le Ber's beauty is still reassuring in its familiarity, but it is immediately undercut as Charron tells the story of their second meeting many years later, when he hides in the church, waiting for her to emerge from her cell for her solitary midnight prayers:

> She came in, carrying a candle. . . . The candle shone up into her face. It was like a stone face; it had been through every sorrow. . . . At first she prayed aloud, but I scarcely understood her. My mind was confused; her voice was so changed,—hoarse, hollow, with the sound of despair in it. . . . And once a groan, such as I have never heard; such despair—such resignation and despair! (182–183)

Shorn of markers of femininity, Le Ber's face is no longer rosy and soft, and her formerly gracious voice has become "harsh and hollow like an old crow's— terrible to hear!" (180). The change in Le Ber's voice confuses Charron and marks Le Ber as irredeemably changed, as radically "Other." While defiant, even joyful otherness couched in mystical and miraculous descriptions marks Cécile's story and makes up the legend of Le Ber in public circulation, Charron's sharply contrasting story of Le Ber enacts a verbal mourning, for him, of the female beauty he has lost. His speech forwards the despair he represents Le Ber as embodying, and it is Charron's grief that masquerades as Le Ber's when he tells his story to Cécile's father.

As the epilogue to *Shadows on the Rock* reveals, Cécile eventually substitutes for Le Ber, marrying Charron and performing what was to be Le Ber's role as wife and as mother of "four little boys, the Canadians of the future" (278). In Charron's story of Le Ber, the beautiful hostess is transformed into the incoherent prisoner, while in the novel's story of Cécile, the child who takes to creating a home for her father with such enthusiasm is eventually transformed from daughter to wife, exchanged from father to husband. By leaving unresolved the conflicts presented in the alternate stories of Le Ber, Cather cautions against claims of religious authority or transcendence as methods of defining autonomous subject positions for women. Further, by suggesting in the epilogue that Cécile's growth to maturity culminates in her substitution for Le Ber in marriage to Charron and in the fulfillment of her national duty to Canada by producing sons, Cather insists that spaces—whether domestic or religious—have costs for women attached to their apparent safety.

Shadows on the Rock reveals that the subject positions available to women undergo continual reinterpretation, both public and private, and the struggle for meaning lies not only with the story's teller, but also with its audience. The stories in the text not only refuse the illusion of coherence, they are in direct conflict with one another, and the subject positions available for women are always polarized in the text: Cécile's story is one of adulation, and Charron's story is infused with loss and the desire to possess Le Ber. Women become the object of desire and the currency of exchange; their serviceability enables his illusion of wholeness. Charron dismisses the importance of Le Ber's lost dowry, but announces that "I care about defeat" (177). As Cécile realizes, even Mother Juschereau, who avoids the cultural "entombment" of Le Ber, finds her stories of faith contradicting Cécile's father's stories of advancing science. When Mother Juschereau tells Cécile a story where a bit of bone from a beloved priest was mixed with gruel and made an ill sailor into a Christian, "Cécile could only hope it would never happen that her father and Mother Juschereau would enter into any discussion of miraculous cures. Her father must be right; but she felt in her heart that what Mother Juschereau told her had certainly occurred, and the English sailor had been converted by Father Brébeuf's bone" (127). In each of these stories there is no final interpretation left for the reader to privilege as the text's meaning.

An implicit argument throughout this chapter is that the text of Shadows on the Rock, which insists on fixity and the absence of change through the final page, wears its insistence on stability like a mask. Stories and storytelling repeatedly undercut these qualities and reveal them as illusionary. Like several other critics who examine Cather's use of storytelling, Sharon O'Brien reads Cather's storytelling as a narrative strategy to claim authority by forming literary connections with the storytellers of her childhood:

> Listening to women's talk as she crouched under the quilting frames, the young girl heard the unwritten history of the community that never entered written records or public history. When Cather became a writer of fiction, she likewise practiced an art of connection: she retold and reworked some of these community stories, passing them on to her readers, weaving together oral and written narratives, farm women and artists, past and future in her fiction. (29)

The art of connection O'Brien sees Cather practicing may result more from critical desires for feminist recovery of texts, and expectations regarding what women's writing must do, than from the way storytelling functions in this text. In Shadows on the Rock, storytelling questions, challenges, and in some instances—such as in the story of Jeanne Le Ber—even resists the expected "woman's work" of connection.

The practice of writing as the creation of safe space also has its parallel in Cather's biography. Cather knew the inevitable failure of an artist to control interpretation and was concerned about future interpretations of herself, about the ways in which she would become a story. She limited as much as possible the range of interpretations critics—who also tell stories—could make: Cather and her partner, Edith Lewis, retrieved and burned many of her letters to friends, and their efforts to destroy a lifetime of personal communication were particularly effective in regard to the exchange of letters between Cather and Isabelle McClung Hamborg, a crucial love relationship in Cather's life. In her will, Cather forbade publication of any surviving letters, and she refused to allow film or recorded versions of most of her novels. Despite her efforts, James Woodress estimates that 1,500 of Cather's letters survive in various university collections. Ironically, her testamentary prohibition on the direct quotation or publication of her letters insures that scholars must paraphrase her words— itself a form of interpretation. Moreover, besides simply making her personal correspondence less accessible to readers and critics, Cather's actions have fueled abundant speculation about her sexuality.

In her literary biography, *Willa Cather: The Emerging Voice*, Sharon O'Brien argues persuasively that Cather was a lesbian and had sexual as well as emotional attachments to the women whose lives she shared. Conversely, James Woodress argues in his biography of Cather, *Willa Cather: A Literary Life*, that, because there is no external evidence, claims for Cather as a lesbian are unfounded. At this point in time, Cather's lesbianism has become something of an academic "open secret," a scholarly closet with parallels to the concept of home desired and challenged in *Shadows on the Rock*. Although I find O'Brien's arguments regarding Cather's lesbianism convincing, efforts to definitively position Cather as a lesbian are always vulnerable to challenge and may even run the risk of acquiescing to a paradigm of sexuality that posits heterosexuality as normative and locates Cather outside of that paradigm. On the other hand, attempts to refute Cather's lesbianism may rely on the same illusionary paradigm of a stable and normative heterosexuality. Further, heterosexist presumption and homophobia undergird claims that, because no "proof" exists, Cather must have been, can only have been, heterosexual. As critics, we interpret Cather much as the characters in *Shadows on the Rock* interpret Jeanne Le Ber: through the public legend about her or by entering the protected space of personal letters and testamentary prohibition in order to carry out contradicting stories that reveal as much about her interpreters' desires as they do about Cather.

Shadows on the Rock concludes with an epilogue set fifteen years in the future. Carlin aptly describes the epilogue as "almost . . . an extended musing on the idea and the fact of change, what I believe is *the* central concern, both formal and thematic, of this text" (86). Initially, the epilogue seems to cap the ambivalence of the foregoing pages with happy homecomings. Humbled and aged, Saint-Vallier returns to Quebec after an absence of thirteen years, while Cécile has found a domestic home in marriage and motherhood. The novel concludes as Cécile's father rejoices that "he was indeed fortunate to spend his old age here where nothing changed; to watch his grandsons grow up in a country where the death of the King, the probable evils of a long regency, would never touch them" (279–280). But Saint-Vallier's return is notable precisely because he is changed, and Auclair's final words cannot drown out the stories preceding them, stories which relentlessly refuse certainty and fixity even as they seek to establish stable homes. Nor can readers dismiss Charron's substitution of Le Ber with Cécile, an apparently satisfactory and tractable Other, given Le Ber's extreme struggle to elude just such a home as Cécile now occupies. Carlin argues that "in the brief dialectic about change with which the epilogue closes then, what we read is nothing less than a discussion by the text about itself" (86). What's more, even the ambivalence of the epilogue might be read as Cather's commentary on the possibility of safe space. *Shadows on the Rock* is an extraordinarily challenging novel, one that presents its readers with an examination of the desire for safe space that acknowledges the enormous power and consolation of that desire, while at the same time investigating its costs, particularly for women. The tensions between the desire for a safe space to call home and the fundamental questioning of the possibility that such a space can exist present us with an opportunity to unsettle our own homes and interrogate their creation.

Notes

1. "Feminist Politics: What's Home Got to Do With It?" *Feminist Studies / Critical Studies*, ed. Teresa de Lauretis (Bloomington: Indiana University Press, 1986), 208.

2. For well-edited selections of Cather's early writing, see *Kingdom of Art, Willa Cather's First Principles and Critical Statements 1893–1896*, ed. Bernice Slote (Lincoln: University of Nebraska Press, 1966) and *The World and the Parish, Willa Cather's Articles and Reviews, Vols. 1 and 2*, ed. William M. Curtin (Lincoln: University of Nebraska Press, 1970).

3. In her article "Modernism: The Case of Willa Cather," Rose argues that "when Cather suppressed herself, she did it more completely than any writer I can think of." See *Modernism Reconsidered*, ed. Robert Kiely (Cambridge: Harvard University Press, 1983), 139. Rose advocates Cather's pursuit of anonymity as one of the aesthetic qualities aligning her with the Modernist movement and producing some of her "best" work. In "The Room Beyond, A Foreword on Willa Cather," *Willa Cather: On Writing* (New York: Knopf, 1949), Steven Tennant also urges Cather's greatness be found in

universalizing aesthetic anonymity, with his belief that "A great writer should always have an anonymous quality, something remote like a pregnant silence—which is silent, and yet contains all sound, all time, all things" (xv). Tennant's metaphor for anonymity, the "pregnant silence," renders anonymity a suspicious desire for female authors. And silence, pregnant or otherwise, reiterates an unresolvable problem for women: when to write is also simultaneously to include everything in silence, the authority to speak is a moot issue. Nancy K. Miller has argued more recently that anonymity, even if it were possible, might not be desirable for women authors, who have a structurally different relationship to authority. In other words, it may very well matter, not only that the writer is a woman, but who that particular woman is. See "Changing the Subject: Authorship, Writing, and the Reader," *Feminist Studies/Critical Studies*, ed. Teresa de Lauretis (Bloomington: Indiana University Press, 1986), 102–120. I agree that Cather sought anonymity, especially as it is yoked to universality, and perhaps for a woman writing during Cather's time and place, hers was an effective strategy toward the goal of publishing and its rewards. But I also see her as constantly undercutting the possibility of anonymity through her use of storytelling.

Works Cited

Carlin, Deborah. *Cather, Canon, and the Politics of Reading*. Amherst: University of Massachusetts Press, 1992.

Cather, Willa. *Death Comes for the Archbishop*. New York: Alfred A. Knopf, 1927. Rpt. Vintage Books, Random House, 1971.

———. *The Kingdom of Art: Willa Cather's First Principles and Critical Statements 1893–1896*. Ed. Bernice Slote. Lincoln: University of Nebraska Press, 1966.

———. *Shadows on the Rock*. New York: Knopf, 1931. Rpt. Vintage Books, Random House, 1971.

———. "On *Shadows on the Rock*." *Willa Cather on Writing: Critical Studies on Writing as an Art*. New York: Knopf, 1949.

Fryer, Judith. *Felicitous Space*. Chapel Hill: University of North Carolina Press, 1986.

Martin, Biddy, and Chandra Talpade Mohanty. "Feminist Politics: What's Home Got to Do With It?" *Feminist Studies/Critical Studies*. Ed. Teresa de Lauretis. Bloomington: Indiana University Press, 1986, 191–212.

Miller, Nancy K. "Changing the Subject: Authorship, Writing, and The Reader." *Feminist Studies/Critical Studies*. Ed. Teresa de Lauretis. Bloomington: Indiana University Press, 1986.

O'Brien, Sharon. *Willa Cather: The Emerging Voice*. New York: Oxford University Press, 1987.

Pratt, Minnie Bruce. "Identity: Skin Blood Heart." *Yours in Struggle: Three Feminist Perspectives on Anti-Semitism and Racism.* Brooklyn, NY: Long Haul Press, 1984.

Rose, Phyllis. "Modernism: The Case of Willa Cather." *Modernism Reconsidered.* Ed. Robert Kiely. Cambridge: Harvard University Press, 1983. 123–145.

Rosowski, Susan J. *The Voyage Perilous: Willa Cather's Romanticism.* Lincoln and London: University of Nebraska Press, 1986.

Russo, Mary. "Female Grotesques: Carnival and Theory." *Feminist Studies, Critical Studies.* Ed. Teresa de Lauretis. Bloomington: Indiana University Press, 1986. 213–229.

Tennant, Steven. "The Room Beyond, A Foreword on Willa Cather." *Willa Cather: On Writing.* By Willa Cather. New York: Knopf, 1949. v–xxiv.

Woodress, James. *Willa Cather: A Literary Life.* Lincoln and London: University of Nebraska Press, 1986.

Thriving

While mid to late twentieth-century women's writing certainly runs a wide gamut, it is tempting to identify it at least partially as writing which jumps into the breech, speaking words heretofore denied women, breaking taboos about language and subject matter. The blues lyrics of a writer like Alberta Hunter demonstrate a sexual frankness and playfulness previously rare in women's writing. In pleasing her audience with this play, she also earns artistic and economic sustenance. The fiction of Anne Rice breaks every sexual and social taboo imaginable. Its immense popularity speaks for its timeliness, but also raises questions about how women are currently using this new freedom of expression.

The goals of contemporary writers seem at once more personal and more public than those of nineteenth- and early twentieth-century writers examined in this anthology. Joy Kogawa and Sandra Cisneros, for instance, speculate within their fiction on individual and communal enhancement. They are politically motivated in their concern about violence against women, people of color, and children, but they are also concerned on a personal level with finding, through narrative, means of thriving in the aftermath of that violence. Both express, in their own ways, a concern for personal integrity, particularly for women of color who face prejudice daily from both mainstream and ethnic communities. While these two authors are not speaking for larger groups of women, they are in many ways representative of the contemporary renaissance of writing by culturally diverse women in the United States and of women's commitment to healing themselves and their communities.

Another way of considering this newfound expression might be in looking at the languages of the body that emerge within the writing considered in this section. Hunter's playful doubling of language engages both mind and body; Rice's graphic depictions of sex and violence replay, and in some ways control, the moment of trauma; Cisneros explores a girl's developing consciousness of her body as female through multiple linguistic lenses; and Kogawa creates passages of lyrical prose to bridge the mind and body. While certainly some writers appear to replay the moment of rupture, other contemporary women writers seem compelled to find a language that will validate the self—as a mind/body whole—and reintegrate that self into a world made safe for it.

163

"The Chicana Girl Writes Her Way In and Out: Space and Bilingualism in Sandra Cisneros' *The House on Mango Street*"

Tomoko Kuribayashi

Sandra Cisneros' young Chicana character/narrator in *The House on Mango Street* is oppressed in United States society in at least three senses: she is non-white, poor, and female. But the character Esperanza draws her strength from the very sources of her oppression. Her ability to speak two languages with equal fluency and her compassion for the socially weak and neglected, especially women of her community and of other ethnic origins, give her a unique spatial vision which enlivens her imagination as a writer and as a social critic. Having mastered two languages, Esperanza knows the two different worlds that the two languages construct and represent. She is able to travel back and forth between the two languages and the two worlds, creating, in the process, new space for herself and for the people she wishes to help out—women, the poor, and minorities, with whom she has something in common. This chapter highlights how bilingualism helps the narrator create a safe space for herself and other Mexican-American women in a society full of violence towards women and minorities.[1]

As a young Chicana growing up in a Mexican-American community in Chicago, Cisneros' narrator-protagonist, Esperanza, is keenly aware of the economic and cultural oppression of the people of her ethnic background in American society, including the oppression of Chicana women within the minority community. Esperanza shares Gloria Anzaldúa's sense of the danger that women of color face from day to day in the United States as well as in other places:

> Woman does not feel safe when her own culture, and white culture, are critical of her; when the males of all races hunt her as prey.
>
> Alienated from her mother culture, "alien" in the dominant culture, the woman of color does not feel safe within the inner life of her Self. Petrified,

she can't respond, her face caught between *los intersticios*, the spaces between
the different worlds she inhabits. (Anzaldúa 20)[2]

Cisneros' narrative illuminates the linguistic, spatial and sexual oppression
that racist society imposes on minority—more specifically Chicana—women,
but also offers a somewhat hopeful perspective on future possibilities. Architecture is a central means by which society as well as Cisneros express and
experience oppression as well as hope for change. In the beginning of Cisneros'
novel, Esperanza yearns for acquisition of cultural ideals of the white society,
most specifically the white, middle-class house widely displayed in mass media.
Esperanza's architectural craving recreates the author Cisneros' childhood experiences in a Mexican-American ghetto in Chicago. Cisneros recollects her
family house, "crowded as the nine of us were in cramped apartments where
there were children sleeping on the living room couch and fold-out Lazy Boy,
and on beds set up in the middle room, where the only place with any privacy
was the bathroom" ("Notebook" 69). She also remembers wondering "why
our home wasn't all green lawn and white wood like the ones in 'Leave It To
Beaver' or 'Father Knows Best' " (72).

These television programs played a significant role in aggravating the
Chicana girl's sense of her family's architectural deficiency. Cisneros' narrator,
Esperanza, also wants a house just like the ones she sees on television and all
her family members share her dream:

> [My parents] always told us that one day we would move into a house, a real
> house that would be ours for always so we wouldn't have to move each year.
> And our house would have running water and pipes that worked. And inside
> it would have real stairs, not hallway stairs, but stairs inside like the houses
> on T.V. And we'd have a basement and at least three washrooms so when we
> took a bath we wouldn't have to tell everybody. Our house would be white
> with trees around it, a great big yard and grass growing without a fence. This
> was the house Papa talked about when he held a lottery ticket and this was
> the house Mama dreamed up in the stories she told us before we went to
> bed. (4)

Despite the parents' hopeful tone, it is unlikely that they will ever have such
a house, as the narrative soon makes clear. When socioeconomic conditions
render it so difficult—almost impossible—for Chicano/as to acquire such houses,
mainstream culture's architecutral ideal, which purportedly inspires cultural
and economic aspirations in every viewer, only helps oppress the minority
populations further.

Young Esperanza is keenly aware of how houses define and represent the
resident's social status; so simply having a roof over one's head is not enough.

Esperanza remembers how ashamed she felt when she pointed to a third-floor flat where she lived, to a nun from her school. The nun asked, "You live *there*? The way she said it made me feel like nothing. *There*. I lived *there*. I nodded" (5). She then resolved that she would have to have "a real house. One I could point to" (5), to be accepted into mainstream society. When her family moves to Mango Street, she still knows that the house is not respectable enough and yearns to escape to a better place.

But later her vision changes and she contemplates the possibility of housing the poor in her future house:

> People who live on hills sleep so close to the stars they forget those of us who live too much on earth. They don't look down at all except to be content to live on hills. They have nothing to do with last week's garbage or fear of rats. Night comes. Nothing wakes them but the wind.
>
> One day I'll own my own house, but I won't forget who I am or where I came from. Passing bums will ask, Can I come in? I'll offer them the attic, ask them to stay, because I know how it is to be without a house. (87)

Owning and controlling her own space is to own her self. One cannot become oneself without having one's own place. As Cherríe Moraga asserts, the "anti-materialist approach [that some white, middle-class feminists take] makes little sense in the lives of poor and Third World women" (129), when material conditions are so much a part of their oppression that coming into possession of material necessities is a must for becoming one's own person. But Esperanza does more than owning herself in the quoted passage. In other words, she does not unquestioningly embrace white, materialist beliefs in earthly possessions and financial security as a priority in and by themselves. First, Esperanza challenges mainstream society's definition of the family. Secondly, and more importantly, taking the socially rejected and oppressed—regardless of their gender, ethnicity, and other differences—into her own space is an expression of Esperanza's defiance of the dominant culture which bases itself on a rigid socio-economic hierarchy and on dichotomous thinking. Her act turns the condition of exclusion of social outcasts into that of inclusion. Moreover, her gesture connects her future to her origin, her future self to Mango Street: "I won't forget who I am or where I came from" (21). Merging the public and the private, or the inside and the outside, is moving toward liberating women of her ethnic background as well as liberating any women who are confined indoors while men move much more freely outside houses. Once the distinction between the inside and the outside collapses, there is no more confining anybody indoors. Merging the two seemingly separate spaces, then, means doing away with rigid gender differentiations as well.

In *The House on Mango Street*, as sociocultural oppressions and future hopes are architecturally expressed, so are the female characters' experiences of social and sexual violence inseparably linked to their spatial experiences. The text, for example, offers a definition of what public space—space outside houses—means to the women characters, which in turn determines the meaning of the indoor space and of the female body. The best illustration of this is how, to Cisneros' young narrator, space outside houses stands for young women's freedom as well as ostracism from the Chicano/a community. Esperanza envies women a little older than herself who dare roam the night streets in search of romantic adventure. But she also knows how little chance for social acceptance these women will have both in the Chicano community and in mainstream American society.

Esperanza sees possibilities in the female bodies that float, or almost float, around in the streets. Marin, an older girl Esperanza admires, is one of them. When her baby-sitter's duties are done in the evening, Marin comes out of her aunt's house. Though "she can only stay out in front, ... What matters, Marin says, is for the boys to see us and for us to see them" (27). When boys passing by tease her, "Marin just looks at them without even blinking and is not afraid" (27). Later, speculating on the relationship between a neighborhood boy she fancies and his girlfriend, Esperanza wishes she could be as bold as the girl, Lois. "Everything is holding its breath inside me. . . . I want to sit out bad at night, a boy around my neck and the wind under my skirt" (73). This desire on the young narrator's part and her daring to make an explicit statement about it are what can possibly enable her to form her own, less inhibiting view of the female body.

Esperanza, however, knows too well what would be the community's judgment on such behavior by young girls. Marin will soon be sent back to Mexico because her aunt thinks she is too much trouble, and Esperanza's mother criticizes Lois, "those kinds of girls, those girls are the ones that go into alleys" (73). Much as she hungers for street life and is aware of her body's potentials, Esperanza also fears "outdoors" and her own female body because of the social sanctions waiting for women who venture out too far. In the vignette "Red Clowns," Esperanza experiences this danger firsthand when she is sexually assaulted by strangers at a carnival.

In *The House on Mango Street* the female body becomes another kind of the space outside, a prohibited space that women fear and yearn to reconnect to. Yet, ironically, society demands that the female body not go out into the literal "space outside." If it did, the "inside" would become the "outside," and the social order would collapse. True, some female bodies are allowed outside domestic space—or excluded from it—to satisfy certain kinds of male sexual desires, but these women are "public women," deemed unfit for the home and subject to violation and exploitation without limits. Except for these women, the female body must be kept indoors so that the status quo of the public/ private division is maintained with men in public space and women in private space. Chicana women in Cisneros' text are allowed no space of their own, with the streets off limits and their bodies made inaccessible. Domestic space is not safe either, as exemplified by the abuse Esperanza's Chicana neighbors endure at the hand of their fathers and husbands.

Esperanza, however, also has another vision of space outside, that is, a space that her imagination and her writing—and bilingual ability—will create for her outside and beyond the limits of her Mexican-American community and of the dominant white culture of America. This last kind of "outdoors"— based on her bicultural and bilingual experiences and abilities—has the potential of redefining the "indoor" space as well as the female body for Cisneros' adolescent narrator. Cisneros' text demonstrates how being bilingual makes Esperanza aware that there is more than one way to interpret what is spoken and written; bilingualism brings her the realization that she can choose what suits her purpose best.

Esperanza's name, which comes from her grandmother, who resented but could not undo the confinement brought on her by her marriage, means "hope." "In English my name means hope. In Spanish it means too many letters. It means sadness, it means waiting" (10). Cisneros' narrative suggests that Esperanza's hope for the future lies in making the most liberating linguistic choices, beginning with her own name. Taking control of language will enable Esperanza to avoid being trapped inside houses and inside Mango Street, where her culture confines women and the white culture confines her people, and to go out to find her own house, her own space. Where she goes to, which space she will fit in, is yet unknown. She will not go into white society as it is. She will instead have to find, or rather create, her own space. Reminiscing about her grandmother, who "looked out the window her whole life, the way so many women sit their sadness on an elbow," Esperanza says, "I have inherited her name, I don't want to inherit her place by the window" (11). The window, which could be an in-between space, established on the very border-line of private and public, and therefore can be subversive, remains a space of oppression and fruitless yearning in Cisneros' text. For example, a beautiful neighbor woman, Rafaela, is only allowed to talk to the children from her window, because of her husband's irrational jealousy. Not only does Esperanza decide to escape the limitations of the window space, she also considers re-naming herself: "I would like to baptize myself under a new name, a name more like the real me, the one nobody sees" (11).

Cisneros' narrative highlights how language—and taking control of it— is a determining factor for Esperanza's future. Taking control of language means taking control of one's spatial experiences. The narrative of *The House on Mango Street* is a linguistic manifestation and product of the process in which Esperanza creates a new self and a new world. The text also testifies how she can do this through giving herself a new name and discovering a new language, without disowning the cultural background from which she comes.

The text emphasizes how the narrator's further dream is to come back to where she is from, after successfully venturing out and securing her own space outside Mango Street: "I have gone away to come back. For the ones I left behind. For the ones who cannot out" (110). This movement envisioned by Esperanza suggests spiraling, as opposed to the linearity often espoused by Anglo-Saxon cultures, and thus constitutes another challenge to the white society and its culture. The text indicates that Esperanza "will always be Mango Street"(104), as the three sisters have prophesied. Although the narrator is ashamed of the house on Mango Street, that she is also fond of it is shown in the way she anthropomorphizes the building: "It's small and red with tight steps in front and windows so small you'd think they were holding their breath" (4). Her vision is of becoming a somewhat free (that is, freer than the women she sees suffering around her) agent, perhaps transcultural or culturally mobile, who can translate herself and what happens to and around her from one language into another, from one place to another. She hopes to be able to write her way both out and in. In and out of the Mexican-American world where people speak Spanish. In and out, also, of the mainstream American world where English is the linguistic medium.

Author Cisneros herself sees two voices in two languages speaking in her writing:

> These two voices at odds with each other—my mother's punch-you-in-the-nose English and my father's powdered-sugar Spanish—curiously are the voices that surface in my writing. What I'm specially aware of lately is how the Spanish syntax and word choice occurs in my work even though I write in English. ("Notebook" 72)

Like Esperanza, Cisneros sees herself as "a translator. I am an amphibian. I can travel in both worlds. What I'm saying is very important for the Latino community, but it is also important for the white community to hear" ("Solo Traveler" B2).[3]

Having two languages at one's command may enable a person to avoid being locked into one specific value system, or in one specific identity. As Chris Weedon in *Feminist Practice and Poststructuralist Theory* has asserted, our "conditions of existence . . . are at one and the same time both material and discursive" (8). If language—the "discursive"—as well as architecture—the "material"—defines/confines people's bodies and thoughts, Esperanza, as a bilingual and bicultural person (and female in addition), may be able to "swim" between the two languages/two spaces, and to create her own stories and spaces.

Patricia Yaeger in *Honey-Mad Women* suggests that being bilingual can emancipate women (and women characters). One of the ways "the writer can bring a subversive multivoicedness into her text," she says, discussing Charlotte Brontë's novels, is "that the second language can operate as a form of interruption, as a way of dispelling the power of the myth systems represented by the text's primary language" (37). In Esperanza's case, both Spanish and English are patriarchal languages and are not in themselves subversive. However, the two languages multiply her options. For example, English gives her a way out in the instance of her first name. Thus, Esperanza is able to deconstruct the Anglophone world from a Spanish-speaking person's viewpoint as well as question the Mexican-American community's values from an English-speaker's point of view. Moreover, she can deconstruct and question the patriarchal value system(s), whether Anglophone or Mexican-American, from a woman's point of view.

Belonging to a culture means knowing what outsiders don't, or at least understanding the same phenomena differently—more accurately. The vignette "Those Who Don't," for example, illustrates how cultural and linguistic outsiders and insiders view Esperanza's neighbors differently. Outsiders come into the neighborhood scared, while Esperanza and her friends feel comfortable because they know who is who. When Louie's cousin brings a Cadillac and drives the community kids around before he gets arrested for a car theft, the children do not share the police's definition of him as a criminal. Rather, he is the cousin of their friend: "They put handcuffs on him and put him in the back seat of the cop car, and we all waved as they drove away" (25).

Member of two different worlds, Esperanza may be able to establish her own hybrid values to support her visions for new life, for a new world. Gloria Anzaldúa calls this creation "the lifeblood of two worlds merging to form a third country—a border culture" by "those who cross over, pass over, or go through the confines of the 'normal' "(3). It is also "a synthesis of duality, and a third perspective—something more than mere duality or a synthesis of duality" (46). In her 1994 article "Purity, Impurity, and Separation," María Lugones also closely examines the position of a "mestiza" and warns against the mainstream society's attempt to attain "Control over creativity" (460) by breaking a "hybrid" person into separate components. Lugones stresses the need to protect "hybrid ways of creation" (471). To do so, "mexican/americans" should not withdraw into their communities, Lugones continues, nor should they assimilate into "the anglo domain" (471). Mexican-Americans' becoming their own "requires that the language and conceptual framework of the public become hybrid" (471). Esperanza's sally into the Anglophone world, as well as Cisneros' writing this book, is a manifestation of the hybrid modes of creation and the hybridization of the public world that Lugones speaks of.

Virginia Woolf once wondered which was worse, to be confined or to be excluded: "I thought how unpleasant it is to be locked out; and I thought how it is worse perhaps to be locked in" (24). In a way, Woolf herself was culturally bilingual, in that she was at once an educated, upper-middle class person—and female. Despite her dichotomous view of being both on the inside and on the outside of privilege, Woolf was already starting to break down the barrier between the two, or to realize that the barrier/distinction is arbitrary and can be defied. Because of her cultural placement, Cisneros' character, Esperanza, may have an even more flexible vision than Woolf's of what may be possible, when it comes to discerning borderlines and crossing (or stretching) them. Esperanza explores and then rejects the dichotomy of inside/outside, and posits new alternatives. She will attempt to find, create, and/or establish her own identity and her own space, which will be in both white and Mexican-American cultures and societies, but which will also be in neither. And she can do so well only if she knows who she is and if she believes in what she is and does.

Esperanza's sense of self and freedom and its affirmation come from her writing. Her disabled aunt, Lupe, listening to Esperanza's poems, encourages her to keep on writing, her advice again embodying the strength Esperanza's culture and older women around her can give her:

> That's nice. That's very good, she said in her tired voice. You just remember to keep writing, Esperanza. You must keep writing. It will keep you free, and I said yes, but at that time I didn't know what she meant. (61)

Just as Woolf wrote to create space for women to write in, Esperanza creates space through writing. Just in the same way, I think, the novel, *The House on Mango Street*, has created a unique kind of space for its author in the American literary scene, by transforming, or hybridizing, the literary world.

But Woolf asked for a room and good-sized income before she could write. She was keenly aware of the constraints economic and spatial deprivation could impose on a woman writer's imagination. This awareness is not absent from Cisneros' text nor from Chicana critics' writings. Rather, literary freedom is inseparably linked to material liberation in both instances. Yvonne Yarbro-Bejarano discusses how "The exclusion of Chicanas from literary authority is intimately linked to the exclusion of Chicanas from other kinds of power monopolized by privileged white males. Their struggle to appropriate the 'I' of literary discourse relates to their struggle for empowerment in the economic, social and political spheres" (139). Esperanza's narrative and Cisneros' writing, then, pave the way for Chicanas to come into their own economically, socially and politically in United States society. As Yarbro-Bejarano writes, "In telling these stories [about themselves and other Chicanas], Chicanas reject the dominant culture's definition of what a Chicana is. In writing, they refuse the objectification imposed by gender roles and racial and economic exploitation" (141). Establishing their identity free of oppressions by racist patriarchal society through writing becomes the foundation for Chicanas' gaining control over all aspects of their lives. María Lugones also stresses the importance of taking control of "the production of material life" in a manner of hybrid creativity ("Purity" 471).

In light of the creation of such a self-image, it is significant that the narrator of Cisneros' book speaks from a young female child's point of view. Of course, such a point of view, presented as malleable and naive, is artificially constructed. Cisneros' adoption of a youthful perspective may, however, suggest the sort of subjectivity a woman needs if she is to embark on deconstructing the world around her—a more open, vulnerable, imaginative subjectivity that some cultures attribute to children. Needless to say, such an endeavor can be undertaken only at a tremendous cost to the agent, and it may very well be questioned whether such a thin-skinned subjectivity can survive this ordeal.

Perhaps more importantly, taking on a child's or an adolescent's point of view is a literary strategy that facilitates Cisneros' narrator's questioning of what is around her and what has been imposed on her or taken away from her. It also enables her to deconstruct and reconstruct her society, her language, and her body which society and language forcibly define. In other words, Cisneros may have chosen a girl's point of view so that the deconstructing process is literarily facilitated. As Chris Weedon says, "Conscious subjectivity, acquired in language, is seen as inherently unstable and subjectivity itself as constantly in process" (87–88). Cisneros' young narrator, through telling stories and writing, through discovering and/or creating her own language between two established linguistic systems (English and Spanish), will be able to feel and see the flexibility of her subjectivity, which will let her more easily remold herself and her world view.

Cisneros' novella also follows the coming-of-age formula. Even though people are constantly in process, some cultures, including that of the United States, affirm the state of being in process only for a specific growing-up time. As adults, people are supposed to be finished. In such a culture, puberty/adolescence becomes a kind of borderline, a third kind of space. Conveniently, in the case of Cisneros' text this view of the narrator's age as an in-between-but-in-neither sort of space matches her positioning as a bilingual and bicultural being.

The last vignette of Cisneros' novella, "Mango Says Goodbye Sometimes," addresses the crucial question of whether Esperanza will be able to come back to where she is from, once she gets out of Mango Street, or of her Mexican-American community. The viewpoint is of a grown-up writer's, not a young girl's:

I make a story for my life, for each step my brown shoe takes. I say, "And so she trudged up the wooden stairs, her sad brown shoes taking her to the house she never liked."

I like to tell stories. I am going to tell you a story about a girl who didn't want to belong.

We didn't always live on Mango Street . . .

I put it down on paper and then the ghost does not ache so much. I write it down and Mango says goodbye sometimes. She does not hold me with both arms. She sets me free. (109–10)

The rest of the vignette suggests that she will not totally desert Mango Street. She will definitely come back, just as Cisneros has by writing this novella. Through the very text of *The House on Mango Street* the narrator moves back to her native community. The narrative is a textual documentation of the homeward movement of her body as well as of her spiritual homecoming.

The narrator's leaving home is necessary, though, for her to find her self. Anzaldúa says of herself, "I had to leave home so I could find myself, find my own intrinsic nature buried under the personality that had been imposed on me" (16). Esperanza is taking tremendous risks, and she is fortunate to be able to choose to do so, since so few of her group of people can afford it. As Anzaldúa says, "As a working class people our chief activity is to put food in our mouths, a roof over our heads and clothes on our backs" (17). While most women of her ethnicity have had to choose between "three directions . . . to the Church as a nun, to the streets as a prostitute, or to the home as a mother," Esperanza is making the newly and sparingly available fourth choice, "entering the world by way of education and career and becoming self-autonomous persons," or claiming a public identity (Anzaldúa 17). She can do so because she has visions, and also because she has language skills and the energy which she inherits from the Chicana women around her.

Acquiring education and a career, a minority in a white, racist society risks making compromises and being assimilated into the white world. But retaining one's own perspective is still possible. In her article, "Playfulness, 'World'-Travelling, and Loving Perception," María Lugones discusses what it means to travel to different worlds:

Those of us who are "world"-travellers have the distinct experience of being different in different "worlds" and of having the capacity to remember other "worlds" and ourselves in them . . . the experience is of being a different person in different "worlds" and yet of having memory of oneself as different without quite having the sense of there being any underlying "I." (11)

According to Lugones, one of the ways of being at ease in a world is "being a fluent speaker in that 'world.' I know all the norms that there are to be followed, I know all the words that there are to be spoken" (12). At least linguistically, then, Esperanza can be at ease both in the Anglophone and Mexican-American worlds. Lugones recommends that we (women) travel to other people's (women's) worlds so that we can look at things, including ourselves, from a different point of view. Cisneros' character, Esperanza, travels from one world to another and creates a third space of her own. She is not trapped in any one of them. Even the new space she creates for herself will welcome other travellers, just as her dream house will shelter passing bums. Similarly Cisneros' narrative invites her readers into a new fictional space.

It is important to note that such a straddle as Esperanza assumes can just as easily stifle her voice because the narrator/writer may feel out of place in both systems, instead of being at home in both. Gloria Anzaldúa finds the in-between space both liberating and murderous to Chicana women, as testified by the two conflicting points of view quoted from her in this chapter. The balance Esperanza must maintain to preserve the liberating element is extremely delicate. What helps her keep the just right posture is, as has been pointed out above, her strong connection to the Chicana/o community of her childhood. Yarboro-Bejarano points out the connection between Cisneros' and Esperanza's writing and their connections to the Mexican-American community:

> The House on Mango Street captures the dialectic between self and community in Chicana writing. Esperanza finds her literary voice through her own cultural experience and that of other Chicanas. She seeks self-empowerment through writing, while recognizing her commitment to a community of Chicanas. Writing has been essential in connecting her with the power of women and her promise to pass down that power to other women is fulfilled by writing and publication of the text itself. (141)

Cisneros' emphasis on her narrator's ties to the Chicana/o community is another challenge that her narrative issues against the mainstream American individualism.

Nina Auerbach, discussing women outcasts in Victorian England in *Romantic Imprisonment*, says that "culture takes inspiration from its outcasts" (xvii). Anzaldúa argues that outcasts tend to have highly developed sensitivity, what she calls "La facultad," "the capacity to see in surface phenomena the meaning of deeper realities, to see the deep structure below the surface" (38). By being an outcast from the dominant society and temporarily "becoming" an outcast also from her own ethnic group—exiling herself from the Chicano/a community—Esperanza may become the source from which societies/cultures derive their energy and their future. By definition, for an outcast, boundaries are not permeable. However, as outcasts force society and culture to change and grow, the borderlines shift and expand, creating in the process third spaces in which the oppressed can live and speak out in relative safety.

In *The House on Mango Street*, at least three elements combine to generate a strategy for creating new, safer spaces which will accommodate women's desires, including the desire to write: Cisneros' central character's bilingualism, her cultural placement as a minority person within the dominant white culture of the United States and as a young woman within the segregated Mexican-American community, and her ability as a writer. Cisneros' text suggests that women's writing taking place in these new spaces will lead to creation of more new spaces where women—more specifically, Chicana women—can develop their abilities and cherish their dreams.

Notes

1. One important way in which Cisneros' text reaches the audience most in need of the encouragement it offers is the public readings the author often gives. For example, see the January 7, 1993 *New York Times* article, "A Solo Traveler in Two Worlds," which reports on her reading at a tiny branch of The Brooklyn Public Library.

2. Anzaldúa's language can connote essentialism, as in the case of the first word "Woman" in this indented quote.

3. Cisneros uses more Spanish in her poetry, especially in her most recent poetry collection, *The Loose Woman*, than in her fiction.

Works Cited

Anzaldúa, Gloria. *Borderlands/La Frontera: The New Mestiza.* San Francisco: Spinsters/ Aunt Lute Book Company, 1987.

Auerbach, Nina. *Romantic Imprisonment: Women and Other Glorified Outcasts.* New York: Columbia University Press, 1986.

Cisneros, Sandra. *The House on Mango Street.* 1986; New York: Vintage Books, 1991.

———. "From A Writer's Notebook—Ghosts and Voices: Writing from Obsession." *Americas Review* 15.1 (Spring 1987): 69–73.

———. "A Solo Traveler in Two Worlds." Interview with Mary B.W. Tabor. *The New York Times.* January 7, 1993. B2.

Lugones, María. "Playfulness, 'World'-Travelling, and Loving Perception." *Hypatia* 2.2 (Summer 1987): 3–19.

————. "Purity, Impurity, and Separation." *Signs* 19.2 (Winter 1994): 458–479.

Moraga, Cherríe. *Loving in the War Years*. Boston: South End Press, 1983.

Weedon, Chris. *Feminist Practice and Poststructuralist Theory*. Oxford: Basil Blackwell, 1987.

Woolf, Virginia. *A Room of One's Own*. 1929; London: Grafton Books, 1977.

Yaeger, Patricia. *Honey-Mad Women: Emancipatory Strategies in Women's Writing*. New York: Columbia University Press, 1988.

Yarbro-Bejarano, Yvonne. "Chicana Literature from a Chicana Feminist Perspective." *Chicana Creativity and Criticism: Charting New Frontiers in American Literature*. Eds. María Herrera-Sobek and Helena María Viramontes. Houston: Arte Público Press, 1988. 139–169.

Abuse and Its Pleasures:
Compensatory Fantasy in the Popular Fiction of Anne Rice

_____

Annalee Newitz

"I don't want to think of witches as some sort of rare commodity to those who know how to use them."

—spoken by Ash, a character in Rice's *Taltos*

The story behind the movie *Interview with the Vampire,* based on Anne Rice's first novel, dramatizes an issue which has plagued Rice as an author for a long time: she is a marginal cult figure confronting what it means to have a mainstream audience. Rice, whose screenplay for *Interview* had been kicking around Hollywood since the late 1970s, had very specific ideas about how the movie should be made. She felt it ought to be something like a low-budget European art film, starring Rutger Hauer or Jeremy Irons. Hollywood had other ideas and hired all-American movie star Tom Cruise to play the aristocratic Lestat. At first, Rice was appalled, telling anyone in the press who would listen that mainstream Hollywood stars like Cruise would ruin her work. She appealed to her fans to boycott the movie, and would not relent until she finally saw an early cut that changed her mind. Taking out a full-page ad in *Variety,* Rice proclaimed that Cruise had done a wonderful job and retracted her earlier comments. Later, she told *TV Guide* in an interview that she would never again scorn her status as a popular author with a mass audience.

Rice, like her cultish vampire heroes, finally gave up lurking in the shadows and cashed in on monstrosity—or, to put it simply, she got used to the idea of selling out. While Rice wanted to claim initially that she was "victimized" by Hollywood, clearly she was hardly the victim in this situation—not only did she make a small fortune off the movie deal, but she was also able to use her story of "abuse" to nearly crush the movie project with bad publicity. Although Hollywood and the demands of its mass audience had supposedly "traumatized" Rice, she finally decided to "join" Hollywood, helping to make the movie version of *Interview* a smash hit of the Christmas season in 1995.

179

In an ironic mirroring of Rice's own "selling out," the heroes in Rice's novels have in common one basic trait: they feel marginalized or abused, but learn to use their victimhood as a form of empowerment. Her characters often become powerful, wealthy, or famous by taking up the tools of their oppressors—and revaluing their victimization as something pleasurable and special. Rice's best sellers, for which she is most widely known, include novels about vampires, witches, mummies, and demons (the five Vampire Chronicles, three novels in the Witch Cycle, *The Mummy* and *Servant of the Bones*). In recent years, as she has grown progressively more famous, Rice has revealed that she also writes sadomasochistic pornography and "bodice ripper" romances under the names A. N. Roquelaure and Anne Rampling (the Sleeping Beauty trilogy, *Belinda* and *Exit to Eden*); she has also written two historical novels.

I want to suggest that Rice's novels—like her brief anti-Hollywood publicity campaign—can function to simultaneously arouse and dismiss her audience's feelings about various kinds of social abuse. By representing abuse within a contained, fictionalized setting, one might say that Rice generates a therapeutic "safe space" in which readers can experience and master their anxieties about abuse. And to a certain extent, I want to allow for this possibility in my analysis. But there is also something deeply troubling about the way Rice invites readers to deal with their anxieties. For ultimately she offers what I will call an "anti-therapeutic" resolution to abusive situations: her abused characters gain power by sustaining and even celebrating their trauma. Usually this means that they become abusers themselves, learn to enjoy abuse, or wreak violent revenge upon their abusers. Rice reproduces—often symbolically—the terror and anguish of the abusive situation, but the only way out is "getting on top" rather than escape from abusive relationships altogether. In other words, she dismisses or limits the possibilities of "safe space" readers might seek in her fiction by suggesting that nowhere is "safe" from abuse. Rather than safety, she offers her readers compensatory sadomasochistic fantasies and the promise of unlimited, vengeful power.

Recently, feminists have begun to ask what it might mean for women to have pleasurable fantasies about rape, or violence, or hurting children—fantasies which are, by and large, associated with a stereotypically "male" imagination in popular culture. In her landmark work *Loving with a Vengeance*, Tania Modleski looked at female-authored "taken by force" scenarios in romance novels and concluded that "we have seen that the desire to be taken by force (manifest content) conceals anxieties about rape and longings for power and revenge (latent content)" (Modleski 48). What I want to focus on in this chapter is what Modleski calls the "latent content" of these kinds of fantasies. In Rice's fiction, which often blurs the boundaries between gothic horror, romance, and sadomasochistic pornography, we find anxiety about transgressive sexual acts coupled with a desire to perform them for the sake of "power and revenge." Fredric Jameson, whose work on popular culture heavily informs

Modleski's analysis of the romance, suggests that popular narratives struggle to generate allegories adequate to explain social reality (Jameson 281–299). That is, popular narratives can be understood as allegorical representations of certain social truths, such as the ubiquity of domestic violence, or the terrifying results of class warfare. I would suggest that there are two such social allegories working together—or perhaps against each other—in Rice's fiction. One, which I will discuss first, understands Rice's fantastical monsters as figures for sexually abused children and their families. The other allegory, which gets told in her erotic fiction, understands gendered sexual relations to stand in for specifically economic power relations. That is, I will be offering two allegorical pathways through Rice's work; if we follow one after the other, we will reach a point where we can see that understanding what is at stake in Rice's fiction means finding a way of reading traumatic sexual violation together with what might be called traumatic economic violation. Rice's writing functions as an allegory for and symptom of many people's experiences with abuse: as children, as gendered beings, and as adults who are trying to negotiate their class identities in a capitalist economy.

The Abused Child as Monster

Rice's Vampire Chronicles are comprised of five novels about the relationships between several vampires who form a series of "families." Most notably in the first two novels, *Interview with the Vampire* and *The Vampire Lestat*, we find eroticized, romantic relationships between parents and children. The point-of-view character in *Interview* is Louis, a vampire who recounts his experiences during the nineteenth century to a boy who interviews him in contemporary San Francisco. Louis is made a vampire by Lestat, the point-of-view character in the following four novels. Conversion into a vampire—in which Louis and Lestat exchange blood—is both erotic and reminiscent of breast feeding, according to Louis:

> Lestat whispered to me, his lips moving against my neck. I remember that the movement of his lips raised the hair all over my body, sent a shock of sensation through my body that was not unlike the pleasure of passion.... He pressed his bleeding wrist to my mouth.... I drank, sucking the blood out of the holes, experiencing for the first time since infancy the special pleasure of sucking nourishment.... I heard the night as if it were a chorus of whispering women, all beckoning me to their breasts. (*Interview* 18–21)

In this scene, part of Louis' pleasure is predicated on his "infantile" response to Lestat, who later takes on the role of Louis' neglectful parent and lover. To keep Louis from fleeing what becomes an increasingly antagonistic relationship, Lestat makes a "vampire child" out of a five-year-old girl named Claudia. To produce her, Lestat tempts Louis to drink her blood. Rather than let her die, Lestat feeds her his own blood and makes her a vampire who will remain in a little girl's body forever. Later, he threatens Louis by pretending he might kill or harm Claudia if Louis disobeys him. Louis and Claudia become inseparable, and Louis considers their relationship to be a union between "Father and Daughter. Lover and Lover" (*Interview* 102). Rice offers many descriptions of Claudia's childish sensuality, heightening our sense that it is precisely her status as a child that makes her so sexually alluring to her "parent" Louis. In *The Vampire Lestat,* we discover that Lestat himself has engaged in an eroticized relationship with his biological mother Gabrielle during and after transforming her into a vampire. Lestat describes:

> I leant forward and kissed the blood on [Gabrielle's] open lips . . . [then] came the thirst, not obliterating but heating every concept of her, until she was flesh and blood and mother and lover and all things beneath the cruel pressure of my fingers and my lips, everything I had ever desired. I drove my teeth into her, feeling her stiffen and gasp, and I felt my mouth grow wide to catch the hot flood when it came. (*Lestat* 157)

These graphic representations of incestuous desire are palatable —and even erotic—because they appear within the context of fantastical narratives about vampires. When I have taught these books in English classes, students unfailingly observe that the vampires could not possibly be incestuous because "they're not human, so human rules don't apply." One characteristic of Rice's vampires, moreover, is that they are absolutely unable to engage in sexual intercourse. All of their erotic pleasure is directed toward drinking blood (that is, killing people). Rice hints that converting into a vampire causes the genitals to cease their sexual functioning, although she is quite vague on this point. In other words, Rice provides readers with two ways to disavow that what they are enjoying is a story about parents and children having sexual relations. First of all, these are monsters, and therefore somehow not parents and children. And second, these monsters cannot have sex anyway. Built into this double denial is in fact a covert admission that indeed these characters *are* engaging in incest—for certainly one would not need to utterly discount the sexuality of these vampires if indeed there were no problematic aspects to the way they choose to act on their erotic desires. Put simply, the kinds of relationships we find Rice's vampires engaging in are highly *suggestive* of incest. Yet there is a certain plausible deniability built into any reading that wants to claim the vampires' relations are *strictly* incestuous.

It is in this plausible deniability that one finds the Vampire Chronicles offering a way of remembering and understanding child abuse, because Rice's representations of abuse are safely contained within the realm of pleasurable fantasy. The idea that people come to terms with memories of abuse through fantasy is a common one in therapeutic and psychoanalytic work. Judith Herman, in her book *Trauma and Recovery*, explains how this kind of fantasy could operate in what she calls "post-traumatic stress disorder." Incest or child abuse victims often suffer from this disorder, a mental state in which people imaginatively—sometimes pathologically—attempt to come to terms with massive physical and emotional trauma suffered in the past. One of the key ways people experience post-traumatic stress is through "reenactment":

> Adults as well as children often feel impelled to re-create the moment of terror either in literal or disguised form. Sometimes people reenact the traumatic moment with a fantasy of changing the outcome of the dangerous encounter . . . traumatized people find themselves reenacting some aspect of the trauma scene in disguised form, without realizing what they are doing. (Herman 39–40)

By reenacting, or repeating, the traumatic scene in a context over which they have imaginary control, trauma survivors are able to confront terrifying memories without always remembering them *as they really happened*. This is what Herman means when she says trauma victims may reenact memories in "disguised form" or "without really realizing what they are doing."

Reading Rice's fiction works something like a fantasy reenactment of traumatic sexual child abuse: a reader confronts issues surrounding eroticized encounters between family members, but she encounters these threatening issues in a romantic, fantastical context. Thus people are invited to endure terrifying memories and feelings in response to incest or child abuse without having to admit that in fact these memories and feelings are "real," in their own lives or the lives of others. One need not actually have been an incest or child abuse victim in order to need fantasy reenactments of this sort. As Modleski notes about romance readers, fantasies about being "taken by force" help alleviate anxieties about rape for women in general, not just rape victims. Likewise, people who are anxious about their own parenting skills or problems with child abuse might seek representations of these traumas "in disguised form."

Having established that post-traumatic stress disorder might play a part in readers' enjoyment of Rice's horror fiction, we need to look more closely at how Rice's horror narratives resolve problems of incest and child abuse. Partly, as already stated, Rice situates these problems in the realm of fantasy. But she also chooses a fantasy realm in which parents and children are vampires, creatures who survive by murdering other people and each other. *Interview* concludes when Louis and Claudia murder Lestat because he has mistreated

them routinely. Lestat survives this "murder," and ultimately tracks them down
for a final confrontation. In Paris, having joined a group of European vampires,
Lestat helps to murder Claudia for being an "abomination," a vampire child.
According to vampire law among the European vampires, vampire children are
strictly forbidden because they cannot survive on their own. While *Interview*
seems to claim Claudia is killed merely for being a child, she is more importantly a *seductive* child. Louis himself, who mourns Claudia's loss, notes that
Claudia has become a child who seems to solicit pedophilic, or pseudo-
incestuous, desire in her victims:

> I was never very far away [from Claudia], and was always uncomfortable . . .
> because I feared her. She'd always been the 'lost child' to her victims, the
> 'orphan,' and now it seemed she would be something else, something wicked
> and shocking to the passers-by who succumbed to her. (*Interview 208*)

It is this kind of "daughter," who seems aware of the implications of her
relationships with Louis or other adults, who is an "abomination" and must be
killed. Thus the seductive child is eliminated because she is a "forbidden"
monster. A similar fate meets Akasha, "Great Mother" of all vampires, in *Queen
of the Damned,* part three of the Chronicles. Akasha, the ancient Egyptian
queen who began the vampire race thousands of years before, goes insane and
tries to murder all men on Earth to make the world a perfect matriarchy.
Subsequently, a "family" of vampires—including Lestat and Louis—must murder
Akasha, ostensibly to protect all the men in the world from certain death. But
Akasha is more than an exceptionally violent vampire. In *Queen,* we discover
that a "demon" lives in vampire blood who links all the vampires together—
this demon is especially strong in Akasha's blood, and if Akasha is killed all the
vampires will die as well. This problem is solved when twin vampire sisters,
Akasha's "first daughters," kill Akasha and eat her heart and brain (*Queen* 456).
What I would point out here is that Akasha serves as the emblem and reminder of the fact that all the vampires share the same blood. They are all
Akasha's children—with the same blood in their veins—and they are all therefore "related" in some way. This information calls attention to the incestuous
overtones in many of the vampires' relationships. Like Claudia, Akasha becomes an abomination to the vampires and must be eliminated. Characters
such as Claudia and Akasha who threaten to make the incestuous fantasy of
the Chronicles too literal become "monsters to the monsters" and must die.

But this kind of "kill the bad guy" resolution is far more complicated
than it might seem at first glance. Killing off the "really bad" (or too-literally
incestuous) vampires is another form of denial at work in this fantasy. For all
the vampires are pseudo-incestuous monsters (like Claudia), and all of them
routinely kill human beings (like Akasha). Blaming, then eliminating, individual

vampires for being "abominations" calls attention away from the ordinary abominable acts Rice's other vampires engage in nightly (killing humans and having romances with their "family members"). Most importantly, it calls readers' attention away from violence and incest in the human world. This fantasy structure—in which bad individuals take the blame for general misery—resembles "internalization," another symptom of post-traumatic stress disorder. Herman writes that child abuse survivors often cope with their trauma by blaming themselves for what others have done to them, thus allowing their families to appear blameless and worthy of love. People who blame themselves for their abuse do so by generating fantasies in which they are inherently bad or evil and therefore "deserve" everything that has happened to them:

> The language of the self becomes a language of abomination. Survivors routinely describe themselves as outside the compact of ordinary human relations, as supernatural creatures or nonhuman life forms. They think of themselves as witches, vampires, whores, dogs, rats, or snakes. . . . By developing a contaminated, stigmatized identity, the child victim takes the evil of the abuser into herself and thereby preserves her primary attachments to her parents. (Herman 105)

In the Vampire Chronicles, there is no single "self" who takes the blame away from a single family perpetrating incest or abuse, but there is an entire community of monsters who can take the blame for human crimes. These monsters are "outside the compact of ordinary human relations," and therefore cannot help the fact that they are perverse by human standards. By generating a series of sympathetic and monstrous "selves" readers can identify with, Rice sets up a version of internalization in her fiction. Readers are reassured that human families are not "bad" because "only vampires would act like that." Whenever these vampires come too close to reminding us of human family dysfunction, they are eliminated anyway—*because they deserve it.*

Internalization fantasies—in which bad monsters deserve the abuse they get—come up repeatedly in the Witch Cycle, which contains three of Rice's more recent books. These lengthy novels chronicle the history of the Mayfair family through thirteen generations. Each generation contains one "witch" who can communicate and have erotic encounters with a polymorphous demon named Lasher. (Lasher, by the way, is the same type of demon we saw in the Vampire Chronicles living in the vampires' blood.) The Witch Cycle contains the only literal representations of incest we get in any of Rice's fiction, and it also contains some of the most graphic portrayals of violent monsters as well. Before I discuss the literal incestuous relations in these novels, I want to lay out the fantasy incest monster scenario. Lasher, who yearns to become human, is finally "born" at the end of *The Witching Hour* when his spirit "merges" with the fetus inside the thirteenth generation witch, Rowan Mayfair. Rowan, Lasher's "mother," is kidnapped, held prisoner, and raped by Lasher in the second novel *Lasher* and is forced to bear his daughter, with whom he also copulates and plans to have a child. One of Lasher's monstrous properties limits his ability to father children unless he can find a person who has genetic material compatible with his own. Only Rowan and Lasher's daughter Emaleth have that genetic material. *Lasher* ends with one of the most startling pseudo-incestuous fantasies I have ever encountered, which mirrors the "eating the mother" scene at the end of *Queen of the Damned*. Rowan, nearly dead, is revived when she kills Emaleth and then drinks her dead daughter's breast milk:

> [Rowan] shot three bullets into the girl's face . . . "Oh, Emaleth, oh, baby, oh, little Emaleth," she sobbed. The girl lay dead, her arms out, her shirt open, face a soft mass of blood. . . . And then [Rowan] closed her mouth again on the girl's breast. The room was still. No sound but the sound of suckling. Rowan drank from the left breast and then moved to the other, sucking as ravenously as before. . . . At last she sat back, wiping her mouth, and a low sad groan came from her, and another sob. (*Lasher* 557–8)

Emaleth is killed because she is unable to do anything but give birth to more monsters like her father. But I would argue that, like Claudia, Emaleth must be eliminated because she is a reminder of incest.

The Witching Hour, which is primarily the story of Rowan and her witch ancestors, introduces us to the Mayfair family and Lasher's relationship with them. A great deal of *The Witching Hour* is a "case file" on the Mayfair family compiled by the Talamasca, a secret society which has been investigating paranormal phenomena since the Middle Ages. Descriptions of Rowan's own deepening relationship with Lasher are intercut with passages from this "case file," which begins in the early fifteenth century with the first Mayfair witch who can summon the demon Lasher. In Rice's mythology, demons are beings who are only dimly intelligent, and often appear self-aware only because they are able to mimic the human beings who summon them. Rice makes it clear that Lasher is attracted to the Mayfair witches because, in mimicking them, he becomes self-conscious and human; in other words, Lasher's identity can only be a reflection of the Mayfair family he emulates. Like other demons in Rice's work, the mostly invisible Lasher is able to cause small rainstorms, move objects, and appear to the women who conjure him (whom he can also "touch," particularly in a sexual manner). Because the ability to summon demons is an inherited trait, Lasher is passed down from generation to generation in the Mayfair family. Once the family has amassed great wealth on a colonial-era plantation, they begin a tradition of incest and inbreeding which seems to culminate with Julien Mayfair, the only man to whom Lasher ever appears. Julien lives during the nineteenth and twentieth centuries and is Rowan's great-great grandfather. He has a daughter by his sister Katherine named Mary Beth, and also has a daughter by Mary Beth. Rowan's grandmother is a product of the union between Mary Beth's daughter Stella and Mary Beth's brother Cortland. Rowan, in other words, is the result of several generations of incest. And Lasher seems to follow the most incestuous strain in the family, attaching himself to Julien's own incestuous forebears and later serving Julien's offspring in particular.

Lasher is also fond of imitating Julien's appearance; when he does "appear" to the Mayfair witches, he takes on the guise of Julien as a young man. That is, Lasher is strongly identified with Julien, who has a predilection for incestuous relationships. Lasher's significance as a figure who stands in for the family's incestuous relations becomes particularly clear in a description of Julien's sister Katherine. The narrator of the Talamasca "case file" writes, "But other than the tales of incest, which characterize the Mayfair history since the time of Jeanne Louise and Pierre [Mayfair], there are no occult stories about Katherine" (*Witching Hour* 393). What is noteworthy about this passage is the slippage between "tales of incest" and "occult stories." Here we see the extent to which Rice tends to conflate incest and the occult, a move which robs incest of its reality while at the same time strongly associating it with a mythical figure who is destroyed by the end of *Lasher.*

I would point out that Lasher, besides being a supernatural monster, is also Rowan's child. He is therefore associated with an entire family history of incest *and* he becomes the final product of that family when Rowan helps him to merge with the body of her unborn baby. Lasher is both perpetrator and progeny of incest. One might attribute Lasher's dual role to the effect of internalization fantasies at work in the Witch Cycle, where Lasher becomes the child who takes the blame for his family's abuse. Lasher performs a function similar to Rice's vampires: he is the fantasy figure who acts out both the crimes and the guilt of an abusive family. Lasher's position as child and perpetrator of incest, I would argue, is not necessarily a locus of identification for child abuse victims engaging in internalization. He might just as easily be a figure for the kind of projection that goes on in abusive families when a parent blames his child for being "seductive" or "bad" and therefore deserving of rape or beatings. That is, Lasher is the kind of "child" we might find in the fantasies of a parent who wishes to disavow guilt or responsibility for having abused a child. Furthermore, we discover in *Taltos,* the third book of the Witch Cycle, that Lasher is a deviant and unnaturally evil member of a race of good beings known as the "Taltos." Ash, a benevolent Taltos, tells Rowan and her husband the history of his race, who are nothing like the violent and hypersexual

Lasher. This further confirms our sense that Lasher, like Claudia or Akasha, is a monster among monsters who deserves any punishment he might get.

In fact, Lasher's rape and abuse of Rowan make it possible for Rice to convert the Witch Cycle into a story about a parent's revenge upon a child who has abused her. At the conclusion of *Lasher*, when Rowan kills both Lasher and Emaleth, it would seem that Rowan has in fact come to occupy the position of child in relation to her own children. Rowan nurses from Emaleth after killing her, as if Emaleth were in fact a "parent" to her mother. Lasher and Emaleth's instantaneous growth into adults directly after being born underscores my point. By blurring the line between parent and child, Rice generates a fictional space in which children can be cast as perpetrators of child abuse. Rice's representations of parents and children help to explain her habit of inviting readers to identify with characters like Lasher and Lestat, who repeatedly abuse their "families." The Witch Cycle and the Vampire Chronicles begin with books told from the point of view of individuals who are hurt or abused by characters who later become sympathetic protagonists. While Lasher is the frightening, overwhelming monster in *The Witching Hour*, he tells his own story in *Lasher* and explains why it is that he has behaved so ruthlessly. *Lasher* is certainly a story about how Lasher abuses Rowan, but it is more importantly a story of Lasher's own history of abuse; we discover he has been "born" to human parents before who forced him to participate in humiliating pagan rituals, neglected him, and scorned him. In fact, Lasher believes he is a reincarnation of "Saint Ashlar," who Rice connects to a pagan-influenced Protestant church in Scotland. We discover that Lasher is no monster, but actually a saint who cannot help but desire to reproduce—his need to reproduce incestuously, it turns out, is built into the rituals of Saint Ashlar. Lasher is represented as a victim of the very sexuality which he has used to victimize his mother and daughter. He is adult and child, perpetrator and victim.

Likewise, the Vampire Chronicles begin with Louis' story in *Interview*, but the second novel *The Vampire Lestat* is told from Lestat's point of view (and, like *Lasher*, is named for its protagonist). While Lestat is a cold and manipulative character in Louis' story, we discover in *The Vampire Lestat* that Lestat has himself been used and hurt. Like Lasher, Lestat tells a story about his painful intimate relationships which is intended to solicit readers' sympathy and make his crimes against Louis and Claudia both understandable and forgivable. In these monster stories about child abuse, all of the characters ultimately appear to be victims in the end. Rice invites readers to feel deeply ambivalent about characters who are abusive: at any moment, we might discover that these abusers are victims too, and therefore we cannot hold them responsible for their cruelty to others. The safe space where Rice stages and masks sexualized child abuse is therefore a safe space for both perpetrators and victims. It is a space where the line between victim and perpetrator is impossible to draw, and therefore Rice makes it impossible to judge whether or not child abuse is in fact abusive at all.

Sexual and Economic "Safe Spaces"

While Rice's explicitly supernatural narratives tend to disavow abusive sexuality or relegate it to the realm of the occult, her pornography, erotica, and historical novels do precisely the opposite. The Sleeping Beauty trilogy (*The Claiming of Sleeping Beauty, Beauty's Punishment,* and *Beauty's Release*) and *Exit to Eden* are Rice's most explicit sadomasochistic novels, and all offer graphic representations of what might be considered "perversity" or "obscenity" to their readers. The erotic romance *Belinda* and historical novel *Cry to Heaven* are not about sadomasochism, but nevertheless fall into the category of "perversity." I use the terms "perversity" and "obscenity" advisedly, to designate sexual acts which do not conform to an admittedly narrow definition of mainstream heteronormative sexuality.[1] These novels celebrate coercive sexuality, and hinge upon erotic fantasies variously involving rape, bondage, castration, and pedophilia. What connects the erotica and historical novels to the Witch Cycle and the Vampire Chronicles is Rice's use of "safe" fantasy spaces, and a broadening investment in the idea that victims and perpetrators of abuse can achieve a measure of freedom by switching positions with each other.

Exit to Eden serves as a kind of commentary on the way safe fantasy space gets set up in the Sleeping Beauty trilogy, and in fact the Sleeping Beauty novels themselves are referred to by a character in *Exit to Eden* as "erotic classics" (*Exit* 16). *Exit* is the story of Lisa, a young woman who works as a trainer at "The Club," an exclusive, private resort where people pay to participate in sadomasochistic fantasies of their choice. The Club is divided up into masters, slaves, and trainers, and each group performs a different role. Masters are The Club's "clients," the wealthy patrons who come to be erotically serviced. Slaves are paid—by contract—to be trained as people who will service the masters. Lisa describes how The Club works as a safe space:

> The Club frightens the slaves at first. It terrifies them. But in a real way, The Club is a great womb. It's an immense community where no one is ever abandoned, and the lights never go out. No real pain or damage is ever inflicted. There are never any accidents at The Club. (11)

Lisa describes The Club as a place where "no real pain or damage is ever inflicted," and yet notes that its slaves are terrified by it. That is, while The Club does not "really" hurt its slaves, it certainly arouses genuine emotions in them. Here we see Rice setting up a boundary between ritualized (that is, pleasurable) abuse and "real" abuse or "real" sexuality. But no such boundary exists between emotions experienced in sadomasochistic ritual and emotions felt in "reality." This is a telling contradiction that recurs throughout Rice's pornography: "real" violence may not be occurring, but real emotions of terror and pain may result.

One of the ways Rice builds her insular pornographic spaces is through the super-abundant wealth her characters often take for granted. The Club caters to the richest and most well-connected people in the world; or rather, its masters are wealthy, while its slaves are paid (though we understand that they may simply "choose" to be paid and perhaps do not really need the money). That is, The Club is a safe space mostly because characters *pay* to make it so. Located on a privately-owned island off the Florida coast, The Club is an extremely elite and expensive vacation spot. Understood this way, s/m sex at The Club is just another high-priced diversion with fashion accessories. Furthermore, its inhabitants are not only safe from "real" sexual violence, but also the kind of violence motivated by poverty they might encounter in crime-ridden urban areas. The Club is "safe" for s/m, but more importantly it is a "safe" enclave for the upper-class.

In the fairy tale style aristocrats of the Sleeping Beauty trilogy, we find another demonstration of how class relations tie into s/m safe spaces. Slaves in these novels are young aristocrats (princes and princesses mostly) who are being "trained" in brutally erotic ways to prepare them to take their places in the ruling class. To become a truly gifted queen, the princess Beauty must first be degraded and abused by "the Queen" of the s/m castle where the first two novels take place. Here, "private" and "safe" forms of sexual abuse are intended to prepare young people to exercise public power as members of the aristocracy. Furthermore, the most "unsafe" and terrifying punishments the characters endure take place "in town," where they are sold to commoners who sexually assault them and force them to work at menial jobs tending bar or grooming horses. It is clear that the menial jobs are far worse punishment than the sexual assaults.

Robert Stoller describes sadomasochistic sexual fantasies as revisions of early traumatic experiences in which people learn to convert remembered pain into pleasure. "The trauma in each perversion script . . . is converted to a triumph. The attackers of earlier times are defeated, undone, unable to persist in their attack. . . . Now the victim is the victor and the trauma a triumph. . . . If the story is well-constructed, one feels guiltless and without anxiety" (Stoller 32). Stoller's observations offer a way of understanding how Rice's pornography might work as a psychological defense against the kinds of abuse it reenacts. Part of the purpose of these fantasies for readers might be, as Stoller suggests, symbolic mastery over remembered experiences of domination (sexual or otherwise) which they did wish to participate in and which certainly did not afford them pleasure. Furthermore, Rice's tendency to confuse sexual and economic subordination would lead readers away from naming one possible source of their trauma: having to perform the kinds of menial jobs which, for characters in the Sleeping Beauty trilogy, are merely another part of an s/m sex game.

Readers' ability to feel pleasure—and even have an orgasm—while reading about sexual humiliation and subjugation might be considered one way of masking painful feelings about their class and social positions. Class division generates many forms of social abuse which might seem to mirror the polarized roles and abuse we find in s/m gaming. However, the "bottom" in s/m abuse ultimately gets as much—if not more—pleasure as the "top." Rarely do we find the "bottom" class in a capitalist society getting anything other than abuse from "tops"; certainly there is no pleasure in an underclass position. Conflating class division with s/m role division invites us to believe that the underclass gets just as much gratification from its position as the ruling class does. The Sleeping Beauty trilogy, of course, promises that all "bottoms" will eventually be "tops" both sexually and as a class.

Additionally, Rice's pornography and erotica suggest that romantic "liberation" from sexual gaming comes when male and female sexual roles can be made fluid and interchangeable. For example, in *Exit,* Elliott falls in love with Lisa when she puts on a "double phallus" and has anal sex with him as if she were a man. Rice is careful to represent Elliott responding to Lisa's female/male body as particularly seductive:

> She lowered the phallus and pushed one end of it up and into herself . . . the other end curving outwards, and toward me just exactly as if she were a woman with an erect cock. The image was stunning: her delicate form and the gleaming cock rising so perfectly from the tangled curly hair. . . . Then came that exquisite feeling of penetration, of being opened, that gorgeous violation as the oiled cock went in. (*Exit* 121)

Later, the two reverse positions and Elliott says, "I went on fucking her harder . . . than I ever fucked anything or anyone—male or female, whore or hustler, or powerless phantom of my imagination—in my life" (*Exit* 123). He is able to experience a kind of sexuality with Lisa that transcends gender and even material reality. This lays the foundation for their emotional bond. Of course, Lisa and Elliott's "trading off" is largely sexual, and within the context of role playing. Nevertheless, it might be said to offer readers a sense that liberation from traditional gender roles is possible, and therefore to make the space of sadomasochistic fantasy all the more alluring. To the extent that gender roles can be compared to class positions, this fantasy about fluid identity can be said to hide another fantasy about cash fluidity.

There is even a degree to which Rice's position of authorship defies traditional gender roles, and makes her pornographic representations seem not merely "safe" but "liberatory." Pornography, as critics like Andrea Dworkin have argued, is most often considered a "male genre." Dworkin writes that "strains of male power are intrinsic to both the substance and production of pornography" (Dworkin 24). But what happens if a woman is responsible for the "substance and production of pornography"? Many contemporary feminists would argue that Rice is in some ways "subverting" the structure of domination Dworkin criticizes in pornography, and that by occupying an authorial voice so often reserved for men Rice challenges the idea that women are different from—and subordinate to—men. Theorist Judith Butler argues that when women take on or imitate aspects of male identity "both [genders] lose their internal stability and distinctness from each other" (Butler 123). What Butler consistently ignores in her analysis is the way certain forms of "distinctness" get maintained even as gender roles wither away. Not only is Rice taking on a "male" identity as a pornographer, but she is also taking on the identity of a capitalist who makes money at it. Pornography is one of the most notorious "spaces" in which sexuality and economics intermingle. Thus, "subverting" gender identity in the context of pornography does not necessarily mean subverting power and authority in general. One form of hierarchy (gender) may simply be swapped for another (class). Specifically, we might understand Rice's fluid gender roles as a simultaneous repetition of and protest against class roles—particularly abusive ones.

Cry to Heaven, Rice's historical novel about castrati opera singers in eighteenth-century Italy, speaks directly to the way non-traditional gendered identity is bound up with an absorption/rejection of ruling class authority.[2] Tonio, the main character, is a young man from a family of statesmen whose father Carlo has him castrated and sent away to live among eunuchs for political reasons. Subsequently, Tonio becomes a famous opera singer who can play both male and female parts on stage. In large part, this novel is a celebration of Tonio's ambiguous sexuality, his love affair with his singing teacher Guido (another eunuch), and late Renaissance Italy. At the same time, its plot is something like a "rape revenge" narrative, for the novel's climax comes when Tonio is able to confront and kill his father for having mutilated and abandoned him. Carol Clover has described the rape revenge narrative in film as a genre in which male audience members identify with a female hero who stalks and often kills her former rapists. The rape revenge narrative can be understood as a site in which gender role swapping is foregrounded: male audience members identify with its heroine because she takes on a "masculine"—that is, violent—role in order to avenge her own abuse (Clover 114–165). Tonio's castration is described as a form of rape: "He felt his legs forced apart, hearing the cloth rip before the cold air touched his nakedness.

'NOOOO!' he was roaring between clenched teeth" (*Cry* 136). Moreover, in a telling reproduction of the terms of Clover's argument, Tonio is able to get revenge upon Carlo by dressing up as a woman and posing as a prostitute to seduce him. Although Tonio reveals his true identity while dressed as a woman and kissing Carlo on the lips, he changes into men's clothing before killing him. Carlo interprets Tonio's actions as "too clever," for the only times Carlo is unguarded are when he visits prostitutes.

What Tonio has lost in his castration, besides his literal maleness, is also his "male entitlement," or rather the money and social position he might have inherited had he remained both a man and Carlo's son. He has been violated economically as well as sexually. To recover, Tonio finds a "safe space" in which he can gain a form of wealth and prestige which is comparable to his father's. He becomes a famous and sought-after opera singer, who travels in the same powerful circles as political figures. Tonio's ability to perform as both a man and a woman is not specifically what enables him to wreak violent revenge upon his abusive father. Tonio can only be a man/woman because he is already a member of the privileged "artist" class, with access to money and powerful social connections. These connections, and the money required to maintain them, are most importantly what help Tonio enter Carlo's territory undetected, armed, and prepared to escape quickly. Tonio rejects his father's authority, but he does it by imitating it in nearly every way: Tonio uses political power and violence to destroy his father, just as his father once used these methods to destroy him.

Making Money

Revenge upon authority—this time maternal—returns in Rice's erotic romance novel *Belinda*. This is Rice's only novel in which adult-child sexual relations are explored in a literal sense. Belinda is the sixteen-year-old lover of forty-four-year-old Jeremy Walker, an author of children's books about little girls. Jeremy is wrestling with the influence of his dead mother, a writer of historical romances who requested that he continue to write under her name after her death. We discover Jeremy's deepest secret is that he wrote his mother's last two novels, which were both smash hits. Belinda meets Jeremy while on the run from her mother, a suicidal, neglectful actress named Bonnie who has tried to shoot Belinda for sleeping with her current husband. During the course of their affair, Jeremy begins to paint nude portraits of Belinda, occasionally putting her in settings reminiscent of his children's books (in one portrait, she is surrounded by dolls). His representations of their sexual relationship in these paintings become an act of revenge for both of them; Jeremy wants to use them to "commit suicide" as a children's author and escape from having to identify with and paint little girls, while Belinda wants to get revenge upon her mother, who has tried to ruin Belinda's career as an actress.

Jeremy and Belinda wish to use the "Belinda paintings" to embark upon new career paths. That is, their revenge will be fame and fortune. Just as Tonio's revenge upon Carlo was a simultaneous embodiment and rejection of parental authority, so too is Jeremy and Belinda's. They are enslaved by the memories and authority of their mothers because their mothers are famous and wealthy artists. Furthermore, both—but particularly Belinda—have been unable to escape their mothers' authority because they have been dependent upon an inheritance (or payments) for their livelihood. In Jeremy's case, this is somewhat more complicated, for his children's books have made him independently wealthy; however, as Belinda points out to him, the content of his children's books— which are about little girls who live in huge Victorian homes—demonstrate that he feels like a little girl trapped in his mother's house. Jeremy's mother has even left him her name in her will so that he can continue to write her books after she is dead. He therefore struggles with the burden of having inherited not only her money, but also her identity as a writer.

What I would point out about *Belinda* is that it, of all Rice's books, comes closest to literally representing what is at stake in her pornography, historical fantasy, and gothic horror fiction: that is, the way class identity is the foundational trauma against which Rice defensively generates fantasies of fluid parent/child and male/female roles. In effect, what I want to argue is that Rice's fantasies in which abusive relationships become pleasurable or ambiguous are ways of thinking through the abuse and pleasure generated by capitalism. I do not wish to claim that all trauma in Rice's work is strictly economic, but I do want to call attention to the way class returns again and again as the buried term around which all other forms of abuse coalesce and become coherent. Because *Belinda* comes so close to admitting how salient class issues really are to its main characters, it is also the novel in which we confront most explicitly the results of child abuse and sexual transgression. You might say *Belinda* is a novel markedly without a "safe space": it does not take place in a fantasy realm, or within an occult story, or in history. I would suggest that the fantasy of adult/child sexual relations, which informs Rice's gothic horror and erotica, must become explicit in *Belinda* as a kind of distraction from the narrative about class trauma, and upward mobility as a form of reenactment and revenge.[3] The moment at which the repressed term of economic class threatens to become conscious is also the moment at which we are invited to become utterly shocked and absorbed by a flagrantly literal fantasy of pederasty.

Now I want to backtrack for a moment and reexamine abusive relations in Rice's horror and erotic narratives as figures for capitalist class relations. I contended earlier that one might characterize the "family units" in the Vampire Chronicles as abusive, and in particular as incestuous. *Interview*, the first novel, is Louis' firsthand account of the way Lestat abused him and their "child" Claudia. But what cements the bond between Lestat and Louis? What is it that has brought about their abusive relationship in the first place? Quite simply, Louis' money. Louis is the son of a wealthy plantation owner, and Lestat is an impoverished noble's son from France. Lestat has no idea how to manage his finances, and for this reason he chooses to make Louis into a vampire: Louis can be his companion, and quite literally, his accountant. Louis says:

> Lestat had always known how to steal from victims chosen for their sump-tuous dress and other promising signs of extravagance. But I suspected that beneath [Lestat's] gentleman's veneer he was painfully ignorant of the most simple financial matters. But I was not. And so he could acquire cash at any moment and I could invest it . . . and so for that he had ushered me into the preternatural world that he might acquire an investor and manager for whom these skills of mortal life became most valuable in this life after. (*Interview* 38–39)

Later, Louis says that Lestat "could persuade me to kill a child, but not to part with my money" (*Interview* 96). Integral to their "family," then, is not just Lestat's abusive emotional power, but also Louis' control of their money. Fur-thermore, when the vampire "family" triumphs over Akasha at the end of *Queen,* they declare their solidarity with one another—and celebrate their triumph over the kind of abuse perpetrated by Akasha—by opening an elite, expensive mall in Miami together where they can shop and hunt for mortals. In the last chapter of *Queen,* we follow Lestat as he walks through the mall, which is connected to a mansion where the vampires live together. As he gazes at the stores and the items for sale, he also watches people walk by and hungers for their blood. Finally, he has to leave the mall because he realizes "somebody is going to die" (*Queen* 474) if he keeps shopping. What I would want to point out is that Rice's vampires are not just a kind of projection of the dysfunc-tional family into the realm of fantasy; for this fantasy hinges on their identities as capitalists who steal money and blood from their victims to become rich and remain immortal. The idea that capitalists become wealthy through rob-bing and killing is as traumatic—and, in many ways, as true—as the idea that families can be sources of abuse and violation. That these kinds of traumas get spoken together in Rice's work is therefore not surprising. That both ideas must remain mystified by their association with fantastical monsters is equally unsurprising.

The Witch Cycle figures the intertwined traumas of economic and family relations in the demon Lasher. Lasher, as I noted above, is both source and result of the Mayfair family's history of incest. He is also the source of their enormous wealth, and in fact the Mayfair witch that he chooses to consort with in each generation is dubbed inheritor of "the legacy." "The legacy" is the Mayfair fortune. Therefore, Lasher represents what is popularly called "the cycle of abuse," which gets handed down from generation to generation in dysfunctional families *and* he represents a vast amount of money handed down as well. In fact, what has held the Mayfair family together in spite of its incestuous and violent tendencies is its accumulation of money. Like the capitalist vampires, Lasher has made the Mayfairs wealthy through stealing and spying on their business competitors. To a certain extent, the Witch Cycle is a fantastical rendering of the same issues at stake in *Belinda:* characters are locked into abusive family relationships because they depend upon an inheritance to maintain their class identities.

Taltos, the third novel of the Witch Cycle, provides another example of the way class seems to structure supernatural monstrosity. As I mentioned earlier, a "good" Taltos named Ash is introduced in this novel; he ultimately explains that Lasher is a Taltos who has become a vengeful, insane spirit. Rice convinces us that Ash is different from Lasher in two basic ways: he abstains from sex, and he is the impossibly wealthy CEO of a corporation that mass-produces children's toys. Ash speculates that capitalist mass production might even be a form of salvation, and thinks to himself that "This commerce, this endless multiplicity of beautiful and useful things, could save the world, ultimately" (*Taltos* 8). Rather than producing children, as Lasher does, Ash produces things for them to buy. The message seems to be that monsters are good if they are independently wealthy. Lasher's wealth is parasitic upon the Mayfairs—he has had to attach himself to a family in order to make money, and to inherit that money he has to make sure he is born into the family at some point. While Lasher is demonized and killed, Ash is rewarded: finally, Ash ends up "marrying" a Taltos born to Mona Mayfair, the young witch Rowan has named the next "designee" of the Mayfair fortune. *Taltos* ends with an exultant, mystical sex scene in which Ash and Morrigan Mayfair (Mona's Taltos baby) are joined at last. The distinction between human and monster ends up appearing far less important than the distinction between rich and poor: a wealthy monster can marry into a wealthy human family.

While both Rice's horror fiction and her erotic fiction contain numerous depictions of fluid family and gender roles, her characters exist in a rigidly hierarchical class framework. In some sense, Rice's vampires, witches, and sexual adventurers toy with their identities precisely because they are securely positioned as upper middle-class. Lisa, of *Exit to Eden,* has simultaneously taken up sadomasochistic role-playing games and achieved an upper-middle class status. Telling the story of her affiliation with The Club, she says:

> I'd made more money at twenty-seven than I'd ever dreamed I'd make in a lifetime. Now and then I'd try to remember what it was like when I wanted

all those gold-covered lipsticks at Bill's Drugs on Shattuck Avenue, and only had a quarter for a pack of gum. (*Exit* 5)

Her money and her sexual role-playing are inextricably linked. I would also point out that in the fourth installment of the Vampire Chronicles, *The Tale of the Body Thief,* Lestat switches bodies with a human being and becomes impoverished. As soon as he is in a mortal body, he is rendered powerless (and violently ill) because the "body thief" who has taken Lestat's vampire body has also seized control of Lestat's bank accounts. Lestat, without money, nearly freezes to death because he has no place to sleep. Becoming human, in *Tale,* is to surrender economic power. This solidifies an already-existing connection between Rice's vampires and a fantasized capitalist class. Economic identity is fluid in Rice's novels (to the extent that characters like Lisa and Lestat do rise and fall in class status), but only in a limited sense. Unlike the fluidity of family and gender roles, class fluidity is accompanied by disaster. Becoming poor is associated with mortality, desperation, and horror. Rarely do her characters become poor; in fact, nearly all of Rice's characters are upwardly mobile or already wealthy. *The Feast of All Saints,* for example, is the chronicle of a community of people trying to become middle-class. Characters in *Feast* who do not make it out of poverty die or become "kept women."

Finally, Rice's portraits of fluid power relations in families and sexual couplings take place within the context of abuse and sadomasochism because they represent an effort to come to grips with (and yet deny) the painful intractability of class identity. Lynn Chancer has postulated that:

> The relationship between capitalist and worker is analogous to a sadomasoch-istic one: sadomasochism may be a social fact of life under capitalist systems like that in the United States. Like sadomasochism, U.S. capitalism is based on a conditional form of social psychology that brings severe repercussions— the potential loss of livelihood, itself symbolic of the ability to live—should it be questioned too independently. (Chancer 122)

That is, sadomasochism is itself installed in our economic relations. Further-more, family relations (abusive or not) can in large part be conducive to sadomasochistic relations. Jessica Benjamin suggests that the bond between parent and child sets up a relationship in which one person—the parent—is always dominant, and the other—the child—always submits. She attributes people's absorption with sadomasochistic role playing to their early desire (as children) to be recognized as the parents' equal. Having failed at this, the child becomes invested in forms of recognition which are sadomasochistic: the sadist is always recognized, and the masochist is always the bestower of recognition. In other words, sadomasochism is a crippled desire for mutuality, in which the labor of recognition is divided up between two people. Certainly, as we find in Rice's work, the task of recognition can be traded back and forth between partners, but "pleasure is still viewed as something to be negotiated within an acknowledged structure of power" (Williams 171).

Rice's work functions so exceptionally well as compensatory fantasy because she portrays all social roles as fluid and interchangeable. Yet, the identities meted out to individuals within the family, gender, and the economy are often static: rarely do children have the power or the ability to abuse their parents; rarely do women dominate men sexually as often as men dominate women sexually; and rarely do members of the underclass become wealthy capitalists. Her fantasies speak directly to a painful problem people encounter in hierarchical culture, particularly when hierarchy makes possible sadomasochistic and abusive relationships. Rice's fictional narratives offer fantasy compensation to readers who may feel themselves constrained by their identities, and particularly if their identities have made them vulnerable to abuse. But the safe spaces in Rice's work, while they certainly offer a kind of liberation from constraining roles, tend to reproduce the abuser-abused binary. That is, the "hook" in Rice's narratives is a fantasy of fluidity within hierarchy, rather than a fantasy of dismantling of hierarchy altogether.

Notes

1. I would point out, however, that in recent years (particularly during the late 1980s and early 1990s), s/m sexual gaming has entered the mainstream, and in particular has become a hotly-debated issue among feminists. Post-feminist icon Madonna has represented herself in videos and her book *Sex* as a participant in s/m scenarios, and feminist critics from Camille Paglia to Jessica Benjamin have acknowledged its importance for understanding contemporary sexual arrangements.

2. Anne Rice's book, *The Feast of All Saints,* tells a similar story, in which gendered and sexual ambiguity gets replaced by racial ambiguity. The characters in this historical novel are all of mixed racial descent, and their fluid or dual identities seem to give them the same kinds of properties as Rice's bisexual characters (and, in fact, some of the characters in *Feast* are bisexual). These mixed-race characters also challenge parental authority by simultaneously embodying it and rejecting it.

3. In "Family Romances," Freud writes that part of the structure of a "family romance" involves a child's search for a family "grander and more aristocratic" than his own with which to identify. This is, Freud postulates, partly an act of revenge and partly an act of transcendence: "the child's imagination becomes engaged in the task of getting free from the parents of whom he now has a low opinion and of replacing them by others who as a rule are of higher social standing" (Gay, *The Freud Reader* 299). Freud is suggesting a connection between fantasies of upward mobility and revenge upon one's family.

Works Cited

Benjamin, Jessica. *The Bonds of Love: Psychoanalysis, Feminism, and the Problem of Domination.* New York: Pantheon, 1988.

Butler, Judith. *Gender Trouble: Feminism and the Subversion of Identity.* New York: Routledge, 1990.

Chancer, Lynn. *Sadomasochism in Everyday Life: The Dynamics of Power and Powerlessness.* New Brunswick: Rutgers University Press, 1992.

Clover, Carol. *Men, Women, and Chainsaws: Gender in the Modern Horror Film.* Princeton, NJ: Princeton University Press, 1992.

Dworkin, Andrea. *Pornography: Men Possessing Women.* New York: Plume, 1979.

Gay, Peter, ed. *The Freud Reader.* London: Norton, 1989.

Herman, Judith Lewis. *Trauma and Recovery: The Aftermath of Violence—From Domestic Abuse to Political Terror.* New York: Basic Books, 1992.

Jameson, Fredric. *The Political Unconscious: Narrative as a Socially Symbolic Act.* New York: Cornell University Press, 1981.

Modleski, Tania. *Loving with a Vengeance: Mass-Produced Fantasies for Women.* New York: Routledge, 1982.

Rice, Anne (writing as Anne Rampling). *Belinda.* New York: Jove, 1986.

———. (writing as A. N. Roquelaure). *The Claiming of Sleeping Beauty.* New York: Plume, 1983.

———. *Cry to Heaven.* New York: Pinnacle, 1982.

———. (writing as Anne Rampling). *Exit to Eden.* New York: Dell, 1985.

———. *The Feast Of All Saints.* New York: Ballantine, 1979.

———. *Interview with the Vampire.* New York: Ballantine, 1976.

———. *Lasher.* New York: Knopf, 1993.

———. *The Queen of the Damned.* New York: Ballantine, 1988.

———. *The Tale of the Body Thief.* New York: Knopf, 1992.

———. *Taltos.* New York: Knopf, 1994.

———. *The Vampire Lestat.* New York: Ballantine, 1985.

———. *The Witching Hour.* New York: Knopf, 1990.

Stoller, Robert J. *Observing the Erotic Imagination.* New Haven and London: Yale University Press, 1985.

Williams, Linda. *Hard Core: Power, Pleasure, and the "Frenzy of the Visible."* Berkeley: University of California Press, 1989.

On Blues, Autobiography, and Performative Utterance: The *Jouissance* of Alberta Hunter

Kari J. Winter

Throughout the twentieth century, African American women blues artists have been rich sources of feminist and African American self-affirmation. Hazel Carby, in her path-breaking essay "It Jus Be's Dat Way Sometimes: The Sexual Politics of Women's Blues," argues that because women blues singers have existed outside the pale of respectability, they "frequently appear as liminal figures that play out and explore the various possibilities of a sexual existence; they are representations of women who attempt to manipulate and control their construction as sexual subjects" (12). Building on Carby's analysis and focusing on the work of the great blues performer Alberta Hunter, I will investigate three issues. First, does it make sense, in the context of blues culture, to connect writing to safety? Second, in what ways does Alberta Hunter's work trouble the entrenched feminist belief that a woman artist's "I" is autobiographical (self-written, self-disclosing, and self-authorizing)? And finally, if Alberta Hunter sought neither safety nor autobiographical expression, what did her artistry achieve for her?

Blues

In his influential essay, "The World and the Jug," Ralph Ellison signifies on the image of the world as an imprisoning jug:

> [Irving] Howe seems to see segregation as an opaque steel jug with the Negroes inside waiting for some black messiah to come along and blow the cork. . . . But if we are in a jug it is transparent, not opaque, and one is allowed not only to see outside but to read what is going on out there; to make identifications as to values and human quality. (116)

If, as Ellison argues, liberal white northerners have seen blacks as trapped in a jug of racists' creation, African Americans have created self-empowering metaphors for their lives even from within the prison of oppression. Ellison is playing with an image he inherited from a blues song written forty years earlier by Alberta Hunter. Called "Down-Hearted Blues," the song launched both Hunter and Bessie Smith on the road to international fame in the 1920s. The song began: "Got the world in a jug, got the stopper in my hand." While Ellison images the blues artist as trapped in a glass bottle, looking out to read the world and assign value, Hunter images the world as trapped within a jug and the blues artist as the creator or at least the ruler of that jug. "[I]f you want me," Hunter sings, "you must come under my command."

At first glance, Hunter's conception of the power of the blues artist may seem overblown, romantic, and naive. She certainly was an unlikely candidate to claim such power. Few childhoods appear more desolate than hers. Born black, female, and frail in Memphis in 1895, Alberta Hunter was abandoned by her father before she was old enough to remember him. Her mother, Miss Laura, supported herself and her two daughters by working as a maid in a brothel. In later life, Hunter described her childhood as haunted by neglect from her mother and mistreatment at the hands of men, ranging from the selfishness of a grandfather who ate "all the good chicken and [left] us the feet and the neck" (Taylor 4) to sexual molestations and abuse by various men throughout her adolescence. Relatives and friends nicknamed her "Pig," alleging that she was always dirty. Hunter's response to suffering was twofold. First, she said that men's abuse "just made me stay away from men" (Taylor 14). Second, familial injustice made her "want to go to the top and stay there" (Taylor 5).

Hunter succeeded in both determinations. For the rest of her life, she resisted men's sexual advances and committed herself to lesbian friendships. She made it to the top of the blues music industry by becoming one of the most creative blues artists of this century. As music critic Melvin Maddocks observes, "of all the blues singers, Alberta Hunter may have been the most versatile" (23). Hunter's career as a blues performer spanned seventy years. At the age of seventeen, she ran away to Chicago and began singing in bordellos. Before long, she had worked her way up to night clubs like the Dreamland and then began touring nationally. Like most jazz musicians, she flourished on improvisation. Her approach to writing lyrics appeared casual; "different little things would come to me that rhymed," she explained offhandedly (Taylor 53). She wrote songs successfully for decades, but she was more possessive about what she called her "tricks" and "style" than her lyrics.

Hunter's inimitable style had a formative impact on the development of blues music in the crucial decade of the 1920s, when she began selling her songs to other artists as well as recording them herself. She sang throughout the United States, Europe, and Asia in the 1930s and 1940s. When her singing career ebbed in the 1950s, she demonstrated her skill at improvisation by deciding to become a licensed practical nurse, even though she was sixty years old and had never finished elementary school. She took equivalency examinations in 1955 in Chicago and applied to nursing school, secretly shaving twelve years off of her age. She succeeded. After twenty-two years of devoted nursing, Hunter was forced to retire in 1977 because the hospital personnel office thought she was seventy years old. She was actually eighty-two. Never one to give up, Hunter went to New York to launch her second musical career. She became more popular and famous than ever before. She was particularly pleased when "her" President Jimmy Carter asked her to sing in the White House. She sustained her second international singing career until her death in 1984, at the age of eighty-nine.

One remarkable aspect of Hunter's career is how much she endangered herself—that is, literally put her life at risk—in order to make money and to sing. At the age of sixteen, Hunter was so physically underdeveloped that she could travel on trains on a child's pass, which is exactly what she did when she ran away from Memphis to Chicago. Learning quickly that working as a maid or restaurant drudge would trap her permanently in poverty, Hunter decided to sing. For months she was routinely thrown out of the brothel where she aspired to perform. She had to fight not only to claim an audience but also to avoid omnipresent pimps. Once her career was launched, she was at risk from police raids, pickpockets, confidence men, and thugs. One night at a blues bar in Chicago, the lights went out and when they came back on, Hunter discovered that a man sitting near her had been shot. In 1922 when Hunter went on a southern tour, "the body of a young black boy, lynched because he supposedly talked back to a white man, was thrown into the lobby of a theatre where she was to appear" (Taylor 52).

The danger Hunter faced throughout her life was not atypical; it was part and parcel of everyday life for most African Americans. Writing and singing could be associated with safety only in very limited, particular ways. Since its origins in the eighteenth century, African American writing has been connected primarily to freedom and to the decolonizing of identity—processes undertaken at tremendous risk. In a historical context where literacy was outlawed, African Americans who wrote literally endangered their lives with the same strokes whereby they claimed ownership of their lives. After formal emancipation in 1864, art continued to be a danger-ridden activity. As James Baldwin puts it, the blues artist risks "ruin, destruction, madness, and death, in order to find new ways to make us listen" (86). In Baldwin's formulation, the blues artist encourages his or her listeners "to leave the shoreline and strike out for the deep water" (85). Safety is invoked only in the sense that the artist stands as "witness that deep water and drowning [are] not the same thing" (85).

African American cultural theorists widely agree that the blues infuse the heart and soul of African American culture. Houston Baker defines the blues as the matrix of African American discourse, the fertile womb of "ceaseless input and output, a web of intersecting, crisscrossing impulses always in productive transit . . . the multiplex, enabling _script_ in which Afro-American cultural discourse is inscribed" (3–4). Resisting unitary or binary ideological narratives, Baker argues, the blues refuse "to be pinned down to any final, dualistic significance. Even as they speak of paralyzing absence and ineradicable desire, their instrumental rhythms suggest change, movement, action, continuance, unlimited and unending possibility" (8). In Alberta Hunter's blues, the lyrics as well as the instrumentals often empower the singer toward feminist self-affirmation, agency, movement, and change. For example, in "I've Got a Mind to Ramble" (written in 1949 and first recorded in New Jersey, January 11, 1950), Hunter expresses an angry determination to leave a humiliating love affair. She describes how gossip is circulating "all over town" because the higher she tries to raise her lover, the lower he tries "to drag [her] down." Fed up with begging him to mend his "low-down dirty ways," she has made up her mind to leave. In face of his disbelief that she will actually leave, she responds, "Just count the days I'm gone."

In case the no-count triflin' man didn't get the point, Hunter drives it home in multilingual play in her song "I've Had Enough" (alternately named "I'm Tired of Being Your Football" and "Alberta's Blues"; written around 1978 and recorded in New York, July 28, 1981, when Hunter was eighty-six years old). After declaring that she has had enough of being kicked around like a football, the singer expresses her determination to leave on the nine o'clock train. She concludes with verbal fireworks, displaying the six languages— Italian, French, Danish, Yiddish, German, and English—that she was proud to sing in and adding a little Japanese for good measure: "If I never, ever, see you again, brother, / Good-bye. Or, sayonara. Au revoir. See ya see ya" and so on— multilingual excess sure to intimidate many a brother. In this song, as in many others, Hunter participates in the blues philosophy that, resisting Master Narratives, inspires energies that undermine, bypass, subvert, and exceed patriarchal logic.

Defining the blues as mournful music about victimization is a common but uninformed mistake. Through multiple artistic media such as music, writing, and painting, the blues articulate a hard-won affirmation of life and self. The blues artist "fill[s] the air with life," with his or her own life, which the artist understands contains the lives of many other people as well (Baldwin 140). Through the blues, Baldwin argues, the artist and the audience lament the tragedies of their lives, but also discover "how we could cease lamenting" (140). Freedom is imagined and expressed in the blues: the audience finds freedom through listening and the artist finds freedom when the audience listens, in a reciprocal movement. Blues theorists have shown that blues art must be created afresh every generation because "reaffirmation is precisely the contingency upon which the very survival of man as human being, however normally unsatisfied and abnormally wretched, is predicated" (Murray 6).

In his influential essay on Richard Wright's autobiographical masterpiece *Black Boy*, Ralph Ellison defines the blues as "an impulse to keep the painful details and episodes of a brutal experience alive in one's aching consciousness, to finger its jagged grain, and to transcend it, not by the consolation of philosophy but by squeezing from it a near-tragic, near-comic lyricism. As a form, the blues is an autobiographical chronicle of personal catastrophe expressed lyrically" (78–79). Every piece of this definition signally illuminates the achievement of blues artists like Richard Wright. It may also work well to describe the music of a mournful singer like Billie Holiday. However, unlike Wright or Holiday, most African American women who have sung the blues have joined feminist politics with the transformative powers of the blues matrix. Part of their power, I would argue, comes from their insistence on *exceeding* what Ellison calls "an autobiographical chronicle of personal catastrophe." To understand why women artists empowered themselves by stepping outside of autobiography, we need to re-examine the feminist quest to tell a free story.

Feminism and Autobiography

The history of women's writing as we know it is a history of struggle against patriarchal scripts that inscribe women in silence. In the recent wave of the feminist movement, classic texts from Anglo-American and French feminists have continually exhorted women to claim their voices and write their stories. For example, in her inspiring 1976 essay, "The Laugh of the Medusa," Hélène Cixous declares:

> Woman must write her self: must write about women and bring women to writing, from which they have been driven away as violently as from their bodies—for the same reasons, by the same law, with the same fatal goal. Woman must put herself into the text—as into the world and into history— by her own movement. (245)

Similarly, in 1980, in *Diving Deep and Surfacing*, Carol Christ called on women to write their stories because "Women's stories have not been told. . . . Without stories she cannot understand herself" (1). Responding to these and other feminist calls during the past two decades, thousands of women around the world have gotten personal and political through writing autobiographically.

What, then, did Shoshana Felman mean when she asserted in 1993 that "*none of us, as women, has as yet, precisely, an autobiography*" (14)?

In *What Does a Woman Want?* Felman cautions against what she calls "the mere stylistic trend" of "getting personal" in one's writing. She argues:

> "Getting personal" does not guarantee that the story we narrate is wholly ours or that it is narrated in our own voice. . . . Trained to see ourselves as objects and to be positioned as the Other, estranged to ourselves, we have a story that by definition cannot be self-present to us, a story that, in other words, is not a story, but *must become* a story. (14)

Felman continues her provocative analysis by arguing that women can engender or access their stories only indirectly, through "the *bond of reading*, that is, through the *story of the Other* (the story read by other women, the story of other women, the story of women told by others)" (14). She suggests that women need to conjugate "literature, theory, and autobiography together through the act of reading and by reading, thus, at once our sexual difference and our autobiography as missing" (14). Like Felman, I believe that feminists need to problematize our current, often untheorized enthusiasm for autobiography. Because our identities have been written in and by patriarchal scripts, telling the stories of our lives is not necessarily a liberating act. We may, almost as if by instinct, compulsively repeat femininity or rewrite ourselves as men. As Felman asks, "*from where* should we exorcise this male mind, if we ourselves are possessed by it?" (5). Following Felman, I would argue that we must return to the site of possession— that is, we must read and reread the stories that have written us. Before we can write ourselves out of determined and determining patriarchal scripts, we must teach ourselves to read differently, vigorously, and dangerously.

Although not an academic theorist, Alberta Hunter found her own ways— in a hurry and at a very young age—to read, reread, and theorize about patriarchal, white supremacist scripts. She saw that marriage and fame were mutually exclusive for women, and she chose fame (Taylor 15). With characteristic pragmatism and a determination to forge success in a tremendously unjust world, Hunter recognized the futility in her context of testifying to sexual abuse. As she said near the end of her life,

> People think a child is a liar. Children can scream and cry and do everything to try to impress the person of the fact that they are being mistreated, that they're not lying, and still, they would not be believed. It's a crime. Oh, it's a crime. (Taylor 14)

Whereas Richard Wright was able to chronicle his personal catastrophes in lyrical form and to find an audience, Hunter had stories to tell that the world was not ready to hear in her lifetime. The way she created safety for herself was not by baring her soul but by protecting her privacy:

> I never shared my private life with anybody in the world, not even with my mother. I've always been a loner. The only thing that anyone knew about my private life was what they tried to guess. But nobody ever knew. I never sat around and told stories on myself. (Taylor 30)

Although this personal privacy contradicts the narrative trajectory of late twentieth-century feminist models of healing and wholeness, Hunter created a woman-centered private life (she sustained several sequential long-term lesbian relationships and supported her mother through old age) at the same time that she created a rewarding artistic career. Her achievement dramatizes the non-identity—the shifting identities—of she who was written, she who reads, she who writes, and she who sings. If Hunter had attempted to integrate her various private and public selves into one single, sexually-specific, sincere, "realistic" self, her ability to perform would have been inhibited and her musical legacy impoverished.

A problem that undermines many feminist attempts to tell a free story and to author a free self is that women writers have often failed to free themselves imaginatively from the phallocentric ideal of a unified self. "Integration," "authenticity," and "wholeness" have been catchwords of liberal feminist self-concepts. I argue that far from being free, this unified self, this "I" of autobiography, tends to be constrained and contained in a patriarchal, self-indulgent solipsism. We need to author new concepts of self that take bliss in multiplicity. The power of Emily Dickinson and Emily Brontë, for example, stems from their non-identity with the voices and personae of their writing; they write themselves in multiple voices and figures not contained in autobiographical facts. Such, too, is the case of Alberta Hunter. She cannot be limited to a singular voice; she imagines into existence countless voices and infinite possibilities.

Despite Hunter's remarkable accomplishment, only one book (a biography), a handful of scholarly articles, and a few documentary videos have been published analyzing her work. The relative inattention granted to Hunter compared to a singer like Billie Holiday may stem, it seems to me, from the fact that Holiday was as dramatic in her tragic failure as a drug and alcohol addict as she was gifted in her musical performances. In many ways, Holiday's early death serves as a warning and punishment for transgressions, in step with the discourse repeatedly aimed at African Americans in the recent decades of the "wars on drugs" and "just say no" reductive moralism. In contrast to Billie Holiday, Alberta Hunter's long, successful, exuberant life suggests that transgression *does* sometimes pay. Her transgressive conduct does not fit stereotypes of black behavior. Asked her secret to longevity, Hunter replied: "Lookit, honey, I never smoked, drank, cussed, took drugs, owed nobody nothin' and never did musical exercises to warm up. All I ever did is open my mouth and sing" (Taylor 267). She took care of her voice, got plenty of rest, travelled around the world when she felt like it, and kept a low profile except when performing. She had a reputation for being tight with money and taking care of business. She did not break rules carelessly; she was a disciplined worker and a strong-willed rebel who did things deliberately the way she believed they ought to be done—breaking rules on principle and for good reason.

The primary social conventions Alberta Hunter set out to break were the narrative conventions that told blacks and women how to lead their lives. After witnessing the desperately circumscribed lives that white American society assigned to blacks and experiencing molestations as a child, Hunter was determined to create new life stories for herself. She recalled "losing" men to other women. With the ironic twist that characterizes much of Hunter's speech and music, she lamented the way other women took her men away: "Oh, I lost them all. Oh, Lord. God is so good. They got their marriage. And I got the fame." Having rejected the marriage plot, Hunter then rejected idealizing images of motherhood, saying: "No, I'm glad I don't have to sit around and hold them babies. No, Lord, look at me, stepping off one plane and getting on another, going up, up, up. But I love children. I like them, but I don't want them around me" (Taylor 15). Hunter provided a home for her mother, made women friends the sexual centers of her life, and developed long-lasting friendships with male musicians. Most importantly, she devoted herself to living and singing new stories. Positioning herself as a blues messiah, Hunter explained: "The story is love. A lot of people need it and want it badly but they haven't had it. . . . It's a great pleasure to be able to spread love and to be a participant in it, to be one of the messengers. I came to bring a message and I'm trying to deliver that message. I'm waiting for you to accept it" ("Alberta Hunter" 252).

III. Performative Blues

If Alberta Hunter did not author an "autobiographical chronicle of personal catastrophe" or strive to express an authentic, integrated self, what did she achieve in her blues performances? The safety she created for herself was the kind of safety that comes from financial stability. The freedom and power that she claimed were the freedom and power that come from giving voice not necessarily to autobiographical "facts" but to the entire human range of emotions and selves. How good it is to sing and dance, at the age of nineteen, at the age of eighty-three. Whereas Ellison's invisible man keeps searching for his illusory "I/eye," Hunter shows little interest in an autobiographical "I." She desires to bring on stage a performing, performative "I" whose very presence is the sign of her triumph.

In July 1922 Alberta Hunter recorded the first song that she herself wrote. As mentioned above, the song was called "Down-Hearted Blues." When Bessie Smith selected it for her first recording, it sold over a million copies, making both Bessie and the song famous. Hunter herself continued singing "Down-Hearted Blues" for sixty years, and she said that she collected royalties on all recordings of it for the rest of her life. Hunter was twenty-seven years old in 1922 and squeezing out a precarious living from various jobs. She was invited to New York for a recording session for the first time that summer. When she wrote "Got the world in a jug, got the stopper in my hand," she was not reporting a pre-existing truth. The lines did not function as a description of autobiographical reality. Rather, "Down-Hearted Blues" functioned performatively as a speech act to bring a new reality into being. In the beginning was the Word—or, as J. L. Austin puts it, "to utter the sentence (in, of course, the appropriate circumstances) is not to *describe* my doing. . . : it is to do it" (6). By singing "got the world in a jug," Hunter put the world in her jug.

In place of the anger and vengeance that Richard Wright so forcefully expresses and in place of the Oedipal struggle to kill the Father that Ellison's invisible man enacts and later rejects, Alberta Hunter positions herself in her music as what Roland Barthes would call an "intractable lover." Hunter described her jazz this way:

> Personally, it means to do unto others as I wish to be done to at all times. It's my music, I love it. I can touch a person. I can touch different people that never paid any attention to me before through my jazz. Yeah, touching. It's a language. Jazz has a language all its own. Naturally it's an expression of love. ("Alberta Hunter" 251)

As Barthes has shown, love (*jouissance*) is an anti-ideological force that cannot be manufactured, governed, managed, or directed; it tends to slip away just when one catches on to it and to explode just when one thinks it has been contained. Love is unruly, gratuitous, excessive, and serendipitous; it is not easily manipulated, placated, or cured. While anger and protest make one tired, love unleashes energy (Barthes 23).

Barthes observes that in love there is sometimes an "explosion of language during which the subject manages to annul the loved object under the volume of love itself: by a specifically amorous perversion, it is love the subject loves, not the object . . . it is my desire I desire, and the loved being is no more than its tool" (31). In Hunter's music, she performs multiple fictive heterosexual postures:

an abandoned lover, an insatiable lover, a vengeful lover, and so on. What becomes clear in watching her perform is that her passion is perverse precisely in the sense that it turns away from the loved object. Her love is so excessive that, intoxicated by her own desire, she annuls the (male) lover's voice and exorcises his desire. She desires her own desire.

Like dozens of other women who sang the blues, Alberta Hunter refused to buy into the bourgeois "goodness" that traps so many women in variations of miserably virtuous martyrdom. In her conclusion to "I've Got a Mind to Ramble," the singer celebrates leaving an unhappy marriage and returning to a lusty, expressive self with the sense and the will to suck the juice out of life. Hunter confides in the audience: if we see her stealing, don't tell on her because she's stealing back "to [her] used-to-be," her former assertive, sexual, fulfilled self, the one who can have "two men, make it three." One man is good for money, but the other man arouses her heart and her lust. With bright eyes and a wide smile, an eighty-year-old Alberta swayed night after night in front of a dazzled audience. Wearing a red dress and gold hoop earrings, she cackled about the beauty of her long, tall lover and licked her lips while repeating the classic blues line: "The blacker the berry, the sweeter is the juice."

Perhaps the song that best dramatizes the pleasure Hunter takes in erotic linguistic play is "My Handy Man Ain't Handy No More." This song was recorded in New York on December 17, 1979, when Hunter was eighty-four. She begins by asserting that "whoever said a good man was hard to find / Positively absolutely sure was blind / Cause I just found the best man that ever was." She proceeds to titillate the audience by listing "just a few of the things" her handy man does. The sexual metaphors include: shaking her ashes, greasing her griddle, churning her butter, and stroking her fiddle. With a suggestive grin and raised eyebrows, Hunter continues to pun on her man's handy skills while the audience laughs and claps. The handy man threads her needle, creams her wheat, heats her heater, chops her meat. Hunter cackles that she doesn't care whether or not the audience believes her; her man is "mighty nice . . . to have around / 'Cause when my furnace gets too hot—unnh— / He's right there to turn my damper down." Improvising with a seemingly endless supply of oral and tactile sexual metaphors, Hunter continues for several more minutes listing the man's skills at cooking, cleaning, and caretaking. The poor man works so hard and so intently that "he never has a single word to say," Hunter croons, shaking her head. She concludes with a testament to the man's prowess: he makes sure she gets "a nice fresh piece *every* day." To skeptics who might doubt the veracity of the singer's claims to have found the superman who keeps her so abundantly satisfied, I can only repeat Hunter's own assertion of her impeccable honesty: "You know I don't lie— / Who me? Not much now."

Sixty years after writing "Downhearted Blues," Alberta Hunter still had the world in a jug; at the age of eighty-five, she was singing "Down-Hearted

Blues" five nights a week to captivated New York audiences. She explained to reporters that although blues lyrics describe women beaten up by men, the blues are not about love troubles or people who "just have a few worries." She continued:

> Many people think a woman sings the blues only when she is in love with a man who treats her like a dog. I never had the blues about no man, never in my life, honey. If a man beats me, I'll take a broomstick and beat him to death.
>
> But that's not the blues. We sing the blues because our hearts have been hurt. Blues is when you're hungry and you don't have money to buy food. Or you can't pay your rent at the end of the month. Blues is when you disappoint somebody else: if you owe some money to your best friend, and you know he needs it, but you don't have it to give him. (Taylor 263)

As this passage indicates, Alberta Hunter's blues may be about love in a large sense, but they do not chronicle her personal suffering or describe her sexual identity. They do not make her safe or establish an authentic, integrated self. Rather, her blues are performative acts that empower her to play with multiple selves and put money in the bank. The *jouissance* she takes and gives—the bliss that makes her rich—is bliss in storytelling, bliss in creation, and bliss in the audience that responds "Amen."

Works Cited

"Alberta Hunter." *Particular Passions: Talks with Women Who Have Shaped Our Times.* Eds. Lynn Gilbert and Gaylen Moore. New York: Clarkson N. Potter, 1981. 245–53.

Austin, J. L. *How to Do Things with Words.* Cambridge: Harvard University Press, 1975.

Baker, Houston A. *Blues, Ideology, and Afro-American Literature: A Vernacular Theory.* Chicago: University of Chicago Press, 1984.

Baldwin, James. "Sonny's Blues." *Fiction 100: An Anthology of Short Stories.* Ed. James H. Pickering. New York: MacMillan, 1988. 66–87.

Barthes, Roland. *A Lover's Discourse: Fragments.* Trans. Richard Howard. New York: Hill and Wang, 1978.

Carby, Hazel. "In Body and Spirit: Representing Black Women Musicians." *Black Music Research Journal* 11 (1991): 177–92.

———. "It Jus Be's Dat Way Sometimes: The Sexual Politics of Women's Blues." *Radical America* 20 (1986): 9–22.

Christ, Carol. *Diving Deep and Surfacing: Women Writers on Spiritual Quest*. Boston: Beacon Press, 1980.

Cixous, Hélène. "The Laugh of the Medusa." *New French Feminisms*. Eds. Elaine Marks and Isabelle de Courtivon. New York: Schocken, 1988. 245–264.

Ellison, Ralph. "Richard Wright's Blues." *Shadow and Act*. New York: Vintage, 1953. 77–94.

———. "The World and the Jug." *Shadow and Act*. 107–43.

Felman, Shoshana. *What Does a Woman Want? Reading and Sexual Difference*. Baltimore: Johns Hopkins University Press, 1993.

Maddocks, Melvin. "Alberta Hunter: The Lady Sang More than the Blues." *Christian Science Monitor* October 26, 1984: 23.

Murray, Albert. *Stomping the Blues*. New York: Da Capo, 1976.

Taylor, Frank C., and Gerald Cook. *Alberta Hunter: A Celebration in Blues*. New York: McGraw-Hill, 1987.

" 'In the Center of My Body is a Rift':
Trauma and Recovery in Joy Kogawa's *Obasan* and *Itsuka*

Julie Tharp

In her essay on Joy Kogawa's *Obasan*, Shirley Geok-lin Lim locates the novel within a Japanese-American literary tradition that comments on its predecessors, noting that this complex portrayal of the mother is a direct descendant of Monica Sone's "mother text," *Nisei Daughter*, published in 1953 (298). Identifying her mother with traditional Japanese culture and ethnicity and American culture with the English language, Sone finds it impossible to maintain a "double identity in a repressive, racially homogenizing system" (299). Geok-lin Lim argues that the blending of the two cultures into one "is the repression of that part of the narrator's identity represented by her Japanese mother. Ironically, but not intentionally so, the book ends with the lesson of one for the price of two; the mother's story of a different race is burned, confiscated, imprisoned, and finally engulfed in the mainstream" (300). *Obasan* takes the repression of the mother's story as its central text. Geok-lin Lim argues that Naomi has to learn to use the discourses not just of self-narration and its converse "recessive silence" but also the discourse of "sociopolitical fact" in order to tell the mother's story. The many dream sequences within the novel further develop "the closest approximation to speech from 'that amniotic deep' " that begins to tell the story of the daughter prior to separation from her mother (308).

The discourses of "sociopolitical fact" actually take priority over self-narration and the discourses of silence in several critics' examinations of *Obasan*. Cheng Lok Chua demonstrates how the novel follows a pattern of "processual structure," a theory developed by anthropologists to describe ritual migration. She connects the three stages of separation, liminality, and aggregation to the removal, internment, and reintegration of Japanese Canadians that Kogawa describes in the novel. Donald C. Goellnicht and Marilyn Russell Rose discuss the novel *Obasan* as metafictional history and Naomi as historian. Rose calls the relocation of Japanese Canadians a "sociopathic rape" (222), and, interestingly, in 1988 predicts Aunt Emily's comments in the 1992 novel *Itsuka* where

213

Emily writes, "Over the years, the Japanese Canadian community went into hiding and became silent as rape victims" (208). In point of fact the novel *Itsuka* does illustrate how only in her commitment to political action through her enforced work on *Bridge* magazine does Naomi begin to recover from her stone-like paralysis. These critical essays, however, seem to dismiss too quickly the more personal components of Naomi's experience as well as dichotomize the personal and the political. Rose, for instance, sees in Naomi's affect-less personality the ideally neutral historian.

The process described within the two novels fits as neatly with models of trauma and recovery from sexual assault as it does with processual structure. Furthermore, the second novel, *Itsuka*, is difficult to reconcile in its entirety unless we consider the effects of sexual abuse on Naomi. The symptoms of Posttraumatic Stress Disorder that Naomi exhibits on a number of occasions within the novel seem inconsistent with a reading of her trauma as one stemming only from political disenfranchisement. For example, early in the novel a stranger, who has allegedly molested a girl behind the curling rink, pulls his car up alongside Naomi, who is working in a beetfield. When he comes up to her with a five-dollar bill and asks her name, she turns and walks toward her uncle and brother.

> It's while I'm walking toward them, and not looking backward, that the dizziness and the pain roll through me. I double over.
>
> "Uncle!"
>
> I stumble over the clods of earth, faint and retching. "Hey there, hey there," the stranger keeps blurting out.
>
> "Uncle!"
>
> I have soiled myself. I'm mortified. I'm half crawling as I change direction and head for the irrigation ditch bridge. Uncle with his bowlegged rolling gait comes running across the field to where I lie, hiding under the bridge in the mud where the stranger can't see. I remove my underpants gingerly. Without a word, Uncle squats in the mud and the thistles, taking the foul garment as if it were a handkerchief and swishing it in the brown ditch water.
>
> All that afternoon, Uncle stays with me in the clamminess of the dirt cellar at the far end of the field. (*Itsuka* 31)

Naomi's extreme reaction to the threat of the stranger resembles nothing so much as sexual retraumatization. The soiling of the underpants further suggests a sexual component to her trauma.

In a review essay on the relationship of childhood sexual abuse to adult Posttraumatic Stress Disorder, John B. Murray observes that "The most distinctive signs of PTSD are re-experiencing symptoms such as intrusive memories, avoidance of stimuli connected with the event, a numbing of general responsiveness that may involve loss of ability to have loving feelings, heightened bodily arousal, recurrent nightmares and flashbacks" (666). The nightmares and panic attacks that Naomi experiences and her general emotional numbness throughout both novels—she describes herself on an emotional scale as somewhere between a "cactus and a chimpanzee" (*Itsuka* 133)—and the abdominal pain she experiences when coming into contact with men suggest an inability to move beyond the abuse and separation she suffered as a child.

Naomi's relationships with men throughout *Itsuka* are characterized by panic attacks and dreadful nightmares. Her courtship with Hank is doomed from the start. In reaction to his hand "placed lightly beside [her] shoulder" (51), Naomi spends all night in "a nightmare of snakes" (51). When he tries to kiss her, her "heart is pounding wildly and a slightly nauseous dizziness sends [her] headlong onto the couch" (53). The first time that Father Cedric touches her in friendship, she experiences a similar panic reaction: "The sudden nauseous pain extends from somewhere around my navel and across the abdomen. I bend double and attempt to ride the tide, my mind reeling backward as it does in its efforts to find the source, the cause, the spark" (*Itsuka* 133). Naomi is conscious of the long duration of this illness, but incapable of diagnosing it for herself. "Who knows what the psychogenesis of an illness may be? There are so many mysteries in the past—so many unknowns and forbidden rooms" (*Itsuka* 134).

She does, nonetheless, posit a psychological source for her illness. Murray also points out that studies suggest a strong connection between the "disruption of relationships with primary caretakers" and psychiatric disorders (659). Naomi recalls that, according to Aunt Emily, she only "became sickly after Mother disappeared" (*Itsuka* 134). In the very next line of the novel, Naomi connects the events through word choice: "Something vast as childhood lies hidden in the belly's wars. There's a rage whose name has been forgotten" (*Itsuka* 134). On this occasion, however, she thinks in more reflective terms about the "illness" she has had all her life, the pain she feels in her abdomen on these occasions. In *Obasan,* Naomi has expressly connected the feelings of safety provided by her mother with the belly. It is this safe space that has been invaded and torn in two when she is forcibly separated first psychologically and then physically from her mother. The rage is that of the child silenced by her abuser and of the child whose mother did not keep her safe. "Mothers' lack of support, as described in victims' reports, was often disastrous and contributed strongly to their feelings of helplessness and isolation" (Murray 670). By the time Naomi is an adult, she has held her anger inside so long she cannot summon rage over Canada's injustices, over the manner in which the country tore Japanese Canadians in two, separating families, relocating homes, essentially destroying whatever familial and communal safe spaces they had created for themselves.

King-Kok Cheung provides an insightful reading of the various functions of silence within *Obasan*, arguing that Kogawa differentiates between various kinds of silence, distinguishing among "protective, stoic, and attentive silence" (128). It is only through her attentive silence that Naomi (and the reader) can come to appreciate the protective, stoic silence of the Issei and of others who endure. Kogawa, however, "reveals the strengths and limits of discursive power and quiet forbearance alike; in doing so, she maintains the complementary functions of verbal and nonverbal expression" (Cheung 128). While Naomi is overwhelmed by Aunt Emily's spate of words, she finds her mother and Obasan's messages of silent endurance ultimately inadequate to her needs in overcoming the oppressive circumstances of her young life. Instead Naomi also needs a defiance, which she develops through her rage and grief over her mother's injuries. The reclamation of a family history that was not supposed to be remembered requires this defiance. Lim writes that "the project of memory and writing is also the project of rescuing race history from 'wordlessness' and of healing through poetic language itself the psychosocial wounds caused by the internment and dispersal of Japanese Canadian families. . ." (308).

A. Lynne Magnusson's psychoanalytic view of Naomi's wordlessness helps us to locate her "linguistic anxiety" in the child's separation from the mother, but Magnusson also undermines the role of sexual abuse in *Obasan*, suggesting that it functions more symbolically in the woman's mind than as an actual event linked temporally and psychologically to the mother's disappearance. While I agree that the pre-Oedipal mother/child bond is doubtless broken by either or both events, either one of the events could also have produced the trauma evident in the character. What seems signficant is that they are linked. First, consider the mother's role in Naomi's dilemma.

Obasan explores the problem of the mother who is first absent in the sense that she does not protect Naomi from the neighborhood molester (although Naomi does not consciously blame her for that) and secondly the mother who is absent by choice, leaving to see her own mother and staying to hide her disfigurement. Naomi has to deal with several issues when she learns of her mother's fate: the horror of her injuries and death and the horror of her mother's purposeful detachment. While Kogawa's novel does not seem to blame the mother for these events, Naomi criticizes her mother's silence as ultimately harmful to both of them.

Separated from her mother as a young child, Naomi can only bear to remember a few scenes from her early childhood. Those few scenes suggest that her mother, although Nisei, is a proper Japanese woman: "She is altogether yasashi [soft and tender]" (*Obasan* 51). The only text Naomi remembers her mother delivering to her is the child's song: "How did you, Miss Daffodilly,/

Get your pretty dress?/ Is it made of gold and sunshine?/ Yes, child, yes" (51).
The song reinforces a gentle, almost whimsical femininity without any political
consciousness of ethnic or national identity. Mother's favorite songs are, however, actually western ones, suggesting that she has assimilated at least partially
to Canadian culture.

Naomi does distinguish a certain gender and race consciousness through
her mother's body. She identifies a certain look with her mother:

> Her eyes are steady and matter of fact—the eyes of Japanese motherhood.
> They do not invade and betray. They are eyes that protect, shielding what is
> hidden most deeply in the heart of the child. She makes safe the small
> stirrings underfoot and in the shadows. Physically, the sensation is not in the
> region of the heart, but in the belly. This that is in the belly is honoured
> when it is allowed to be, without fanfare, without reproach, without words.
> What is there is there. (*Obasan* 59)

Unfortunately the mother is not able to protect her daughter from the neighbor man who molests Naomi, who dishonors "this that is in the belly," separating Naomi from the shelter of her mother's eyes. "His hands are frightening
and pleasurable. In the center of my body is a rift. In my childhood dreams,
the mountain yawns apart as the chasm spreads. My mother is on one side of
the rift. I am on the other. We cannot reach each other. My legs are being sawn
in half" (*Obasan* 65). While the issues of childhood sexual abuse loom large
in this passage, transcend cultural identity, they also function metaphorically
since Naomi is seduced over to this Anglo man's house and away from her
Japanese mother's protection.

Naomi envisions herself as a "young branch attached by right of flesh and
blood" to her mother's tree trunk leg. "Where she is rooted, I am rooted. If
she walks, I will walk. Her blood is whispering through my veins. The shaft
of her leg is the shaft of my body and I am her thoughts" (*Obasan* 64). This
pre-Oedipal interdependence expresses in organic, natural terms a powerful
and idyllic connection that allows the child to claim the strength of her parent
as her own. It is Old Man Gower's hands that turn Naomi into "a parasite on
her [mother's] body, no longer of her mind. My arms are vines that strangle
the limb to which I cling. . . . I am a growth that attaches and digs a furrow
under the bark of her skin" (*Obasan* 64). A different kind of body knowledge,
coupled with a knowledge of misused power and exploitation, abruptly rup-
tures the mother/daughter intimacy.

Furthermore, Naomi is never redeemed from this seduction since she reports in the next sentence, the beginning of a new chapter, that "It is around
this time that my mother disappears" (*Obasan* 66). The child is left alone on one
side of the rift, without even her mother's presence to serve as a stabilizing factor.

> I hardly dare to think, let alone ask, why she has to leave. Questions are
> meaningless. What matters to my five-year-old mind is not the reason that
> she is required to leave, but the stillness of waiting for her to return. After
> a while, the stillness is so much with me that it takes the form of a shadow
> which grows and surrounds me like air. Time solidifies, ossifies the waiting
> into molecules of stone, dark microscopic planets that swirl through the
> universe of my body waiting for light and the morning. (*Obasan* 66)

Although Naomi reports that her "five-year-old mind" is not concerned with
the reasons for her mother's departure, it seems likely that a child might blame
herself and her "shameful" behavior for a parent's disappearance. All the same
it is the stillness, with perhaps a measure of guilt and shame lurking behind
it, the waiting and listening, that completely preoccupy the girl. In place of her
mother's happy songs and steady eyes, Naomi is left with her own stillness and
Old Man Gower. " 'Would you like me to tell you a story?' he asks. . . . Is this
where the terror begins?" (*Obasan* 62), she asks. The "terror" refers to the
frequent nightmare she has of three Asian women lying in the dirt, British
soldiers standing over them. The Japanese mother/woman is suppressed in the
dream as in waking life and replaced with the dangerous presence of white
men.

The lack of a story to counter Old Man Gower's, for surely a song about
daffodils holds no strength against his lies, forms the basis for the child's
development. Suppressing his story, rejecting it, Naomi is left only with silence,
a waiting for her mother to reclaim her with her own stories.

Comparable events take place on the international level, as the white men
in the United States federal government permanently and physically separate
Naomi from her mother by bombing Hiroshima and Nagasaki, inflicting grave
injuries on her mother as well as on so many others. She is also separated from
her father and from her home and community by the relocation policies that
forced all Japanese Canadians into relocating to Canada's interior. Both the
bombing and the relocation partially sever Naomi and her family from their
ethnic identity as surely as Old Man Gower has separated Naomi from her
mother. Japan becomes the parasite on the Issei's and Nisei's bodies, strangling
them, but only because the Canadian government has deemed them parasites
on the body of Canada.

Naomi does not have any knowledge of her mother's whereabouts,
however, until she is well into adulthood. Her mother's story is suppressed
by the entire family by the mother's own wish. She imposes silence and
Naomi's aunt, Obasan, maintains that silence. Often compared to a stone in
her taciturnity, Obasan is always enduring and self-sacrificing. She has none
of the beauty, drama, mystery, or horror of the lost Mother. Instead she is
plain and steady, *always* there in the background anticipating family needs:

"She remains in a silent territory, defined by her serving hands" (*Obasan* 226). For Naomi, Obasan is Japan. Obasan espouses a philosophy of endurance, telling the children that people "are made strong and excellent when they go through life's difficulties" (*Obasan* 131). Obasan teaches Naomi how not to be *wagamama* (selfish), how to heed always others' needs. Aunt Emily on the other hand is Canada: articulate, learned, professional, politically active. Words stream out of Aunt Emily's mouth and pen in an endless spate. She encourages Naomi to learn about the terrible things done to Japanese Canadians and to act on her anger.

For a model Naomi seems to choose Obasan, but not wholly out of allegiance to Japan. Rather it seems to come by default; her long silence "solidifies, ossifies the waiting into molecules of stone" (*Obasan* 66). The habit of waiting emotionally paralyzes Naomi. She has no desire for a love life, no desire for family. She lives alone. She has no political conviction. In speaking of Aunt Emily, however, she offers a comment on herself: "People who talk about their victimization make me uncomfortable. It's as if they use their suffering as weapons or badges of some kind. From my years of teaching I know it's the children who say nothing who are in trouble more than the ones who complain" (*Obasan* 34). Her discomfort derives from the threat to her silence. Her observation on the children suggests that she might wear the silence as her own badge, at the very least as a defensive weapon against those who would pry.

In the end of *Obasan*, when Naomi has learned, from her grandmother's words, of her mother's fate, she thinks, "Gentle Mother, we were lost together in our silences. Our wordlessness was our mutual destruction" (243). For Naomi, silence within this crucial relationship, the lack of a story around which to build her self, her love, her anger, is actually destructive. She concludes that Obasan's silence, while abiding in a profound respect for other's wishes, colludes in this destruction. Aunt Emily is the only one who has wanted to tell but was prevented from doing so by Uncle Isamu. Naomi rejects her mother's martyrdom, her desire to protect her children with lies. The depth of that rejection is expressed clearly in a long epigraph, of which I will only quote a portion:

> There is a silence that cannot speak.
> There is a silence that will not speak.
> Beneath the grass the speaking dreams and beneath the dreams a sensate sea. The speech that frees comes forth from that amniotic deep. To attend its voice, I can hear it say, is to embrace its absence. But I fail the task. The word is stone.
> I admit it.
> I hate the stillness. I hate the stone. . . .

Naomi summons forth her mother's voice from that "amniotic deep" in order to free herself from the imposed silence but also to rejoin her mother in the only way left open to her. She concludes after learning of her mother's fate that "for a child there is no presence without flesh,"—the child she was could not heal the rift in her life without her mother's physical presence— "But perhaps because I am no longer a child I can know your presence though you are not here" (*Obasan* 243). She tries to know her mother's presence imaginatively, to heal the rift even though her mother is not physically present. In writing the novel, Joy Kogawa has constructed an elaborate attempt to embrace the absent voice, to contain the mother in some manner useful to Naomi's construction of identity, but we learn from the epigraph that she cannot fully "attend the voice," "to embrace its absence" (*Obasan*).

Naomi solves the dilemma of embracing absence by retreating to the natural world where the novel begins. She concludes that she will only heal the rift with her mother now in death, where "Love flows through the roots of the trees by our graves," when she literally becomes the same flesh as her mother, their bodies become ground nourishing the trees above (*Obasan* 243).

This image of an underground stream of love and nourishment is first broached in chapter 1 of *Obasan* when Naomi recalls the annual walk she and her Uncle take on the prairie. When Naomi asks her Uncle why they come here he cannot answer, but it is clearly significant for him. Naomi does not understand, even though she feels herself a "part of this small forest" (3). She does note the "underground stream," however, which nourishes the wild rose bushes. She stands "for a long time watching the contours of the coulee erode slowly into the night" (4).

In the novel's last chapter, Naomi reveals a transformed perception of this same landscape, a perception which reconciles the issues of silence and separation for her.

> Father, Mother, my relatives, my ancestors, we have come to the forest to-night, to the place where the colours all meet—red and yellow and blue. We have turned and returned to your arms as you turn to earth and form the forest floor. Tonight we picked berries with the help of your sighted hands. Tonight we read the forest braille. See how our stained fingers have read the seasons, and how our serving hands serve you still. (*Obasan* 246)

Naomi needs to claim an erotic or fleshly integrity for her connection to her mother, to all the dead who are with her. The abstraction of grief cannot bear the weight of all their absences. "My loved ones, rest in your world of stone. Around you flows the underground stream" (*Obasan* 246). She is able to conjure up from the stream the concrete and fluid presence of their silence. "Between the river and Uncle's spot are the wild roses and the tiny wildflowers that grow along the trickling stream. The perfume in the air is sweet and faint. If I hold my head a certain way, I can smell them from where I am" (*Obasan* 247). Naomi affirms the living, the sensual in the midst of loss—the mind's desire is for rootedness in the body; the body's desire is to endure in the flesh. The scent of roses here is her uncle's flesh made to live again in the rose.

The measure of the power this reconciliation has provided for Naomi lies in Kogawa's inclusion of a government document at the end of *Obasan*. Heretofore seemingly indifferent to past atrocities, knowledge of her mother's fate seems initially to fuel Naomi's defiance of Canadian politics, even though at the beginning of *Itsuka* we find Naomi more or less paralyzed as always. The memorandum cited there in full is an expression of the governmental struggle over the status of the offending bodies and loyalties of Japanese-Canadian citizens. Read within the narrative of Naomi's life it takes the place of the mother's story, the mother's voice. It more or less becomes Naomi's nursery tale, since it was foisted upon her at the same time that her mother was taken from her by the same institutional powers. Unjust government ideologies of racial discrimination and dehumanization were the lessons she learned in childhood. It is, however, only in being reconciled with her mother, only in knowing her mother's story that she has the strength to recognize this, to claim the damage and to begin over from that starting point.

Knowledge of this formative tale allows Naomi to break her vigil of silence, her waiting for a story that can never come. Although the narrative perspective is oriented to discovery through the present tense, we have to assume that it is crafted by a consciousness who has already been there, who already knows the story from start to finish. She is tracing the protagonist's movement from impotent silence (as opposed to the attentive) to a style of communication that balances the verbal and non-verbal, although the novel *Itsuka* reveals this to be a long and arduous movement indeed. It is primarily because of the protectiveness of Obasan and Uncle that Naomi does not learn her mother's story until the age of thirty-six, presumably because it is not exactly a bedtime story suitable for a young child. The story, however, carries with it the seeds for a radical consciousness.

When Naomi's mother leaves, Naomi's world becomes static, awaiting the mother's return. The child thinks, "If my mother were back, she would move aside all the darkness with her hands and we would be safe and at home in our home" (*Obasan* 69). The "darkness," she explains, is everywhere, threatening them in the streets, in school, everywhere but home. The darkness is the threat of war, but it is also pervasive anti-Japanese sentiment that gets Stephen beaten up at school and ultimately tears the home and family apart. In response to these threats as well as to the threat of Old Man Gower, Naomi moves within herself into a place of emotional stasis, a move Murray maintains is common to childhood trauma survivors.

Naomi's emotional retreat remains complete until the year she learns about her mother's death, described in *Itsuka* as the year "a certain circular spinning stops. A cocoon disintegrates. The knowledge of death follows the knowledge of death and gnaws its way through my shell" (70). Once the shell is disintegrated, Naomi can begin the real work of reintegrating herself, of creating a safe space, a home not just for her mind but for her feelings as well. The illness she has suffered through her life is symptomatic of the splitting off from her body, the being sawn in half. Much later in the novel she reports, "The fact of flesh is new in my life. A simple fact, as commonplace as pebbles on a beach. But I'm a pebble that was lost. Now I've been found. I'm held in a hand that's as warm as song" (*Obasan* 248). She also begins speaking of herself on several occasions as the "body/mind," a conscious assertion of the unified self. The reintegration does not guarantee safety by any means, but, if asserted willfully, it provides a stronger basis from which to respond to the outside world and gives her the tools she needs to build a new home.

One crucial means by which Naomi begins to heal this breach within herself is through her developing relationship with Cedric. Described initially as a priest and called Father Cedric, later in the novel he becomes merely Cedric and the *Bridge* staff speculate about the growing relationship between him and Naomi. Cedric is, then, at once safe and stimulating. The friendship grows between them, however, for a number of reasons: Cedric's conception of place, his connections to nature and to Native philosophy through his mother, and his maternal nurturance of Naomi. Cedric, in a sense, steps in for the missing mother and provides the stories and the safety Naomi has lacked all these years.

Cedric's concept of place exists separately from his recognition of the land as a country called Canada. He sees it as the "place of [his] great-great-grandmother" (*Itsuka* 159), a Native, and derives his identity from that heritage. He conceives of the land as existing independent of national identities and this, in turn, connects for Naomi to her uncle's sense of place, to a vision of the land as prehistoric. In *Obasan* it is this sense of everyone joined together through the earth and its "underground streams" and "sensate seas" that allows her to move beyond her mother's and uncle's deaths, to take comfort in a natural reconciliation. This vision of the place also allows Naomi to claim the land for herself. Canada had stripped her of her official right to belong, but the land has never dispossessed her. In fact, Cedric's ancestors may have more right to it than the Canadian colonizers.

The two are thus joined through a preference for natural surroundings as opposed to the urban world. They both express an organic, even romanticized, connection to the earth. Cedric says that he is released "from the political by the personal and primitive. His mother's gift to him was a capacity to sense sentience. The sense of the Presence, he says, is the most primitive sense, more precious than all the other senses" (*Itsuka* 160). He learned from his Métis mother that " 'The animals that make no sound,' he says '—the rabbits, the deer—they feel as much as the ones that cry out' " (*Itsuka* 158–159), more or less echoing Naomi's own comment about her students. Cedric's ability to listen to the silence, to honor it and keep it safe, gives Naomi a space in which to heal herself, a space *outside* of the imagined, amniotic space in which she is connected to her mother. Cedric's active listening allows her to move beyond the narrow boundaries of self.

Finally, and perhaps most signficantly, Cedric functions as a maternal figure in several ways. He, like Naomi's mother, "makes safe the small stirrings underfoot and in the shadows" (*Obasan* 59). Whenever Naomi has nightmares, Cedric arrives to comfort her. When others ignore her as a cipher, he forces them to see her as a person with intelligence and power. Naomi describes him: "He is soothing as friendship. He cradles me as a mother holds her child, with care and confidence. He is as gentle as the smallest waves from the sea where the rainbow is moored and he does not, he does not invade" (*Itsuka* 298). Whether the reference to invasion be sexual or merely emotional, the safety Cedric provides gives Naomi the space in which to wrestle with her lifelong illness. They are creating a home for themselves built out of mutual trust.

At the same time that this personal relationship has been developing, however, so too has the professional one as they both work on the redress efforts. Naomi's initial reluctance and indifference to issues of redress increasingly develop into a deeply held commitment to the cause. At the end of the novel, when Canada finally agrees to the apology and financial settlement, Naomi realizes a final reintegration: "I laugh. I am whole. I am as complete as when I was a very young child" (*Itsuka* 328). Judith Herman emphasizes the need for the survivor of sexual abuse to reconnect with a community in order to heal. Healing both of the internal rift and the intranational one restores Naomi to her whole self, I would argue in part because the internal body/mind rift is complicated by the body's victimization on two fronts: sexual and racial.

In trying to convince Stephen to use his high public profile to help the redress cause, Aunt Emily argues that Japanese Canadians "will never be at home, in this country or anywhere, unless [they] first achieve redress. . . . What heals people is the transforming power of mutuality. Mutual vulnerability. Mutual strength" (*Itsuka* 220). What Naomi slowly learns within the course of the novel is that mutuality—between family members, political activists, friends—creates the trust needed for a healing home, for safety in the belly. Without that mutuality neither the failures nor the triumphs have meaning; life itself has little meaning.

In placing the childhood sexual abuse and separation from the mother at the center of Naomi's illness, Kogawa invites connections between sexual and nationalist assaults. Kogawa does not explicitly delineate a vision of Canada and the United States as raping Japan; she's more subtle. In Emily Kato's observation that *Isseis* and *Niseis* have behaved like rape victims in their silence, the question begs answering: in what other respects does this trauma and recovery resemble that of rape victims? She answers this question through careful reflection on Naomi's slow and painful reintegration of her self in mind and body, as a Canadian woman of Japanese heritage. Kogawa's meditations on the loss of and struggles to reclaim connection to the mother reverberate with the longing for a home that will make safe "this that is in the belly."

Although it takes two complete novels to create this safe space, Kogawa accomplishes it through a variety of narrative strategies ranging from intensely personal, poetic passages to political discourse. The fragmentation of styles in the first novel eventually merges into one more wholistic narrative by the end of *Itsuka.* This merging reflects Naomi's healing, which can only take place as she learns to construct a narrative for herself—a new bedtime story—that will hold her with as much care and tenderness as her mother did, but with the political shrewdness that Cedric possesses. The voice Naomi develops is one that transcends national boundaries in its Japanese respect for silence and Canadian recognition of the power of discourse. It also synthesizes the logical and emotional, the personal and political. The novels illustrate particularly well that the opposition of the private language and silence of trauma survivors to the official language of government documents is a division full of danger for those who cannot learn to use the whole gamut of expression in order to craft a language that recognizes the whole person within the larger community.

Works Cited

Cheung, King-Kok. *Articulate Silences: Hisaye Yamamoto, Maxine Hong Kongston, Joy Kogawa.* Ithaca: Cornell University Press, 1993.

Chua, Cheng Lok. "Witnessing the Japanese Canadian Experience in World War II: Processual Structure, Symbolism, and Irony in Joy Kogawa's *Obasan.*" *Reading Asian American Literature.* Eds. Shirley Geok-lin Lim and Amy Ling. Philadelphia: Temple University Press, 1992. 97–108.

Goellnicht, Donald C. "Minority History as Metafiction: Joy Kogawa's *Obasan.*" *Tulsa Studies in Women's Literature* 8.2 (Fall 1989): 287–306.

Herman, Judith. *Trauma and Recovery: The Aftermath of Violence—From Domestic Abuse to Political Terror.* New York: Basic Books, 1992.

Kogawa, Joy. *Obasan.* Boston: David R. Godine, 1981.

———. *Itsuka.* New York: Anchor/Doubleday, 1992.

Lim, Shirley Geok-lin. "Japanese American Women's Life Stories: Maternality in Monica Sone's *Nisei Daughter* and Joy Kogawa's *Obasan.*" *Feminist Studies* 16.2 (Summer 1990): 289–312.

Magnusson, A. Lynne. "Language and Longing in Joy Kogawa's *Obasan.*" *Canadian Literature* 116 (Spring 1988): 58–66.

Murray, John B. "Relationship of Childhood Sexual Abuse to Borderline Personality Disorder, Posttraumatic Stress Disorder, and Multiple Personality Disorder." *The Journal of Psychology* 127.6 (November 1993): 657–676.

Rose, Marilyn Russell. "Politics into Art: Kogawa's *Obasan* and the Rhetoric of Fiction." *Mosaic: A Journal for the Interdisciplinary Study of Literature* 21.3 (1988): 215–26.

Wong, Sau-lin Cynthia. *Reading Asian American Literature: From Necessity to Extravagance.* Princeton, NJ: Princeton University Press, 1993.

Contributors

Sonia Colette Apgar has an interdisciplinary background and research interests in composition and rhetoric, English and American language and literature, gender studies, autobiographical narrative, spiritual studies, and psychoanalytic theory—especially that which studies the body/mind connection. She writes and teaches English, composition, and writing courses at Highline Community College in Des Moines, Washington.

Susan Anne Carlson graduated from Ohio State University in 1991, with a Ph.D. in English Literature, and spent a year as a Fulbright Lecturer in Eskishehir, Turkey. She is an Assistant Professor of English at Pittsburg State University, Pittsburg, Kansas. Her current research interest is the Brontës, specifically, the juvenilia of Charlotte Brontë. She is writing a book manuscript on the link between Charlotte Brontë's juvenilia and her four novels.

Brenda Daly, Associate Professor of English and Women's Studies, Iowa State University, teaches courses in contemporary women's literature and English teaching methodology. She co-edited the collection, *Narrating Mothers: Theorizing Maternal Subjectivities* (1991), and her recently completed book, *Dialogic Daughters in the Fiction of Joyce Carol Oates*, is now under review. Daly has also published a number of autobiographical essays, as well as articles on contemporary novels by Ann Beattie, Carolivia Herron, Sue Miller, Joyce Carol Oates, Jane Smiley, and Alice Walker. At present she is at work on two books: *Incest Narratives in Twentieth-Century America* and *Authoring a Life*, an autobiographical-theoretical analysis of her language arts education.

Mary Jo Dondlinger is an M.A. student in Interdisciplinary Humanities at Arizona State University, emphasizing twentieth-century American literature and culture and contemporary feminist theories. This essay was originally a part of her undergraduate honor's thesis.

Linda K. Karell is currently an Assistant Professor at Montana State University in Bozeman, Montana. She received her doctorate from the University of Rochester in 1994 and her dissertation is titled *Literary Borderlands* *and Unsettling Stories: Storytelling and Authority in Willa Cather, Mary Austin, Mourning Dove, and Zora Neale Hurston.* Her article, "*Lost Borders* and Blurred Boundaries: Mary Austin as Storyteller," is forthcoming.

Tomoko Kuribayashi is an Assistant Professor at Trinity College of Vermont, where she teaches American and Canadian literature and Women's Studies. She specializes in contemporary women writers from Great Britain, Canada, and the United States, and has published creative writing.

Lisa Logan, Assistant Professor of English at University of Central Florida, is working on a manuscript exploring the connections among captivity, domesticity, and subjectivity in early American women's popular narrative.

Annalee Newitz is a Ph.D. candidate in English at the University of California at Berkeley. Her dissertation is on monsters, psychopaths, and economic class in American literature and popular culture. She is currently co-editing an anthology, with Matthew Wray, called *White Trash: Race and Class in America*, forthcoming from Routledge Press.

Diana L. Swanson is an Assistant Professor of Women's Studies and English at Northern Illinois University. Her articles have appeared in *Women's Studies Quarterly; Twentieth Century Literature;* and *Sexual Practice/Textual Theory: Lesbian Cultural Criticism*, edited by Julia Penelope and Susan Wolfe.

Mary Sylwester, a doctoral candidate at the University of Iowa, is completing a book-length study of women's nineteenth-century migration narratives. In the spirit of those migratory mothers, she will be moving her family to the Washington D.C. area.

Julie Tharp is an Assistant Professor of English at the University of Wisconsin Center in Marshfield. She has published essays on Louise Erdrich and Helena Maria Viramontes, among others on literature and literary criticism by women of color. A forthcoming article, "When the Body Is Your Own: Feminist Film Criticism and the Horror Genre," focuses on women and film violence.

Kari J. Winter is the author of *Subjects of Slavery, Agents of Change: Women and Power in Gothic Novels and Slave Narratives, 1790–1865* as well as numerous articles on African American culture, gothic fiction, and autobiography. She is an Assistant Professor of English at the University of Vermont.

Susan L. Woods, at the time of this writing, was a graduate student in English at Iowa State University. She has published a bio-bibliography on Sue Miller for *The Dictionary of Literary Biography*. At present, Woods writes for a major insurance company, still traveling the boundaries between creativity and traditionally technical fields.

Selected Bibliography

Ackley, Katherine Anne, ed. *Women and Violence in Literature: An Essay Collection*. New York: Garland, 1990.

Alcoff, Linda, and Laura Gray. "Survivor Discourse: Transgression or Recuperation." *Signs* 18.2 (Winter 1993): 260–290.

Barnett, Ola W., and Alyce D. LaViolette. *It Could Happen to Anyone: Why Battered Women Stay*. Newbury, CA: Sage Publications, 1993.

Bart, Pauline, and Eileen Geil Moran. *Violence Against Women: The Bloody Footprints*. Newbury Park, CA: Sage Press, 1993.

Bass, Ellen, and Laura Davis. *The Courage to Heal: A Guide to Women Survivors of Child Sexual Abuse*. New York: Harper and Row, 1988.

———, eds. *I Never Told Anyone*. New York: HarperCollins Publishers, 1983.

Bell, Vikki. *Interrogating Incest: Feminism, Foucault and the Law*. New York: Routledge, 1993.

Benjamin, Jessica. *The Bonds of Love: Psychoanalysis, Feminism and the Problem of Domination*. New York: Pantheon, 1988.

Buchwald, Emilie, Pamela Fletcher, and Martha Roth, eds. *Transforming a Rape Culture*. Minneapolis, MN: Milkweed Editions, 1993.

Chancer, Lynn. *Sadomasochism in Everyday Life: The Dynamics of Power and Powerlessness*. New Brunswick: Rutgers University Press, 1992.

DeSalvo, Louise. *Virginia Woolf: The Impact of Childhood Sexual Abuse on Her Life and Work*. Boston: Beacon Press, 1989.

Herman, Judith. *Trauma and Recovery: The Aftermath of Violence— From Domestic Abuse to Political Terror*. New York: Basic Books, 1992.

Hirschhorn, Norbert. "A Bandaged Secret: Emily Dickinson and Incest." *Journal of Psychohistory* 18.3 (Winter 1991): 251–281.

Jones, Ann. *Next Time She'll Be Dead: Battering and How to Stop It*. Boston: Beacon Press, 1994.

Maracek, Mary. *Breaking Free from Partner Abuse: Voices of Battered Women Caught in the Cycle of Domestic Violence*. Buena Park, CA: Morning Glory Press, 1993.

Miller, Nancy. *Getting Personal: Feminist Occasions and Other Autobiographical Acts*. New York: Routledge, 1991.

Moraga, Cherrìe. *Loving in the War Years*. Boston: South End Press, 1983.

McNaron, Toni A. H., and Yarrow Morgan, eds. *Voices in the Night: Women Speaking About Incest*. Pittsburgh and San Francisco: Cleis Press, 1982.

Russell, Diana E. H. *The Secret Trauma: Incest in the Lives of Girls and Women*. New York: Basic Books, 1986.

Terr, Lenore. *Unchained Memories: True Stories of Traumatic Memories, Lost and Found*. New York: Basic Books, 1994.

Ward, Audrey. *Gender and Domination: The Problem of Patriarchal Power in the Narratives of Alice Walker, Alice Munro, Gloria Naylor, and Toni Morrison*. Ownings Mills, MD: Watermark Press, 1990.

Yaeger, Patricia. *Honey-Mad Women: Emancipatory Strategies in Women's Writing*. New York: Columbia University Press, 1988.

Author Index

Subject Index

African Americans, 122–123, 202, 203. *See also* Hunter, Alberta

Angel in the House, 82, 83

Asian women, 56. *See also* Kogawa, Joy

autobiographical writing: and academic credibility, 16, 19–20; classroom assignment of, 15, 17–19, 24; and pedagogy, 16–17; risks of, 20, 23, 24n. 1

autobiography: and academic writing, 11–14, 22, 30; and blues music, 205; and feminism, 205–208; and theory, 14–15

backlash, 22–23

battered women, 2

bilingualism: in *The House on Mango Street*, 165, 169–171, 173, 176

blues music, 201–205, 208–211

body, the: 6, 163, 168–169; and landscape, 66–67

Brontë, Charlotte, 61–77; abandoned children in the works of, 66; Angria stories and juvenilia, 61–68, 73, 76; *Ashworth*, 68; Byronic hero in the works of, 73, 74; *Captain Henry Hastings*, 75; *Caroline Vernon*, 68, 69, 70–71; incest theme in the works of, 61, 65, 69, 72; *Jane Eyre*, 61, 65, 69, 75, 76; *Julia*, 69–70; masochism theme in the works of, 61, 65–66, 73, 75, 76; mother-daughter rivalry in the works of, 71–72; *The Professor*, 68; *Shirley*, 75; *Villette*, 61, 75

captivity narrative, 118–119, 123–125. *See also* Spofford, Harriet Prescott

Cather, Willa, 147–162; and cross-dressing, 156; *Death Comes for the Archbishop*, 149, 156; and lesbianism, 159; *My Antonia*, 149; "On *Shadows on the Rock*," 150–151;

O Pioneers!, 149; *The Professor's House*, 156; *Shadows on the Rock*, 148–160

Chicanas, 165, 166, 172, 176; in literature, 169. *See also* Cisneros, Sandra.

Cisneros, Sandra: *The House on Mango Street*, 165–177; "Mango Says Goodbye Sometimes," 173; "Red Clowns," 168; "Those Who Don't," 171

coding. *See* strategies of survivors

coming of age story, 173

community, role in recovery process, 51, 95, 223

confessional mode, 15–16, 25n. 3; in works of Virginia Woolf, 85–86, 88, 91, 94

Courage to Heal, The, 52

dialogism, 29, 36, 43n. 1

diaries, 59; of pioneer women, 131, 133–143

Dickinson, Emily, 101–116; family of, 102–104, 105–106, 108, 114, 115n. 3; first person pronoun in the works of, 105, 115n. 5; and the concept of home, 111, 112; and incest, 101–103, 108–111, 114; "One need not be a chamber to be haunted," 113–114; "Rearrange a wife's affection," 110–111; sexual imagery in the works of, 108–111; and the concept of space, 111–114; the "wife" poems, 103–111

discourse: academic, 17; feminist, 9. *See also* confessional mode

distancing. *See* strategies of survivors

domestic violence: frequency of, 2; and romantic love, 3; and silence, 59

domesticity, rhetoric of, 131–132

false memory syndrome, 7, 22

family: patriarchal, 86; Victorian, 82

fantasy, role in recovery process, 183

father-daughter seduction, theme of. *See* incest